PRAISE FOR
FOOD IS THE SOLUTION

"This book is an important call to action for anyone who eats."
—EMERIL LAGASSE

"As global citizens, we all share in the responsibility of creating a better future. With this book, Matthew Prescott shows us how our food choices can do just that."
—JOSÉ ANDRÉS

"*Food Is the Solution* shares easy ways to look and feel great while also respecting the Earth. Talk about a win-win!"
—ELLE MACPHERSON

"Individual action can lead to collective action, and collective action opens the door for system wide, positive change. So please do all you can, starting at home—where Matthew Prescott's inspiring book can guide you to some healthy and delicious choices."
—FRED KRUPP, PRESIDENT OF THE ENVIRONMENTAL DEFENSE FUND

"*Food Is the Solution* will give you the tools you need to incorporate plant-based eating into your everyday life. Start now, and help the planet."
—MARK R. TERCEK, PRESIDENT AND CEO OF THE NATURE CONSERVANCY

"Devour this book. Eat it up. It might just save your life and the world."
—MICHAEL GREGER, MD, FACLM, BESTSELLING AUTHOR OF *HOW NOT TO DIE*

"Food plays a big part of our identity, and this book will help us align what we eat with who we are."
—KEEGAN-MICHAEL KEY

"There's nothing sexier than saving the Earth—and this book shows you how you can do that through the power of your plate."
—PAMELA ANDERSON

"Eat more plants for a better planet: Easy peasy. Bon appétit!"
—PAUL "PEE-WEE HERMAN" REUBENS

"Food is power, and this book will help you use it."
—DAVID CHANG, FOUNDER OF MOMOFUKU

"Matthew Prescott proves that food can be delicious while also helping mend the social and ecological fabric of our world."
—MICHAEL SYMON, HOST OF ABC'S *THE CHEW*

"Though diet is but one of many things we need to change, we won't be able to save the world without dramatically changing our food and agriculture practices. Matthew Prescott has assembled a detailed and delicious road map to survival."
—MICHAEL BRUNE, EXECUTIVE DIRECTOR OF THE SIERRA CLUB

"*Food Is the Solution* is the guide I wish I had as a young mom. This is the blueprint for anyone who eats."
—LAURIE DAVID, ACADEMY AWARD–WINNING PRODUCER OF *AN INCONVENIENT TRUTH*

"A superb and thought-provoking book about the long-term impact of what we eat on the environment and our health. We need to learn how to vote with our mouths and this is a great guide to help us do so."
—THEODORE ROOSEVELT IV, CHAIRMAN, CENTER FOR CLIMATE AND ENERGY SOLUTIONS

"Eating with the Earth in mind has never been easier, thanks to this important and eye-opening book."
—JOHN MACKEY, CEO OF WHOLE FOODS MARKET

"More people than ever are enjoying plant-based foods as a way to help themselves and the planet. Matthew Prescott's book makes it easy and accessible for anyone to lend a hand—and fork."
—TÉA LEONI

"The planet needs us, and this book can help."
—MOBY

"There's a place at the table for everyone when it comes to environmental eating, and this book can help you find yours."
—BOB PERCIASEPE, FORMER DEPUTY ADMINISTRATOR OF THE U.S. EPA

"The fact is, the more plant-based we eat, the better we feel, the better we are. No more alternative facts."
—ROSIE O'DONNELL

"Each one of us can help protect the planet when we choose what to eat. It's simpler than you may think! This book will give you all the tools you need."
—VANI HARI, BESTSELLING AUTHOR OF *THE FOOD BABE WAY*

"Want to save the world while enjoying great food? This marvelous book shows you how."
—JOHN ROBBINS, BESTSELLING AUTHOR OF *DIET FOR A NEW AMERICA*

"This book is the best thing since sliced bread."
—BRUCE FRIEDRICH, EXECUTIVE DIRECTOR OF THE GOOD FOOD INSTITUTE

"Matthew Prescott has cut through all the confusing information on the food supply to bring us great recipes that are good for us and the planet. A must-read!"
—KRISTIN DAVIS

"*Food Is the Solution* offers moving stories and helpful tips so we can all live more sustainably."
—KEN COOK, PRESIDENT OF ENVIRONMENTAL WORKING GROUP

"The message for the future is really very simple: Get as close to a whole-food, plant-based diet as possible."
—DR. T. COLIN CAMPBELL, AUTHOR OF *THE CHINA STUDY*

"Great cause, great recipes, great read!"
—EVAN SHARP, CO-FOUNDER OF PINTEREST

"This book will help you celebrate Earth Day every day!"
—KATHLEEN ROGERS, PRESIDENT OF EARTH DAY NETWORK

"Matthew Prescott provides a compelling case that most foods that are good for you are also good for the world. Whether you're a carnivore or vegan, you'll benefit from reading this book."
—LAWRENCE WILLIAMS, CEO OF THE U.S. HEALTHFUL FOODS COUNCIL

"We impact the world at each meal, and this book can help us use our plates as a force for good."
—RICHARD LINKLATER

"There's a crisis in our oceans and on our planet. This book offers concrete, easy, and delicious ways to help."
—LOUIE PSIHOYOS, ACADEMY AWARD–WINNING DIRECTOR OF *THE COVE* AND *RACING EXTINCTION*

"We can heal our bodies through the right types of food, and by consuming and producing the right ingredients, food also becomes a medicine for our planet."
—PETRA NĚMCOVÁ

"Great book, great food, better world—what more could we ask for?"
—TAL RONNEN, CROSSROADS KITCHEN

"The world—literally, planet Earth—needs this book!"
—KATHY FRESTON, BESTSELLING AUTHOR OF *QUANTUM WELLNESS*

"For those of us already enthralled by Matthew Prescott's perspective and insight into how what we eat affects who we are and the fate of the world, this book comes at exactly the right time."
—MAYIM BIALIK

"This is one of the most crucial books of our time. It offers amazing, healthy food while being environmentally conscious and informative. A must-read!"
—HIS ROYAL HIGHNESS KHALED BIN ALWALEED, PRINCE OF SAUDI ARABIA

"Use this book as an important tool to help you turn your diet into a force for good."
—KIERÁN SUCKLING, EXECUTIVE DIRECTOR OF THE CENTER FOR BIOLOGICAL DIVERSITY

"Protecting our environment takes all hands—and mouths—on deck. *Food Is the Solution* shows how simple it can be to adopt a more Earth-friendly lifestyle, which is a critical first step to changing our habits as a society."
—MARGIE ALT, EXECUTIVE DIRECTOR OF ENVIRONMENT AMERICA

"Thought-provoking resources and recipes to help you kick-start a more environmentally friendly diet."
—IAN ANDERSON, FRONT MAN FOR JETHRO TULL

"*Food Is the Solution* will help you save the Earth and live more compassionately."
—GENE BAUR, FOUNDER OF FARM SANCTUARY

"Today's chefs are spending more time than ever before on plant-forward foods. As this book proves, culinarians can activate positive change to help us all eat better and diversify our food choices, while also preserving our planet and its precious resources."
—SCOTT GIAMBASTIANI, GLOBAL PROGRAM CHEF AT GOOGLE

"This provocative and valuable book reminds us that a smart diet is good for our health, our soul, and our planet."
—GENE KARPINSKI, PRESIDENT OF THE LEAGUE OF CONSERVATION VOTERS

"When it comes to food and its impact on the environment, animal welfare, and public health, we've reached a fork in the road—and Matthew Prescott's book will help you use yours to choose the right way."
—WAYNE PACELLE, PRESIDENT AND CEO OF THE HUMANE SOCIETY OF THE UNITED STATES

"Matthew Prescott has created an outstanding resource to support global change."
—JULIANAA SATIE, FOUNDER OF THE SCHOOL OF NATURAL COOKERY

"Matthew Prescott has offered a significant tool for anyone who wants to take action for the planet every time they eat."
—LINDSEY ALLEN, EXECUTIVE DIRECTOR OF RAINFOREST ACTION NETWORK

"A menu of ideas to help us eat in a more environmentally responsible and healthy way."
—JANET RANGANATHAN, WORLD RESOURCES INSTITUTE

"For your health, the environment, and animals—this book has everything you need to make a difference!"
—DORON PETERSAN, FARE WELL AND STICKY FINGERS BAKERY

"We can use our plates to help the planet. This book is a giant lightbulb switched on to help us."
—JOHN SCHLIMM, AUTHOR OF *FIVE YEARS IN HEAVEN*

"A timely resource to help us all eat better and tread lighter on the planet."
—JAMIE RAPPAPORT CLARK, PRESIDENT AND CEO OF DEFENDERS OF WILDLIFE

"For anyone wondering what they can do for the climate, this important book proves our everyday choices can have powerful consequences—not to mention, some seriously delicious results."
—KEN BERLIN, PRESIDENT AND CEO OF THE CLIMATE REALITY PROJECT

"As this book shows, even slight changes in diet can help improve water quality."
—WILLIAM C. BAKER, PRESIDENT OF CHESAPEAKE BAY FOUNDATION

"We can fight for the planet and public health in the courts or when we eat. Matthew Prescott shows us how to make a difference with every meal."
—TRIP VAN NOPPEN, PRESIDENT OF EARTHJUSTICE

"We can stand up for the planet when we sit down to eat, and Matthew Prescott has given us straightforward, easy ways to do exactly that."
—TERRY TAMMINEN, CEO OF THE LEONARDO DICAPRIO FOUNDATION AND FORMER SECRETARY OF THE CALIFORNIA ENVIRONMENTAL PROTECTION AGENCY

"I get asked all the time how to do more to help animals, the planet, and people. I always say to start with what you do every day—and we all eat! This book will help you feel better while helping others in an easy, great tasting way."
—KRISTIN BAUER VAN STRATEN

"Food tastes so much better when you know it is giving back to the world. This book highlights how and why."
—CHAD SARNO, COAUTHOR OF *CRAZY SEXY KITCHEN*

"*Food Is the Solution* can help you invest in your health and the health of the Earth at every meal."
—LESLIE SAMUELRICH, PRESIDENT OF GREEN CENTURY CAPITAL MANAGEMENT

"This book is a great guide to a simpler, healthier, and more compassionate way to live."
—WENDIE MALICK

FOOD

IS THE

SOLUTION

FOOD
IS THE
SOLUTION

WHAT TO EAT TO SAVE THE WORLD

80+ RECIPES FOR A GREENER PLANET
AND A HEALTHIER YOU

MATTHEW PRESCOTT

Foreword by Academy Award–winning director James Cameron

FLATIRON
BOOKS
NEW YORK

FOOD IS THE SOLUTION. Copyright © 2018 by Matthew Prescott. Foreword copyright © 2018 by James Cameron. All rights reserved. Printed in China. For information, address Flatiron Books, 175 Fifth Avenue, New York, N.Y. 10010.

www.flatironbooks.com

"Thanks, Giving" by Jesse Eisenberg. Copyright © 2018 Jesse Eisenberg.

Book and cover designed by Amy Sly

Food and cover photographs by Jessica Prescott

The Library of Congress Cataloging-in-Publication Data is available upon request.

ISBN 978-1-250-14445-4 (paper over board)
ISBN 978-1-250-14446-1 (ebook)

Our books may be purchased in bulk for promotional, educational, or business use. Please contact your local bookseller or the Macmillan Corporate and Premium Sales Department at 1-800-221-7945, extension 5442, or by email at MacmillanSpecialMarkets@macmillan.com.

First Edition: March 2018

10 9 8 7 6 5 4 3 2 1

For my sister, Hillary—for opening my eyes and starting me on my path

For my mother, Janet—for my senses of service and justice

For my wife, Lara—for everything else in my world

"To ask the biggest questions, we can start with the personal: what do we eat? What we eat is within our control, yet the act ties us to the economic, political and ecological order of our whole planet. Even an apparently small change—consciously choosing a diet that is good for both our bodies and the earth—can lead to a series of choices that transform our whole lives."[1]

—FRANCES MOORE LAPPÉ, *DIET FOR A SMALL PLANET*

CONTENTS

FOREWORD

JAMES CAMERON

In 2012, my wife, Suzy, and I adopted a plant-based diet. Many people come to plant-based eating through health issues—maybe they're facing a quadruple bypass, or want their family to eat better. For us, it was all about sustainability.

I'd known for several years that the carbon footprint of animal agriculture is incredibly high. But I was under the impression that we need animal protein in our diets. Then I saw the film *Forks Over Knives* and began reading into the topic. I learned that not only do we not *need* animal proteins, but that they're actually *detrimental* to us in many ways.

So, comfortable we were doing the right thing not just for the environment but also for ourselves, we went fully plant-based. We explored the huge variety of vegan foods that are out there. We got recipe books and checked out new restaurants. To our surprise, it was much easier than we thought it'd be.

And we loved the food. When you start eating plant-based, your whole palate opens up—your taste sensitivities change. There are countless species of plants with rich flavor profiles and aromas and nutrients. My diet is so much broader and more varied now than when I was eating a typical meat-based diet. And when we want those old comfort foods that taste like meat, there are so many good substitutes available—and more coming into the market all the time. Plus, there are great ethnic options—vegan ravioli and Thai food, Indian food, Mexican food, noodles—things that we all recognize and love, and that always have plant-based options.

These foods are kinder to the land and kinder to our bodies. The fact is that eating more plant-based foods is the number one thing we can do for the environment—for habitat loss, biodiversity loss, water pollution, and so many other issues. Almost every major environmental problem could be solved by a global shift toward plant-based eating. So the right choices to make for our health are also the right choices to make for the earth.

My recommendation? Read up on the issues. Arm yourself with the facts. There are plenty of good books on the topic of plant-based eating. The more you feel good about how you're eating—that there's a higher purpose to your diet—the more likely you are to stick with it. Program yourself for success. Try a twenty-one-day plant-based challenge. Figure out some recipes you want to make, try new foods and see what you like, find some great new restaurants to eat at. Plan your strategy a bit so you'll be successful with your new diet—the fate of the planet depends on it.

James Cameron is an Academy Award–winning director known for some of the biggest box-office hits of all time, including Titanic, The Terminator, Aliens, Avatar, *and more. He is also an oceanic explorer, having been the first person to reach the bottom of the Mariana Trench on a solo mission, and an environmental activist.*

"Almost every major environmental problem could be solved by a global shift toward plant-based eating."

—JAMES CAMERON

INTRODUCTION

FOOD IS THE SOLUTION

When I was about ten years old, my father and I built a small backyard garden. In a sunny corner of our yard, we dug out a rectangle in the grass. We shoveled a trench along its edges, into which we laid bricks to create a border. We picked out stones and twigs from the dirt, breaking up the clumps with our hands until the soil was smooth and dropped easily through our fingers. We sowed seeds for green beans, carrots, radishes. From a garden center down the street, we bought seedlings for tomatoes, peppers, and eggplants, carefully transplanting them into the ground.

Right around this time, I took an interest in cooking. I learned to make scrambled eggs—albeit via microwave and mug (which tasted about as good as it sounds). I'd take great pride in organizing our spice cabinet, combining half-full jars of cinnamon and paprika, placing the most commonly used spices toward the front. I picked through my mother's favorite recipe clippings and pasted them into a homemade "cookbook."

As my interest in food evolved, I progressed from microwaved eggs to stovetop cooking. I started inventing my own recipes. But my fascination with food mostly focused on growing, preparing, and eating it.

Then, when I was twelve, my sister returned from school one day with an announcement: she had become a vegetarian.

"Mr. Thayer says there are antibiotics in chicken meat," she proclaimed. "He says there are hormones and all kinds of other stuff in meat, too."

Vegetarian? It was the first time I'd ever even heard the word, let alone *known* a vegetarian. No meat? Not even chicken? Fish? Bacon?! As any good little brother would do, I poked fun. At dinner, I'd gleefully place a chunk of bloody steak on the end of my fork and stick it into my sister's face while mooing loudly.

My mother took a different approach. Alongside a pot of beef chili for us, she'd have a bubbling pot of bean chili for my sister—even using separate spoons for stirring. A dish of chicken enchiladas would sit side by side in the oven with a dish of veggie enchiladas.

Because I'd always loved food, I certainly wasn't averse to trying some of these mysterious new dishes. I'd eat one beef taco and one bean taco; I'd add bacon to a veggie burger. Slowly, my palate expanded and my culinary horizons broadened.

Lo and behold, I actually liked many of these new foods. I started ordering dishes with "bean curd" at our local Chinese restaurant—not realizing until much later that bean curd is another term for tofu. I tried vegetarian chicken patties and, to my amazement, loved them. I'd order veggie fajitas at Mexican restaurants instead of meat fajitas. I was no vegetarian, but I liked the food. *Whodathunk it?*

It wasn't until later, in my teens, that I learned more about the social issues associated with food production. I learned that what we eat plays a central role in many of society's deepest problems, and can also help solve them.

What I learned is that food can save the world.

Take our own health, for example. Results from the U.S. Centers for Disease Control and Prevention's (CDC) *2011–2012 National Health and Nutrition Examination Survey* show that nearly 35 percent of U.S. adults ages twenty and older are overweight, more than 35 percent are obese, and nearly 10 percent are extremely obese.[2] For children and adolescents, the numbers are also staggering, with nearly one in every five individuals between two and nineteen years old being obese.[3]

This is a full-blown crisis. The human costs—increased heart disease, diabetes, stroke, and more—are staggering. And the economic costs are overwhelming: an obese individual pays thousands of dollars more in healthcare costs than a non-obese individual, according to one study published in the Journal of Health Economics. All told, that study found, obesity accounts for a whopping $200 billion—more than 20 percent—of all U.S. health expenses.[4]

And even though they can offer some help, we needn't rely on healthcare providers, government, or corporations to solve this crisis. The power to reclaim our health can be found in what we put on our plates.

"A diet higher in plant-based foods," concludes a Scientific Report of the U.S. Dietary Guidelines Advisory Committee, "is more health promoting . . . than is the current U.S. diet."[5]

When we do a deep dive into virtually any major healthcare problem plaguing our population, we see a clear correlation to food and diet.

Heart disease, for example, is the number-one killer in America—responsible for a full quarter of all deaths. The causes of this killer are cholesterol (which is only found in animal products) and saturated fat (high levels of which are found in animal products). When our cholesterol and saturated fat levels rise—through consuming too many foods high in them—our arteries become blocked, leading to heart attacks.

But countless scientific studies have confirmed that plant-based whole-food diets can prevent and reverse heart disease in patients without the use of medical intervention.

For example, in 1948, the National Heart, Lung and Blood Institute and Boston University embarked on an ambitious project to identify risk factors for heart disease.

"The American Heart Association recognizes the role of plant-based foods in a healthy dietary pattern. Use Meatless Mondays as another opportunity to eat a well-balanced diet."[6]

—NANCY BROWN, AMERICAN HEART ASSOCIATION CEO

> "The research shows one thing very clearly: we all need to eat more plants and less meat."[7]
> —AMERICAN INSTITUTE FOR CANCER RESEARCH

Today, their Framingham Heart Study (FHS) continues, making it the longest-running clinical study in all of medical history.

"If Americans adopted a vegetarian diet," said former FHS director Dr. William Castelli in a PBS interview, the heart disease epidemic "would disappear."[8]

Diabetes is another epidemic, with 1.4 million people diagnosed with the disease each year, and one in every ten healthcare dollars going toward treating it.[9, 10]

And yet we know that by eating more plant-based foods, diabetics can get their blood sugar to drop and thus reduce or eliminate their dependence on insulin. In a study published in the *American Journal of Clinical Nutrition*, insulin dependence dropped by about 60 percent—with half the study's participants able to get off of insulin entirely—within just sixteen days of adopting plant-based diets.[11]

The list goes on: cancer, stroke, obesity, autoimmune disorders like rheumatoid arthritis—so many of the health problems that weigh us down as individuals, and that weigh down our nation's healthcare system, can be prevented and reversed by eating more plant-based foods.

Imagine a world in which we all are healthier—where we're happier with our bodies and suffer fewer aches and pains. Imagine a world in which we don't have to spend as much of our money on health services, leaving more to spend on our passions and allowing us all to be more generous and charitable. Imagine a world with less disease, fewer early deaths. That world is a happier world, a better world—and plant-based foods are the solution to creating it.

Such a world is also a much kinder, gentler world—one filled with more empathy and compassion.

Today, nearly 80 billion land animals are raised and killed for food each year.[12] These include mammals like pigs and cows, birds like turkeys and chickens. Of course, there are family farmers out there who provide good living environments for their animals—but virtually all meat, dairy, and eggs eaten today come from factory-farmed animals.

In 1950, the total number of farm animals in the United States was somewhere near 100 million; by 2015, it had mushroomed to roughly 9.2 billion.[13] According to USDA data, during the same period that the number of farm *animals* increased by 9,400 percent, the number of *farms* producing those animals decreased by 60 percent.[14]

That, in a nutshell, is factory farming—and its consequences are catastrophic.

CONTINUES PAGE 7

BETTER YOU, BETTER WORLD

MICHAEL GREGER, MD, FACLM

At sixty-five, my grandmother was given a medical death sentence. Suffering from end-stage heart disease, wheelchair-bound, and out of surgical heart bypass options, her life was basically over.

Then she heard about Nathan Pritikin.

Born in 1915, Pritikin was an inventor, nutritionist, and longevity researcher—one of our country's earliest "lifestyle medicine" pioneers. At forty-two, after being diagnosed with heart disease himself, Pritikin began his search for treatment, eventually publishing his findings in his (now renowned) book *The Pritikin Diet*, and later opening the Pritikin Longevity Center, offering diet and lifestyle coaching with the goal of preventing and reversing disease.

So when my grandmother, nearly on death's door, heard of Pritikin, she reached out, eventually coming to follow his program.

So what exactly was Pritikin's plan? His extensive research centered primarily on a low-fat, plant-based diet rich in fruits and veggies, beans, nuts, legumes, and whole grains. Just as we now know that eating more plant-based foods plays a critical role in preventing and reversing environmental catastrophes, we also know plant-based diets can play a central role in overall health and wellness by preventing and reversing many of the diseases that plague us most.

Topping the list for the leading cause of disability and death in the U.S. is heart disease: America's number-one killer and the same disease that caused my grandmother to reach out to Nathan Pritikin. And high cholesterol levels are thought to be a primary cause of this leading killer.

This may help explain why a plant-based diet, which is free of cholesterol and saturated animal fats, has been so successful in preventing and treating the disease. Indeed, plant-based diets are the only type of diets ever proven not only to help prevent heart disease but also to reverse it in the majority of patients.

Following heart disease is cancer, America's number-two killer. Here, too, the balance of evidence suggests that a whole-foods, plant-based diet may help prevent, treat, slow, and in some cases even reverse cancer progression.

As the American Institute for Cancer Research concludes, "The research shows one thing very clearly: we all need to eat more plants and less meat."

Some reasons why plant-based diets may be so effective include lowering cancer-promoting growth hormone levels, methionine intake, inhibiting angiogenesis, intercepting carcinogens, and increasing fiber and antioxidants. Additionally, eating lots of fruits and vegetables (e.g., nine daily servings) may boost detoxifying enzymes, lower inflammation, and make for healthier bowel movements, ridding the body of excess estrogen and cholesterol. It's no wonder populations eating diets centered on whole plant foods have lower cancer rates.

Another major health threat here in the United States is diabetes. And, as is the case with heart disease and cancer, plant-based diets may successfully prevent, treat, and even reverse type 2 diabetes—including in children.

Excluding meat, milk, and other animal products may reduce the risk of diabetes and gestational diabetes by increasing insulin sensitivity, boosting hormone-binding proteins, helping to prevent obesity, and reducing exposure to heme iron, dioxins, and PCBs.

Eggs may be particularly risky: eating only one egg a week is associated with nearly double the odds of getting diabetes. And fish, especially salmon, is one of the primary sources of PCBs and other industrial toxins, which may also play a role in the development of diabetes.

On the other hand, many plant-based foods appear to be protective. Beans may be especially beneficial when replacing meat or refined carbs, such as white rice. By eating plant-based and living a healthy lifestyle, up to 95 percent of type 2 diabetes cases are avoidable.

Of course, simply preventing disease is not the only goal of good nutrition. Everyone, whether eating a plant-based diet or not, ought to be sure to get enough (but not too much) protein, calcium, and iron, for example.

Vitamin B_{12} is one important supplement for those eating plant-based diets. B_{12} is made by neither animals nor plants, but by microbes. And B_{12} deficiency may occur without supplementation. Thankfully, there are safe, cheap, convenient sources available widely. The simplest regimen is to take 2,500 micrograms of the cyanocobalamin form of B_{12} once a week.

Omega-3 fatty acids are also essential. Plant-based sources of omega-3 include flaxseed or chia seed, walnuts, and algae-based DHA supplements, which are bioequivalent to fish oil omega-3 but without the harmful industrial pollutants often found in fish oils.

Combined with even minimal supplementation, plant-forward eating has been definitively shown to prevent, treat, and reverse some of our nation's biggest killers while improving health, wellness, and longevity.

Nathan Pritikin knew this decades ago—and that would ultimately save my grandmother's life. Pritikin actually chronicled her story in his biography: "Mrs. Greger had heart disease, angina, and claudication," he wrote. "Her condition was so bad she could no longer walk without great pain in her chest and legs. Within three weeks, though, she was not only out of her wheelchair but was walking ten miles a day."

Thanks to Pritikin, she was able to live another thirty-one years—to the grand old age of ninety-six. His plant-based diet extended her life by nearly a full third.

Indeed, debilitating, life-shortening diseases and other ailments don't have be a normal part of aging—and they don't have to be your future. Like many of the most pressing environmental problems, they can instead be prevented, treated, *and even reversed* with a healthier diet rich in whole, plant-based foods. So eat up, live long, and prosper!

A founding member and Fellow of the American College of Lifestyle Medicine, Michael Greger, MD, is a physician, author, and internationally recognized speaker on nutrition, food safety, and public health. He's a graduate of the Cornell University School of Agriculture and Tufts University School of Medicine. His book How Not to Die *became an instant* New York Times *bestseller. He has videos on more than two thousand health topics freely available at NutritionFacts.org.*

THANKS, GIVING

JESSE EISENBERG

At some point in my twenties, my family made the switch.

I'd missed a few Thanksgiving dinners because of work, and when I finally returned home, my family cavalierly told me that they now celebrated Thanksliving. That's not a typo.

Thanksliving is just like Thanksgiving—the fun holiday in November—but with an *L* instead of that fun *G*. Thanksgiving, with the *G*, they explained, *is brutal and sanctifies slaughter. Thanksliving* [with an *L*] *celebrates life. It's vegan and we honor two turkeys we've saved by placing their photos at the center of our table.*

With no time to make other plans, I trudged to my family's house in New Jersey on the final Thursday of November 2009. We took a moment of silence to reflect on the horrors of the poultry industry. We talked about what virtue we were most proud of. And the coup de grace: My sister pulled out Jonathan Safran Foer's *Eating Animals* and opened to a dogeared passage about the slaughter of turkeys. We sat around a plate of tofu, hearing of turkey-cide. She was not only preaching to the converted, she was nauseating them.

Looking around the room—these familiar faces, nodding empathically along to the stories of turkey death—I suddenly realized: *my family has gone nuts.*

The following year, I decided to skip Thanksliving. I wasn't opposed to the food; in fact, I have spent many years as a vegetarian and, of course, know that it's a far better diet for the health of the eater, the animals, and the environment. But I couldn't bear to see my family so earnest. These were funny people! People who would have laughed at the family that made Thanksliving dinner!

I was working near Los Angeles, so I asked a producer friend if he'd have me over for dinner. He told me not to expect much. "We just have a little turkey, stuffing, cranberry sauce—nothing fancy." *Nothing fancy* was exactly what I needed.

This producer—I will call him John Doe—had three young children and a wife who was a pediatrician. I had met the family several times and I always thought they were a perfect group. They were always making inside jokes and traveling as a team. And their dinner was unremarkable, for which I was very thankful. We just sat down and made stupid jokes and ate normal American food.

Halfway through, Jane Doe mentioned going to her parents' house for next year's Thanksgiving. And John—normally a mild-mannered guy—blew up. "I told you a thousand times, I am not stepping foot into that psychopathic house!" This was clearly the middle of an ongoing fight.

Jane threw down her fork. "Then I guess we'll just have to get divorced next year and you can go to your dysfunctional family's house and drink with your father until you pass out again."

I stared at the Doe kids, shocked. They stared back, as if to say, "Welcome to our every day."

Jane stormed into the kitchen. I suddenly longed for the newfound earnestness of my family, their moral eagerness, their progressive idealism. I realized every family is insane. But at least mine cared about the world.

Jesse Eisenberg is an Academy Award–nominated actor and the author of Bream Gives Me Hiccups and Other Stories.

> "Factory farming is not only unacceptably cruel, but unsustainably inefficient."[15]
> —JOHN SAUVEN, EXECUTIVE DIRECTOR OF GREENPEACE UK

At these facilities, animals are routinely abused in ways that would be illegal if they were done to a cat or dog. Egg-laying hens are crammed into cages so small they can't spread their wings. Mother pigs are often forced to live in crates so tiny they can't even turn around. Chickens in the meat industry are bred to be Frankenbirds, growing too fat, too fast for their young bodies to keep up with and suffering crippling injuries as a result.

Then there's fish. Worldwide, an estimated 2.7 *trillion* fish are ripped from the oceans each year for food, suffering decompression as they're pulled from the water or being suffocated or crushed aboard fishing vessels.[16] Countless more are raised on aquatic factory farms, where they're packed gill to gill in disease-ridden tanks; though no firm numbers exist for these aquaculture-raised fish, it's likely in the tens of billions.

All this suffering, on such a massive scale, is antithetical to what we believe about animals. We are a nation of animal lovers. We spend nearly $100 billion on our pets each year.[17] We bird watch. We whale watch. We support, through donations, more than twenty thousand individual animal protection charities across the nation.[18] Caring people in every corner of the country rescue and rehabilitate injured wildlife. People rush into flood zones and other disaster areas to rescue animals in need. We volunteer at shelters. The list of ways in which we share our lives with and help our fellow creatures is nearly limitless.

Our compassion for animals extends to those caught up in the food-supply chain.

The Food Marketing Institute is the leading trade association for the grocery industry. "When it comes to attributes beyond those that render personal benefits," concludes FMI in its "Shopper Trends" report, "shoppers prioritize animal welfare second only to employment practices."[19] And a study by the American Farm Bureau Federation—a major lobbying force for factory farmers—found that 95 percent of Americans believe animals on farms ought to be treated well.[20]

And yet, for some of us, there's a disconnect between what's on our plates and those values of compassion that we hold so dear: millions of us don't want animals to suffer and believe they should be treated well, yet also continue eating products from factory-farmed animals.

If more of us can connect those dots—between what we already want for animals and how our food choices impact them—we can better align our morals with our menus to create a kinder world.

Such a world would also be better for people. After all, at its root, our willingness to eat animals even when we know they've suffered comes down to our proclivity for placing animals in an "other" category—focusing on how they may be different from we humans.

Of course, fish were born with gills instead of lungs, chickens with wings instead of arms, pigs with hooves instead of feet. Humans were born with hair instead of fur and a spark of imagination that other species may lack. But while we humans are dissimilar to other animals in many ways, we also share so much in common with them. We feel pain and joy; we can suffer. So do other animal species. Anyone who's had beloved pets at home knows we share with other animals personal preferences unique to us as individuals (one of my cats is obsessed with peanut butter, while another loves spinach). Humans and other animals share a desire to live our lives according to our best interests, to engage in our natural behaviors, to have social interactions with others of our kind and even with other species.

And if, through our diets, we can learn to focus more on those *similarities* rather than our *differences*, we may foster a deeper sense of empathy—which could have powerful implications on how we treat one another.

Say a person comes to the conclusion that simply because chickens were born with wings rather than arms we ought not to cause their suffering. Say they begin eating fewer chickens, or none at all. In making that switch, that person has widened their circle of compassion. Now, how likely would it be for that person, with their newfound empathy toward another species entirely, to lack empathy for fellow humans who were born, say, gay instead of straight, black instead of white, female instead of male, Middle Eastern instead of American?

Indeed, being kind to animals can also make us kinder toward our fellow man. And conversely, people who are cruel to animals exhibit more dangerous and violent behaviors toward one another.

This is why law enforcement agencies like the FBI, police, and Department of Justice use cruelty to animals as a red flag when profiling violent criminals. One scientific study, published in the *Journal of Interpersonal Violence*, concluded that "animal abuse may be a red flag indicative of family violence in the home." In that study, a whopping 60 percent of participants who witnessed or took part in acts of animal cruelty as children also reported instances of child abuse or domestic violence.[21]

So imagine a world where our relationships with animals were based less on abuse and suffering and more on kindness and respect. In that world, our circle of compassion would include not only the dogs and cats in our homes but also the chickens, cows, pigs, and fish on farms. Imagine that throughout the day, as we decide what to eat, we constantly flex that compassion by making kind choices.

What impact could that constant compassion have on society? Racism, sexism, homophobia, xenophobia, war, hatred—the more empathy we have and exhibit toward others, the more these poisons could begin to fade away.

But at the end of the day, even if we make ourselves healthier, in body and in spirit, we can't have the type of better world so many of us envision and hope for without a healthy planet on which to build it—and it's clearer than ever that our planet is in peril.

Most people are familiar with the mother of all environmental disasters: climate change. Erratic weather, rising sea levels, extreme heat and cold—this catastrophe threatens nearly all life on earth. We're also losing rich, important ecosystems and biodiversity at an alarming rate, with up to one hundred thousand distinct species becoming extinct each year, according to the World Wildlife Fund.[22] Our waterways are being impacted, too: in 2013, the U.S. Environmental Protection Agency (EPA) found that the majority of rivers and streams in America are too polluted to support healthy aquatic life, with 55 percent of our waterways rated as being in "poor" condition and only 21 percent of rivers considered "healthy biological communities."[23]

Soil erosion, air pollution, overfishing, deforestation, water scarcity: The list of ways our earth is in jeopardy is virtually unending. For that reason, I've focused this book on the *environmental* implications of our food choices: because what we eat is not only a major factor in deciding what kind of world we live in, but also in what kind of world we live *on*. And it's become clear that meat-heavy diets are destroying the planet.

"We all need protein," points out a Bill Gates video titled *The Science Behind Plant-Based Proteins*. "But animals aren't the most efficient way to get it."[24]

In fact, producing just one pound of meat means feeding an animal up to fifteen pounds of grains and other crops.[25] That means growing massive amounts of feed, which often means destroying ancient forests to make room for farmland. It means spending huge quantities of fresh water to grow those crops.

Then we take those crops (which we've put all those resources into growing), process them, and feed them to the tens of billions of farm animals used each year in the global agricultural system—animals who themselves also require water to drink, land to live on, and other valuable inputs.

The caloric conversion is weak, too: according to a report produced in collaboration with the World Bank, even the most efficient sources of meat convert only around 11 percent of gross feed energy into human food.[26] That means that even in the best cases, nearly 90 percent of what we put into turning animals into meat is wasted.

It's an inefficient system that taxes our planet's finite resources in incredible ways.

So it's no surprise that the livestock sector is now a leading greenhouse gas emitter, estimated to account for more direct emissions than the entire global transport sector, according to the United Nations Food and Agriculture Organization.[27]

Our animal-heavy diet is also a major contributor to water degradation—impacting fish populations and polluting our global waterways. And it's an incredibly thirsty system, with hundreds of gallons of water needed to produce a single pound of chicken or glass of milk, and dozens of gallons needed to produce a single egg.[28]

This makes sense, considering the inherent inefficiencies that accompany a system in which we funnel massive amounts of grain and water through animals to produce protein, rather than converting plant matter to protein more directly. And they're precisely why global development and environmental advocates encourage a diet more focused on plants and less focused on animals.

"Eating plant-forward dishes can go a long way in reducing diet-related carbon emissions."[29]
—NATURAL RESOURCES DEFENSE COUNCIL (NRDC)

> "The more meat everybody eats, the more polluting it is and the more wasteful it is."[30]
> —BARACK OBAMA

"The reality is that it takes massive amounts of land, water, fertilizer, oil and other resources to produce meat," points out Oxfam America in an article promoting meat reduction. "Significantly more than it requires to grow other nutritious and delicious kinds of food."[31]

Less resource use, more efficient resource allocation, more compassion toward animals, spreading empathy to one another, curing and preventing our most serious health crises: plant-based eating, in so many ways, is the common denominator that can solve many of our planet's problems and create a truly better world.

This is what I came to understand so many years ago, after beginning my own journey with plant-based foods, and it's what I've been fortunate to spend my career working toward. As a professional food advocate, I've helped major food companies extend their corporate circles of compassion by demanding better treatment for farm animals in their supply chains—working with major brands like Burger King, McDonald's, and Walmart to move their suppliers in a more humane direction. I've also worked with the world's largest financial firms, which have invested hundreds of billions of dollars in animal agriculture, to leverage that power as a force for change. And I've worked with the food industry, consumers, and other advocates to share the myriad of benefits of eating more plants and less meat.

Of course, I'm not alone in this quest. Countless other individuals and organizations are spreading these concepts as well. And millions of people are catching on.

In its July 2015 article "Even Carnivores Are Putting More Fake Meat on Their Plates," NPR reported, "Consumers—and not just vegetarians—are also warming up to products like tempeh, tofu, and seitan that can stand in for meat."[32]

The meat industry has noticed. "Plant protein is in," reports *Meatingplace*—an industry magazine. Even Tyson Foods—one of world's largest meatpackers—has taken a stake in a plant-based chicken company and announced a $150 million venture capital firm to focus on plant-based proteins.

"Plant-based protein is growing almost, at this point, a little faster than animal-based," said Tyson's CEO in 2017. "So I think the migration may continue in that direction."[33]

Indeed, Americans are now featuring plant-based foods right smack dab in the center of our plates. And not just because doing so is healthier and better for the planet, but also because these foods taste great.

I've always loved ice cream, for example, but not until I adopted a plant-based diet did I know the joys of eating ice cream made from, say, coconut milk. I was floored the first time I tried buffalo wings made from cauliflower instead of chicken. The first time I sprinkled nutritional yeast—little yellow flakes that have a Parmesan-like flavor—on popcorn, it was like fireworks of flavor were going off in my mouth.

Indeed, once I started exploring this vibrant, rich, diverse array of plant-based foods that existed all around me, my long-standing interest in food only grew. What if my sister had never learned about antibiotics? What if she'd never become a vegetarian? I could have missed out on so much culinary variety, so many incredible foods that I now love and crave and get to enjoy every day.

Of course, one needn't go fully vegetarian or vegan to enjoy these foods. In addition to lessening our environmental footprint, being healthier for us, and avoiding animal abuse, simply incorporating *more* plant-based foods into our everyday diet can help expand our culinary repertoire and introduce us to all kinds of new tastes and flavors and textures.

And we needn't let the perfect be the enemy of the good. Eating for a better world doesn't have to be an all-or-nothing endeavor. Certainly it's true that locally grown, minimally processed, whole, plant-based foods like organic produce and lentils have the least eco-impact of any foods we might choose to eat. But we needn't eat *only* those foods to make a difference. Of course, to keep up any kind of diet—be it for health or the environment—we must find that diet to be attainable and *personally* sustainable. After all, the most effective diet is always the one we stick with.

So while frozen plant-based nuggets are certainly not quite as healthy or environmentally friendly as, say, locally grown lentils, they're far better than chicken nuggets. A prepackaged black bean burger is not a zero-footprint product by any means, but it's much lighter on the planet and our bodies than a hamburger. Yes, almond milk requires land and water and other resources to produce, but compared to cow's milk? No contest.

So do what works for you—what tastes good and is attainable and sustainable in your daily life. Try "flexitarian" approaches like Meatless Mondays. Try doing VB6 (eating vegan before six p.m., the approach suggested by author Mark Bittman). Try simply moving meat from the center of the plate to the side of the plate.

And try new foods! Explore the rich array of colorful produce and interesting, delicious plant-based offerings now available at every turn. On this planet-in-peril—with all the ecological, biological, and sociological problems plaguing our world at so many levels—the more we each recognize that the solutions to these problems can be found in our food, the better off we'll all be. **The power is on our plates— let's use it.** 🌿

"Anchoring a plate with a massive hunk of animal protein is so last century."[34]
—WALL STREET JOURNAL

PART ONE:

OUR PLANET

"The future is about a plant-based diet."[35]

—JAMIE OLIVER

EARTH

Imagine the Earth, spinning in orbit: our 197-million-square-mile, four-and-a-half-billion-year-old ball of nitrogen, oxygen, and carbon amid the quiet blackness of space.

But Earth is much more than that.

●

Zoom in through the outermost thermosphere, through the stratosphere, through the clouds. Pass over the North Pole's stark ice caps. Glide over Siberia, covered in snow-capped pine and birch trees. Watch the landscape move from white to green throughout Eurasia—over Kazakhstan, Uzbekistan—then to browns above the Middle East and northern Africa, and to blue over the Atlantic Ocean. Pass over New York City's gray skyscrapers, through the Shenandoahs, their chestnut and red oaks' brilliant shades of orange and yellow, and across the mighty Mississippi. Now slow yourself above the Midwest, above Missouri. Finally, pause above the tiny town of Arrow Rock—a pixel on the planet.

It's here in Arrow Rock, Missouri, where Day and Whitney Kerr bought a Greek Revival cottage, a fixer-upper. That was in 1980, long before they could have known that purchase would turn their own story into one of an epic battle for their land and livelihoods, for the literal earth beneath their feet.

"It was in terrible shape," said Day, who, along with his wife, purchased and restored the home to its former 1860s glory. "It never had indoor plumbing or central heating. No one had lived there for thirteen years. There were times when we thought we were just crazy, but Whitney and I are both committed to historic preservation. We respect history."[36]

And Arrow Rock's got history everywhere one looks: for over a half century, the *entire town* has been registered as a National Historic Landmark. It was in Arrow Rock that Dr. John Sappington—whose home the Kerrs also restored—created the quinine pill; it was there that the Santa Fe Trail and Missouri River intersected, where lauded Missouri River artist George Caleb Bingham lived and worked.

It was also where, in 2007, hog farmer Dennis Gessling proposed building a massive factory farm that would confine nearly five thousand pigs—ninety animals for each of the town's fifty-six residents[37]—and produce more than two million gallons of waste each year.[38]

And he wanted to build it just a quarter mile north of the Kerrs' home.

"This is a historic site for the state and nation," said local bed-and-breakfast owner Kathy Borgman. "This is a spot where history was made. You can't move it. Who would want to come here if the air stinks so bad you cannot breathe it?"[39]

All across the country, communities are threatened by confined animal feeding operations (CAFOs) like the one proposed by Gessling.

"Factory farms can negatively affect rural historic areas in a number of ways," writes Jennifer Sandy of the National Trust for Historic Preservation.[40] "CAFOs obviously have an immediate and negative impact on the historic rural landscape. They are large in scale, housing thousands of animals, and generally consist of utilitarian metal buildings and manure retaining ponds."

In these facilities, animals are confined by the thousands, tens of thousands, or even hundreds of thousands. In the case of pig-production facilities like the one proposed in Arrow Rock, breeding animals are most often confined inside individual gestation crates—metal cages that are essentially the same length and width of the pigs' own bodies, preventing them from even turning around. These animals endure this confinement day and night for four months, while pregnant. As they're about to give birth, they're moved into another, similar, type of crate—after which they're reimpregnated and put back in a gestation crate for the cycle to repeat. A mother pig lives like this for her entire four years on this earth.

These types of facilities are dramatically changing the American landscape, which was once dotted with more traditional-type farms—indeed, what most of us imagine when we think of a *farm*.

Today, those idyllic places are mostly gone—and that's no accident.

"Forget the pig is an animal—treat him just like a machine in a factory," recommended *Hog Farm Management* magazine in 1976. Two years later, *National Hog Farmer* advised: "The breeding sow should be thought of, and treated, as a valuable piece of machinery whose function is to pump out baby pigs like a sausage machine."

And so it was that factory farms were born—leaving a lasting mark on animals, our planet, our nation, and on individual communities.

"As small- and medium-sized producers are forced out," Sandy reports, "many historic farm structures are abandoned or demolished. Areas with factory farms also often see an increase in truck traffic, which can have visual and auditory impacts."

Tascosa Feedyard, Bushland, Texas (2013). Courtesy the artist and Bruce Silverstein Gallery, New York. CREDIT: MISHKA HENNER

> "Raising meat takes a great deal of land and... has a substantial environmental impact."[41]
> —BILL GATES

The citizens of Arrow Rock, Missouri were not going to have it in their backyard.

"These CAFOs spend as little money as they have to get as much money as they can out of the animal," Day Kerr observes. "In the process, they do not protect the environment and have no regard for how they impact their neighbors."[42]

So the Kerrs and their neighbors banded together and stood their ground, raising a stink with local and state governments about the proposed pig factory.

They incorporated as Citizens to Protect State Parks and Historic Sites. They formed alliances with other communities being impacted by CAFOs. They hired lawyers. They demanded reviews from the U.S. Department of Interior (since Arrow Rock is a national historic landmark). They generated press coverage and statewide buzz. They filed lawsuits—including against the Missouri Department of Natural Resources and its director.

And they won. After a prolonged battle, the people of Arrow Rock—resting stop for Lewis and Clark, and a town nearly crippled by a massive pig factory—claimed victory when Gessling officially withdrew his plans.

But things could have easily gone the other way.

In 2016, years after the controversy had been settled, I spoke to Kathy Borgman. She expressed concern that the same threat Gessling posed to her community still exists elsewhere.

"What we accomplished in Arrow Rock was successful in one regard," Borgman says. "But the CAFO problem continues all over Missouri, all over the country."[43]

Indeed, elsewhere across the entire *planet*, factory farms continue wreaking havoc on the earth beneath us.

In fact, globally, animal agribusiness is by far the single largest user of land, according to the United Nations Food and Agriculture Organization (FAO) report *Livestock's Long Shadow*.[44] "In all, livestock production accounts for 70 percent of all agricultural land and 30 percent of the land surface of the planet," found the FAO.

WHAT EXACTLY *IS* A FACTORY FARM?

Factory farm refers to industrial farm animal production. Other terms—like *concentrated animal feeding operation* (CAFO) and *animal feeding operation* (AFO)—have legal definitions. "AFOs congregate animals, feed, manure and urine, dead animals, and production operations on a small land area," describes the EPA. An AFO may be designated as a CAFO if it's considered "large" or "medium" or through special designation by the EPA. Regardless of terminology, these are all places where thousands or tens of thousands of animals live—often crammed together or confined in cages—and where environmental problems persist.

FROM THE HORSE'S MOUTH . . .

"I moved from Switzerland in 1983, to my part of Missouri because of the wide-open spaces and clean environment. When Premium Standard Farms purchased four thousand acres next to my farm in 1993, I knew nothing about the company. But when I heard about the type of hog facility that they were intending to build there, I immediately opposed them. The facility next to my property has an eighty thousand hog-head capacity, which is replaced 2.8 times a year. This facility and others nearby generate so much waste that they have turned our land into waste-handling facilities, which is an immoral and unethical way to use the land.

I can't describe how terrible the odor from the lagoons, spray fields, and barns often is. We can't keep our windows open, and sometimes you can even smell the odor through the shut windows. You open the door and the smell almost knocks you over. One of the worst parts of it is that the odor hits at unpredictable times so it is a constant threat. Breathing in such a terrible stench makes you feel desperate. One time I was planting soybeans on a field and I got so sick to my stomach that I had to stop planting. My wife has allergies, which are aggravated by the odor. She is in the health field, and she believes that many of her patients are also suffering from worse allergies from the hog odor. A year or so ago, I went on vacation to a beautiful national park; when I entered my house upon my return and smelled the terrible odor, I broke down and cried.

"As farmers and human inhabitants of this planet, we are but caretakers of what has been given to us. The tree in front of my house will be here long after I am gone. Every tree I plant will be for my grandchildren to enjoy. Everything I destroy will be gone forever. So will it be with the land."[45]

—ROLF CHRISTEN, GREEN CITY, MISSOURI

That's right: nearly a third of *all the land on the planet* goes toward producing protein from animals. And that production isn't happening in deserts and on craggy cliffs that might otherwise go unused.

So, leaving Arrow Rock and the Midwest on our global journey, we head southeast—over the Gulf of Mexico and western tip of Cuba, across the brilliant blue Caribbean Sea, eventually finding ourselves in perhaps the epicenter of factory farming's earthly impact: the Amazon rain forest.

Seventy percent of previously forested land in the Amazon is now pasture for farm animals, with animal feed crops covering a large part of the remainder.[46] There's no example in Earth's history of old-growth and primary forestland being more quickly converted to human land use.[47]

In the southeastern Amazon, more than half the woodland-savannah ecosystem of the Cerrado has already been converted to agriculture, mostly for the production of meat and animal feed.[48] And three countries away, in Costa Rica, roughly half the small nation's tropical forest land is now used for meat production.[49] The list goes on: in Africa, Southeast Asia, and elsewhere across the globe, we're losing rich, diverse ecosystems on account of our meat-heavy diets.[50, 51]

"The consumption of animal-sourced food products by humans is one of the most powerful negative forces affecting the conservation of terrestrial ecosystems and biological diversity," reports a study published in *Science of the Total Environment*.[52] That's habitat loss for wild animals and native plant species, soil loss, water and nutrient pollution, and more.

If our diets don't change, things will get worse. Some countries, that same report found, may even require up to *50 percent increases* in land used for meat production.[53]

So how much land does it take, exactly, to produce meat for our diets? Looking squarely at the land impact of *American* meat consumption, researchers from Bard College, the Weizmann Institute of Science, and Yale University found that the animal-based portion of an average American's diet requires over *150,000 square feet* of crop and pasture land annually—that's nearly the area of three NFL football fields used to produce meat, eggs, and dairy for each one of us, each year.[54]

But the good news is, there's a solution. No, we don't all need to do as Day and Whitney Kerr, Kathy Borgman, and the other citizens of Arrow Rock, Missouri, did: we don't each need to take up legal and public battles against individual factory-farm operations.

But we can certainly stop funding the perpetrators.

After all, though Arrow Rock managed to stave off its proposed factory farm, unless we curb our reliance on animal products—by eating more plant-based foods—other communities across the world won't be so lucky.

"They tell you we've got more money than God and will outspend you and outlast you," laments Borgman, referring to the power of industrial agriculture. "So it'll be the tide of the markets and the tide of masses to really change things."[55]

But how does each of us play a part in that growing tide? One way for us to help is dietary—and delicious. Many people are now practicing the "Three Rs" of eating: 1) reducing meat and other animal products in their diets by 2) replacing those products with plant-based foods, and 3) refining our diets so as to avoid products from factory farms.

THE **THREE Rs** OF EATING FOR A BETTER PLANET

1 REDUCE our consumption of meat, dairy, eggs, and other animal-based foods.

2 REPLACE animal-based foods in our diet with plant-based foods.

3 REFINE any animal products we consume by avoiding foods from factory farms.

Cutting down forest land near Ecuador's Napo River in order to grow more livestock feed. CREDIT: TOMAS MUNITA/CIFOR

We can enjoy more black bean burgers and fewer beef burgers, bean-and-rice burritos instead of chicken burritos, BBQ seitan or tofu instead of pulled pork, chick*pea* salad instead of chick*en* salad. We can try almond milk, soy milk, coconut milk, or any other variety of the myriad of nondairy alternatives now available at coffee shops and grocery stores nationwide.

We can participate in programs like Meatless Mondays—enjoying the time-honored tradition of a once-weekly vacation from meat. In fact, it was the U.S. Food Administration that created Meatless Mondays over a century ago to save resources during WWI. The effort

Deforestation vs. the Amazon CREDIT: GREENPEACE/RICARDO BELIEL

70% The amount of Earth's agricultural land used for livestock production.

30% The amount of all Earth's land mass used for livestock.

Three Football Fields The amount of land needed per person each year to sustain the animal-based portion of a standard diet.

50% The amount each of us can decrease our diet-related land use by eating more plant-based foods.

DIRT FIRST!
SHEDDING SOIL BY THE TON

BY DANIEL IMHOFF

Agricultural production is the largest source of soil erosion in the United States, with 90 percent of croplands shedding soil above rates that are sustainable for the long term. Since the majority of the nation's cropland is used for growing animal feed, high rates of soil erosion are a direct consequence of industrial animal food production. By squandering the very foundation of agriculture itself—productive soil—animal factory farming is compromising the ability of future generations to meet their needs.

According to the United Nations Food and Agriculture Organization, the world is losing an equivalent of 10 to 15 million acres of farmland through erosion each year. This is a land area the size of Belgium and the Netherlands combined. Some experts argue that soil loss is humanity's most serious environmental challenge.

Each year, the United States loses nearly two billion tons of soil, making farmlands less fertile and setting off a cascade of destructive consequences. The loss of just a few centimeters of topsoil can reduce the productivity of good soils by 40 percent and that of poorer soils by 60 percent. With the flight of bare soil through wind or rain erosion go valuable organic matter and nutrients needed to grow healthy plants. The ability for soil to absorb, retain, and filter water also drastically declines. Estimates just to replace those nutrients and pump more water onto farmlands due to soil loss are over $30 billion per year.

Increasing demands for cattle feed and corn-based ethanol are putting even more strain on already overstressed farmland. Farmers are foregoing rotations of soybeans (which provide more soil protection) to grow more corn. And to grow corn they are moving land out of the USDA Conservation Reserve Program (CRP), a decades-old economic incentive program that has been fairly successful in protecting marginal soils from the plow.

—FROM *CAFO: THE TRAGEDY OF INDUSTRIAL ANIMAL FACTORIES*

"The nation that destroys its soil destroys itself."[56]
—FRANKLIN D. ROOSEVELT

LIVESTOCK & LAND

Turning animals into food requires enormous amounts of land—to grow the crops to feed the animals, and for the animals themselves to live on.

DEFORESTATION: Rainforests, like the Amazon, are leveled.

➡

CROPS: Forests are replaced with crops grown for animal feed.

➡

ANIMALS: If not used for crops, razed forestland is converted to animal grazing ground.

was brought back during WWII, and then revived in 2003 by the Johns Hopkins School of Public Health as a wellness and sustainability initiative. Countless individuals and even entire school districts (like Houston, Los Angeles, Detroit, and more) are now participating, and the idea has spread like wildfire across colleges, universities, hospital systems, and more.

These types of small actions can make a huge difference. In its 2016 report *Shifting Diets for a Sustainable Food Future*, the World Resources Institute found that by reducing animal protein intake in regions that currently consume the most, like the United States, per-person diet-related land use could be nearly *cut in half*.[57]

Considering the impact factory farming has made and continues to make, the importance of a 50 percent reduction in our diet-related land use can't be underestimated. At this very moment, the Amazon continues burning to accommodate our meat-heavy diets. Right now, communities like Arrow Rock are pushing back against land grabs by would-be factory farmers. Farms are shutting down, replaced with factories. Rural landscapes across the country and world are being industrialized—forever changed because of our diets.

The evidence is clear: for the earth beneath and all around us—composed of rich, varied, important ecosystems and communities—we've all simply got to eat less meat and more plants. 🌱

SLAUGHTER: Those animals are trucked to slaughterhouses.

➡

RETAIL: Their products are trucked to grocery stores and restaurants.

➡

HOME: Where they end up on our plates.

"Many of us feel helpless in the face of environmental challenges, and it can be hard to know how to sort through the advice about what we can do to make a meaningful contribution to a cleaner, more sustainable, healthier world. Having one designated meat-free day a week is a meaningful change that everyone can make, that goes to the heart of several important political, environmental, and ethical issues all at once."[58]

—PAUL MCCARTNEY

Cows grazing on land that used to be forest in Rio Branco, Brazil. CREDIT: KATE EVANS/CIFOR

"Diversify Your Diet. Try to eat an all-veggie meal . . . instead of one meat meal a week. More natural resources are used to provide meat than plants." [59]

—THE UNITED NATIONS FOOD & AGRICULTURE ORGANIZATION

IN A NUTSHELL

- Factory farms are destroying national and global landscapes and communities.

- The introduction of large-scale CAFOs negatively impacts communities' livelihoods and well-being.

- Historic areas and structures are being replaced with large-scale agricultural operations.

- Our alarming loss of soil due to animal agriculture is making farmlands less fertile.

- Producing animal proteins requires huge inputs of land—for the animals, their feed, and more.

- The Amazon is disappearing day by day to make room for more animal feed-crop production.

- This is a major change in the landscape, and also loss of habitat for many native species.

Now for the good news! Eating more plant-based proteins can help us each use less land for our diet, avoid destroying rain forests like the Amazon, and preserve local communities and landscapes. Of course, all types of agriculture alter landscapes, and there is no catchall solution, but plant-based food production tends to be less invasive than factory farms. A simple dietary shift can play a big role in protecting the earth beneath us.

WATER

Continuing our global journey, imagine leaving Arrow Rock, Missouri, and heading east. Pass over the Missouri River, then the Mississippi, their muddy waters flowing south. Pass over Illinois's Carlyle Lake—a 26,000-acre reservoir—and Indiana's Wabash River. Head north, then east again, along the coast of Lake Erie. Take notice of all the communities, from rural towns to major cities, built near these rivers and lakes, so settlers would have clean, reliable sources of water for drinking, bathing, and farming—for sustaining life. Finally, slow yourself over upstate New York's Finger Lakes region, and pause above one of those communities: the small town of Willet, nestled along the banks of the Ostelic River.

●

It was there in Willet, just a few days after Christmas 2008, that twenty-five-year-old Cody Carlson found himself hunched over, scraping frozen cow feces off a thick steel cable.

Carlson grew up in Manhattan, though he had been living in Santa Cruz, earning his degree in community studies from the University of California. Back on the California beaches, it would have been hard to imagine his current position: an undercover factory-farm investigator working for an animal protection organization, freezing his ass off on a massive dairy complex.

After graduating, Carlson landed a job at a Manhattan-based firm that conducts investigative research for corporations. There, he spent much of his time in the firm's pro bono division, offering free services to nonprofits. He'd been reaching out to environmental agencies he thought could use his services when, on the news, he learned about an animal cruelty exposé conducted by the group Mercy For Animals (MFA). Carlson, a vegetarian since the age of thirteen, was intrigued. He got in touch.

"I remember e-mailing them and basically asking if they'd like some free research from us," recalls Carlson.[60] But what the MFA could really use, they told him, was a full-time undercover investigator.

Next thing he knew, he was quitting his job in the city, putting his belongings into storage, and driving upstate in search of work on a factory farm. After an unsuccessful attempt at getting hired at an egg-producing CAFO, Carlson saw a job posting for a "maintenance technician" at Willet Dairy in Locke, New York—nestled in the state's picturesque Finger Lakes region.

Though, as Carlson would learn, Willet Dairy was anything *but* picturesque.

The company's 7,800 cows[61] allowed it to ship about 40,000 gallons of milk every day.[62] Those cows also produced roughly 314 *million* pounds of manure in 2006, according to New York's Department of Environmental Conservation.[63] That's equal, in weight, to almost 78,000 Ford F-150 trucks—from just one dairy facility in one state in one year.[64]

It's a lot of waste—and helping manage it all was central to Carlson's role at the complex.

"When I went in for my interview, really the only substantive question they asked me was if I thought I could handle being ankle-deep in shit all day," he recalls. "'It's not a job for everyone,' they said."

During that interview, farm managers took Carlson on a walk-through to ensure he'd be up for the task.

"That was when I saw how these cows live—basically standing in overcrowded concrete aisles all day long, hock-deep in their own waste," he recounts. "Twice a day, they'd be moved out to a separate area, where they'd be hooked up to machines for milking. After that, they were brought back into the concrete aisles. That's basically their whole lives."

It was in those aisles where Carlson spent most of his time undercover as a farm "technician," documenting this routine abuse.

"Yeah, it was a generous title," says Cody with a laugh. "Basically, you've got all these cows standing there letting loose all day. There's an engine that pulls a V-shaped metal device along a steel cable to collect the manure. Eventually, it's pumped down to these massive lagoons that are basically poop ponds."

His job was primarily to fix the pulling and pumping system as it broke—which happened a lot.

"The cable would fray and hit the cows. It'd get clogged up. It'd freeze. We'd have to scrape the frozen feces off and un-jam the thing—basically like unclogging a gigantic toilet," said Carlson. "It was always something different."

And not just for Carlson.

"I can't even get a friggin' clean glass of water," said neighbor Karen Strecker, who described turning on her faucets only to find liquid manure pouring out. "I've been taking a bath and actually had cow shit pour into the tub," she said. "It's nasty." [65]

And not just to see and smell. For years, Strecker was consistently dosed with antibiotics to treat illnesses caused by her exposure to Willet's waste.

"Do people get sick when manure gets spread?" Strecker's doctor, Ahmad Mehdi, asked rhetorically. "Yes, it's a fact," he said. "When you have ten thousand cows in one place, that's a lot of manure." [66]

Across the country, factory farms house all this manure in massive lagoons, like those at Willet. And those lagoons are often close to rivers, lakes, tributaries, and other waterways, increasing the chances they'll harm local ecosystems and water supplies.

North Carolina has been ground zero for this problem.

On September 16, 1999, Hurricane Floyd struck Cape Fear, along the state's coast, with 105 mph winds. Floyd flooded pig waste lagoons, unleashing millions of gallons of waste into nearby waterways. [67] The county's environmental health director at the time reported that nearly one in ten private wells in the area—families' drinking water—tested positive for fecal bacteria in the storm's wake. [68]

As it was, the Cape Fear area already had much to be afraid of from factory farms: a few years earlier, in New Hanover County, 2 million gallons of liquid hog waste from a lagoon spilled into a Cape Fear River tributary. [69] Then a hole in a Duplin County pig waste lagoon spilled another 1.5 million gallons of manure and urine into a swamp adjoining the Persimmon Branch—also a tributary of the river. [70] In Jones County, 1 million gallons of liquid hog waste spilled into the Trent River. [71] And in Sampson County, nearly 200,000 gallons spilled into Turkey Creek. [72]

Travel across the country and you see a similar trail—or stream—of aquatic destruction: About 1,000 miles northwest of Cape Fear—near Elmwood, Illinois—a dairy operator pumped 2 million gallons of waste from his 40 *million–gallon* lagoon into a ravine, draining into Kickapoo Creek and killing local fish populations; [73, 74] only 250 miles away, a massive spill in Missouri killed *all aquatic life* in an 11-mile stretch of Mussel Fork Creek; [75] about 1,800 miles southwest from there—in Oakdale, California—Pete Hetinga of 3H Dairy Farm admitted that over the course of four years, he had discharged wastewater polluted with cow urine and feces into streams that flow into the Tuolumne River and Sacramento Delta; [76] and roughly 800 miles north of Oakdale, in Washington, two factory farms dumped the *entire contents* of their lagoons, spilling a total of 2 million gallons of manure, near the Yakima River—*in the same week.*

Like the one Cody Carlson worked at, dairy complexes often pollute waterways and threaten communities. CREDIT: JO-ANNE MCARTHUR/WE ANIMALS

> "For every pound of beef produced in the industrial system, it takes two thousand gallons of water. That is a lot of water, and there is plenty of evidence that the Earth cannot keep up with the demand."[77]
>
> —PRINCE CHARLES, FROM HIS *FUTURE OF FOOD* SPEECH

And of course, as the saying goes, all rivers flow to the sea—including those flooded with toxic waste.

After Hurricane Floyd, the tens of millions of gallons of escaped manure—plus tens of thousands of dead pigs who'd drowned inside factory farms—rushed into the Atlantic Ocean's Pamlico Sound, resulting in a "dead zone" hundreds of miles wide.

A dead zone is an area of water where oxygen has been choked out, and thus oxygen-dependent life dies;[78] they're caused by pollution, like from factory farms—and they can be massive.

In 2015, the Gulf dead zone encompassed nearly 6,500 square miles; 2002's record-breaking 8,400-square-mile dead zone could have fit North *and* South Carolina inside it.[79]

At the same time runoff and spills from factory farms inland are crippling our nation's waterways and creeping into the ocean, much farther out at sea, our (meat-heavy) diets are also having a negative impact.

"Of all the threats facing the oceans today, overfishing takes the greatest toll on sea life," reports the Environmental Defense Fund.[80] A whopping 2.7 trillion fish are estimated to be taken from our oceans each year[81]— that's more than thirty times the number of all chickens, pigs, cows, goats, sheep, and other livestock farmed globally each year combined.

So it's no surprise that one study published in the journal *Science* predicts that by 2048, *all the world's fisheries* will have collapsed.[82]

This loss of fish life is devastating in its own right. These trillions of creatures may be dissimilar from pets and other animals we've come to personally know, but they're certainly smart, social beings.

Dr. Culum Brown at Macquarie University's Department of Biological Sciences knows this firsthand. He spent much of his childhood tagging along with his father in Southeast Asia. "Much of that time I was in the water snorkeling," he told me. "It doesn't take much to inspire a kid, and the underwater world was just awesome to me. I never looked back."

Today, Dr. Brown is a professor at Macquarie University's Department of Biological Sciences, specializing in the behavioral ecology and evolution of fishes. "Fish are more intelligent than they appear," he says. "In many areas, such as memory, their cognitive powers match or exceed those of 'higher' vertebrates, including nonhuman primates."[83]

And even putting the fish themselves aside, the seafood trade is also complicit in killing other marine animals—considered "by-catch."

Globally, commercial fishing enterprises ravage the oceans for their "target" catch—like tuna—by dragging massive nets through the sea.[84] In the process, these indiscriminating nets also scoop up innumerable other animals.[85]

"Hundreds of thousands of marine mammals are injured or killed every year by fishermen around the world," reports NPR, because of "our taste for seafood."[86]

ENVIRONMENTAL WORKING GROUP PRESIDENT KEN COOK

Some of my earliest experiences with food production came as a young kid when I spent summers working on my uncle's cattle ranch in Missouri. I then went on to study agriculture at the University of Missouri, where I received my master's in soil science. Since then, I've spent much of my career focused on farm and food policy.

When I started EWG in 1993, our focus was on food. Agriculture is the leading cause of water pollution in this country, for example, and factory farms are one of the leading reasons. EWG recently mapped all the CAFO operations in North Carolina and we estimate that these CAFOs produce more than 10 billion gallons of wet animal waste alone every year.

If we're going to get serious about addressing water pollution, we're going to need to recognize that meat production, globally, is a leading factor. Here at home, Americans eat too much meat. We consume 60 percent more meat than Europeans, and we need to adjust our expectations of how much meat we should be eating way down, and eat less meat and cheese, period.

Throughout my career, I've done my best to raise public awareness and outrage over the disastrous impacts large-scale agriculture has on our water systems and environment. And as each year passes, the sense of urgency only escalates.

With the rise of China and other big, emerging economies, there is a much greater demand for meat, which means more of the world's waterways will be polluted. However, there is good news to highlight, too. Never before have there been so many companies, organizations, and citizens mobilized around the various issues of food production and factory farming and how the industry adversely impacts the environment. And coupled with the power of social media and other tactics to harness and forge pressure, there is a real opportunity for organizations like EWG, its supporters and forward-thinking companies alike to bring about significant and positive changes in the way our food is produced.

Ken Cook is one of the environmental field's most influential critics of industrial agriculture. Under his leadership, EWG has pioneered digital technologies to expose the harm done by misconceived crop subsidies and runaway agricultural pollution, and empowered American families with easy-to-use tools to eat better, healthier, and more sustainably. Cook is a board member (and founding chairman) of Food Policy Action, Organic Voices, and the Amazon Conservation Team, and a former member of the board of the Organic Center.

A catfish factory farm in Louisiana. CREDIT: SCOTT BAUER/USDA

A Natural Resources Defense Council study confirms that over 650,000 aquatic mammals are unintentionally killed each year in the global seafood trade—including New Zealand sea lions, several different whale species, porpoises, dolphins, and more.[87]

Unfortunately, one way the industry has begun tackling this problem is, misguidedly, through aquaculture: fish factory farms.

Picture a major dairy farm or a pig complex: animals packed next to one another, barely able to move, and producing huge amounts of waste. That's aquaculture—and it's the fastest growing form of animal farming on the planet.[88]

Aquaculture operations can either be established inland—using gigantic tanks—or in open waters, using a netting system instead.

In 2013, 155 *billion* pounds of these factory-farmed fish were produced.[89] That's the equivalent of almost 350,000 Statues of Liberty.[90]

And these fish factories come with their own set of ecological disasters.

For one, they often *use* more fish than they produce—by feeding fish to the fish they're farming. It sounds like a tongue twister, and is certainly twisted. It means that even if eating *farmed* fish, one is likely still contributing to all the problems associated with *wild-caught* fish, since wild-caught fish may be used as feed in aquaculture.

These operations can be highly damaging in other ways, too.

"Open net-cage salmon farming," for example, "is currently one of the most harmful aquaculture production systems and poses environmental threats in all

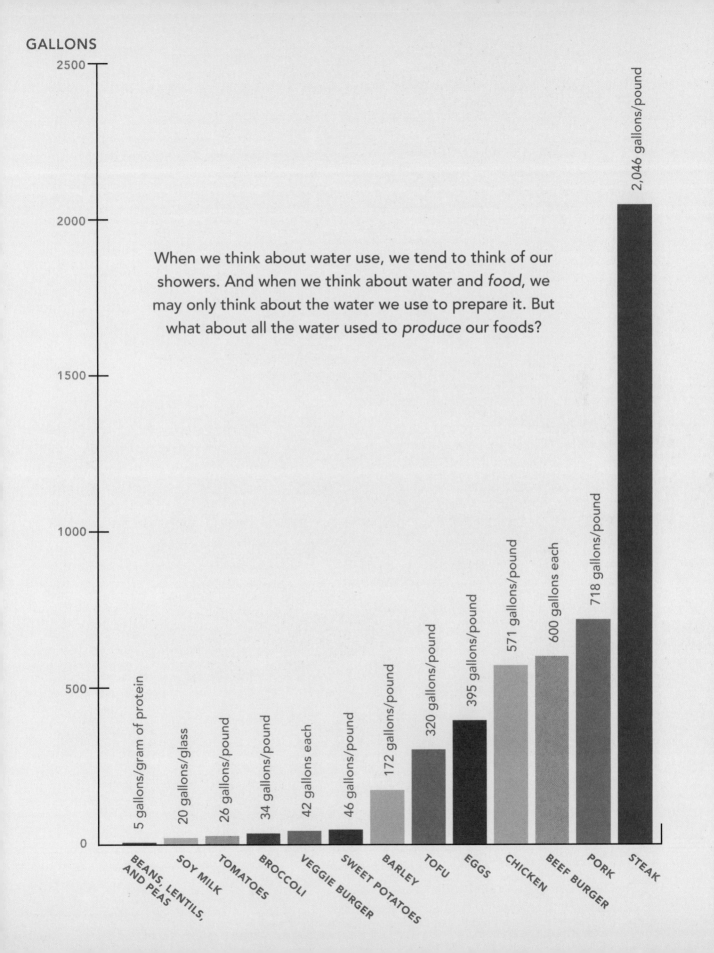

GALLONS

When we think about water use, we tend to think of our showers. And when we think about water and *food*, we may only think about the water we use to prepare it. But what about all the water used to *produce* our foods?

- BEANS, LENTILS, AND PEAS — 5 gallons/gram of protein
- SOY MILK — 20 gallons/glass
- TOMATOES — 26 gallons/pound
- BROCCOLI — 34 gallons/pound
- VEGGIE BURGER — 42 gallons each
- SWEET POTATOES — 46 gallons/pound
- BARLEY — 172 gallons/pound
- TOFU — 320 gallons/pound
- EGGS — 395 gallons/pound
- CHICKEN — 571 gallons/pound
- BEEF BURGER — 600 gallons each
- PORK — 718 gallons/pound
- STEAK — 2,046 gallons/pound

"They may breathe with gills instead of lungs and move with fins instead of feet, but fishes are every bit as intelligent, complex, and social as other animals we may be more familiar with, like dogs and cats."[91]

—JONATHAN BALCOMBE, NEW YORK TIMES–BESTSELLING AUTHOR OF *WHAT A FISH KNOWS: THE INNER LIVES OF OUR UNDERWATER COUSINS*

regions it is practiced," writes the Coastal Alliance for Aquaculture Reform.[92]

Those threats include sea lice (marine parasites that can kill wild fish), algae blooms (which can release toxins into the water), high concentrations of waste—which may be laced with antibiotics—left on the ocean floor, and alien species being introduced into native waters.[93]

So whether on one of the world's many fish factory farms or out in the open seas—it's clear that the over-consumption of animal proteins is unleashing environmental disasters.

That is, of course, unless we continue shifting our diets toward more *plant-based* foods—which is exactly what Cody Carlson would like to see.

It's been more than seven years since Carlson ended his undercover investigation into Willet. In that time, the wind has indeed blown the buying public away from meat, seafood, and dairy—and toward consuming more plants.

"Growing up in New York City, you know, I was raised on food like pizza and pastrami," he says. "I've been vegetarian for almost twenty years now, and the last few years have definitely been, in my opinion, the best time for meat-free options."

Carlson chalks up the increase in those options to the general public shifting more toward plant-forward fare. That added demand is already taking a bite out of factory farms.

"With plant-based diets all the rage in the U.S. currently, milk alternatives—and particularly those from almonds—are seeing strong sales growth and increased innovation, while sales of dairy milk are contracting," reports *Food Navigator*.[94] "In the past five years, sales of almond milk have grown 250 percent to more than $894.6 million . . . [while] the total milk market shrunk by more than $1 billion."

"It's inspiring," says Carlson, of this growth in the plant-based food sector. "When I was working in that hellhole, it was easy to lose hope. But plant-based eating has just become so popular in the last few years. I think about everyone, everywhere, impacted by these factory farms. More people are going to continue making this shift—I know it. Now I've got nothing *but* hope for the future."

A diver for the Philippine fishing vessel *Vergene* at work in and around a skipjack tuna purse seine net.
CREDIT: ALEX HOFFORD/GREENPEACE

"The factory meat industry has polluted thousands of miles of America's rivers, killed billions of fish, pushed tens of thousands of family farmers off their land, sickened and killed . . . U.S. citizens, and treated millions of animals with unspeakable and unnecessary cruelty."[95]
—ROBERT F. KENNEDY JR.

Netted fish off the coast of South Africa. Global fish stocks are collapsing due to seafood-heavy diets.
CREDIT: MATTHEW PRESCOTT

IN A NUTSHELL

- Factory-farm waste causes massively contaminated runoff.

- Storm water can mix with animal waste, carrying it into our rivers and oceans.

- Growing huge quantities of grain and corn to feed animals uses vast amounts of water.

- It can take hundreds of gallons of water to produce a single pound of meat.

- The oceans are being destroyed by seafood overconsumption.

- By 2048, all the world's fisheries could collapse.

- Trawling vessels rip aquatic mammals, sea turtles, coral reefs, and more from the oceans.

- Fish farms may use more fish to feed their fish than the total amount of fish they produce.

- Open-net fish farms may introduce dangerous alien species to the waters in which they operate.

Now for the good news! Eating more plant-based foods can help us tread lighter when it comes to water pollution and overuse. We of course need to use water to produce all foods, but producing plant-based foods is far less water-intensive (plus, no waste lagoons!), and eating less seafood can help us take a bite out of overfishing and destructive fish farming.

Planned
FOR CAFO

— Pine Acres
idential Community

roposed
ken Houses

Wildwood Residential
Development

Sealick
Road

Sealick
Road

Meadow Bridge Road

1 MILE   2 MILE   3 MILE

AIR

Leaving upstate New York on our quest, imagine heading south—across Pennsylvania's Pinchot Forest, across the Delaware River—to the Delmarva Peninsula: a 200-mile-long, 80-mile-wide peninsula wedged between the Chesapeake Bay and the Atlantic Ocean.

●

The Delmarva is almost a world unto itself. Herds of wild horses run on the peninsula's pristine beaches. Its fourteen-thousand-acre Chincoteague National Wildlife Refuge is home to elk and red foxes and ponies and pelicans. Historic farmhouses, quaint communities, cotton fields, and vineyards dot the landscape as you drive north from Virginia Beach into Maryland, then Delaware, up toward Philadelphia.

But life on the Delmarva isn't exactly what it seems.

"We're under attack," said resident Lisa Inzerillo. "I'm afraid to even go outside."[96]

Lisa and her husband, Joe, live on land that's been part of their family for four generations, since Lisa's great-grandparents first built there in 1875. Smack in the middle of the peninsula, between Assateague Island National Seashore to the east and Tangier Sound to the west, the Princess Anne, Maryland, property was idyllic.

In 2010, Lisa and Joe built a new home there. They dug a pond in the back for wildlife, built a small carriage house off to the side. They'd sit out back and relax on their little slice of paradise, breathing in the country air. It was, in a word, perfect. "That is, until about three years ago," Joe told me when I visited them in 2017, "when the chicken factories starting popping up."

It's those chicken factories—and the harmful, putrid gases they emit into the neighborhood's air—that cause Lisa and Joe to live in such fear.

Nowadays, Lisa and Joe are surrounded by dozens upon dozens of these industrial poultry complexes: a mile and a half south is one complex with thirty massive chicken sheds; a mile north, off Peggy Neck Road, there are another nine; three miles southwest, there are yet another nine. The list goes on.

Picture driving through your average American small town—modest split-level and ranch homes with front lawns, one after another, kids' toys in the front yards. But now picture that every fourth or fifth plot is not a house, but a mega poultry farm confining tens of thousands of birds—mixed right in with the homes.

Many of the farms, if you can call them that, are muddy and overgrown. Buzzards constantly circle overhead, ready to pick off dead birds. Huge tractor trailers—carrying birds, feed, and equipment to and from the facilities—now dominate the neighborhood's narrow streets. Ammonia from the birds' waste fills the air, as do flies. And the stench—the stench ranges from sickening on good days to gut-churning on bad ones.

"This property's been in my family almost 150 years," said Lisa. "We built this house ourselves just a few years ago. And now we'll have to sell it, probably at a loss. Who wants to buy a house in the middle of factory-farm hell, where the air smells so bad you can't even go outside?"

Lisa Inzerillo and her map showing the factory farms in her community. CREDIT: MATTHEW PRESCOTT

Stories like Lisa's are common up and down the Delmarva. At any given time, the peninsula is home to nearly *600 million* chickens.[97] Kept in an estimated 4,600 massive warehouses that can reach 600 feet long and that look more like airplane hangars than farms, chickens now rule the region's roost: there are nearly 500 birds for each of the 1.4 million human residents.[98]

And residents are crying foul about it. "I'm sick to death of them saying that these are family farms," said Somerset County's Thomas Kerchner, referring to poultry producers' proclivity for insisting that factory farms are *family*-owned. "They are *farms* like a steel mill is a *blacksmith shop*. There's no comparison."[99]

He and his wife, Sherri, put their home up for sale after deciding they simply could not live among the stench.

"Where you had fifty thousand chickens on a given plot of ground, you've got a half million or two million now—which produces a huge problem of what to do with the manure," said Tom Horton, a columnist for Delmarva's *Bay Journal*.[100]

Horton, who covered environmental issues for three decades at the *Baltimore Sun*, is concerned for the region. "It's too much manure," he says. "Too many animals."[101]

Too many animals indeed. Today, the United States produces nearly nine billion chickens every single year. That means that in this country, every minute of every day—night and day—we slaughter over seventeen thousand birds.

The vast majority of those birds have been genetically manipulated to grow unnaturally fat, unnaturally fast. In 1920, it took a chicken sixteen weeks to reach about two pounds; today's chickens may now reach nearly triple that in only *six* weeks. According to a report in the journal *Poultry Science*, it's the equivalent of a two-month-old human baby weighing six hundred pounds.[102]

Because the birds are so young when they're killed—at about forty-five days old—their bones remain immature. So as they become more and more

A glimpse inside a poultry warehouse. CREDIT: JO-ANNE MCARTHUR/WE ANIMALS

top-heavy throughout their short lives, countless animals suffer broken bones, unable to keep up with their rapidly growing size. They suffer heart attacks and their lungs fail—also a result of their fast growth and enormous size. Nowhere else in the animal kingdom do we see baby animals several weeks old dying from heart attacks in such vast numbers.

And their size isn't the only astronomically large thing about industrially produced farm animals: every single minute of every single day, farm animals nationwide produce 7 million pounds of waste.[103] In Delmarva alone, chickens produce roughly 1.5 billion pounds of manure each year—more than all the annual human waste from New York City, Washington, San Francisco, and Atlanta combined.[104]

Lisa and Joe, Thomas and Sherri—indeed, everyone else dealing with this problem on the Delmarva: they are not alone. Almost a thousand miles away in Calhoun, Kentucky, seventy-six-year-old Bernadine Edwards is surrounded by more than one hundred mega chicken factories within just a two-mile radius.[105]

"There's a horrible odor, a stench, and I have flies and rodents digging in, trying to get into my house," said Edwards. "I'm too old to start over," she lamented. "I can't afford to."[106]

Perhaps not surprisingly, the rural areas where factory farms often set up shop are not wealthy neighborhoods full of luxury cars and new homes; rather, they tend to be concentrated in lower-income areas, particularly with non-white populations.

Environmental justice advocates call this environmental racism. Unsavory and environmentally destructive facilities—landfills, coal plants, toxic-waste dumps, and more—are placed in lower-income neighborhoods, often inhabited by people of color. This goes for factory farms, too, which a University of North Carolina School of Public Health study found "are disproportionately located in communities of color and regions of poverty."[107]

That same study also found that schools with a significant number of white and higher-income students were located, on average, 10.8 miles away from CAFOs;

"Jesus says of the birds of the air that 'not one of them is forgotten before God.' How then can we possibly mistreat them or cause them harm? I ask all Christians to recognize and to live fully this dimension of their conversion. May the power and the light of the grace we have received also be evident in our relationship to other creatures and to the world around us. In this way, we will help nurture that sublime fraternity with all creation which Saint Francis of Assisi so radiantly embodied."[108]
—POPE FRANCIS

The poultry industry confines billions of birds in mega complexes nationwide. CREDIT: FRANCIS LEROY

schools with a significant number of non-white students and roughly half their students on lunch program assistance were located only 4.9 miles away.

"These companies seek rural areas where unemployment, or underemployment, is high and people are desperate," says Aloma Dew, a Sierra Club organizer in Kentucky. "They assume that poor, country people will not organize or speak up, and that they will be ignorant of the impacts on their health and quality of life."[109]

"Quality of life" seems like a stretch here. Bernadine Edwards in Kentucky and the residents of the Delmarva are exposed to a litany of harmful gases in their air—like hydrogen sulfide, which can cause skin, eye, and respiratory irritation; brain and heart disorders; and even death.[110]

Because factory farms can confine hundreds of thousands of chickens or other animals at a single location, these gases may be emitted at high concentrations; that can be detrimental to nearby communities.[111]

In fact, both North Carolina and Iowa—two of our nation's largest factory-farming hubs—have published controlled studies of CAFOs' ill effects on their neighbors. In Iowa, for example, increased instances of eye and upper respiratory problems persisted among people living within two miles of a factory farm.

When I visited with Lisa and Joe on the Delmarva, they complained of respiratory problems. "I'm an ER physician," Joe said. "I'm around sickness all day but never get sick from that. It's the poultry farms that are the problem."

The fans attached to mega poultry facilities often blow "CAFO dust" that threatens communities for miles around. Lisa Inzerillo, on the Delmarva Peninsula, has felt (and breathed) these impacts firsthand. CREDIT: USDA

"Communities near industrial farm animal production facilities are subject to air emissions that . . . may significantly affect certain segments of the population. Those most vulnerable—children, the elderly, individuals with chronic or acute pulmonary or heart disorders—are at particular risk."[112]

—THE PEW COMMISSION ON INDUSTRIAL FARM ANIMAL PRODUCTION, A PROJECT OF THE PEW CHARITABLE TRUSTS AND JOHNS HOPKINS BLOOMBERG SCHOOL OF PUBLIC HEALTH

And with that, he ducked out to pick up his respiratory medication at the pharmacy. He grabbed his keys and jacket and left through the side door. Lisa, saddened, chimed in: "It's because all these mega chicken houses all around us have these giant fans on them. They're blowing God knows what into the air all day long. And we're breathing it in. When it's real windy, you can't even go outside. It's either the stench or the flies. We just stay inside mostly now."

What keeps Lisa and Joe inside is the particulate matter—including of the fecal variety—that escapes from CAFOs and is carried by the wind. What they breathe in when they go outside is referred to as CAFO dust—and it's incredibly dangerous: it's a top cause of bronchitis, can cause heart disorders like arrhythmia, and can even lead to heart attacks.[113]

And these ill effects are nothing new: we've known of them for years.

One report, conducted for the North Dakota Attorney General's office, analyzed fifty-six socioeconomic studies about the impact CAFOs have on local communities.

"Based on the evidence," the study concluded, "public concern about the detrimental community impacts of industrialized farming is warranted." The report continued: "This conclusion rests on five decades of government and academic concern with this topic . . . five decades of social science research which has found detrimental effects of industrialized farming on many indicators of community quality of life."[114]

Fifty years of social science and government concern over this issue; living proof from communities on the Delmarva, in Kentucky, Iowa, and North Carolina; study after study, year after year: how is it that producers have been able to continue ravaging rural communities for so long?

In short, we let them.

OUR POULTRY PROBLEM

34.3

Pounds of chicken eaten
per person in **1960**

108

Pounds of chicken eaten
per person in **2016**

215%

Percentage increase

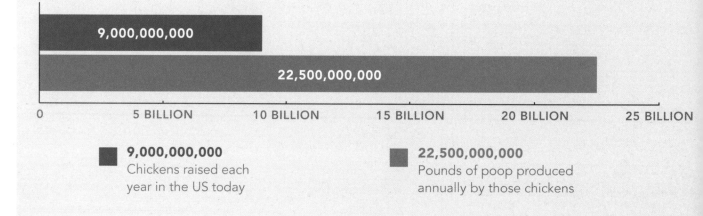

9,000,000,000

22,500,000,000

| 0 | 5 BILLION | 10 BILLION | 15 BILLION | 20 BILLION | 25 BILLION |

9,000,000,000
Chickens raised each
year in the US today

22,500,000,000
Pounds of poop produced
annually by those chickens

0	100 MILLION	200 MILLION	300 MILLION	400 MILLION	500 MILLION	600 MILLION

1,400,000
Delmarva's human population

600,000,000
Delmarva's chicken population

500
Chickens per person on the Delmarva

1,500,000,000
Pounds of poop produced each
year by Delmarva's chickens

OXFAM AMERICA CAMPAIGN MANAGER BEN GROSSMAN-COHEN

Right now, one person in nine goes to bed hungry every night—not because there isn't enough food to go around, but because of deep power imbalances and improper resource allocation. The reality is that eating meat requires way more energy, land, water, and other finite resources than other delicious foods. And individuals can help rectify this imbalance with their own diets simply by eating less meat.

Indeed, our diets are deeply intertwined with a complex food system that greatly affects people all over the world. We've learned over decades of responding to humanitarian crises and working in some of the poorest places on the planet that ending poverty requires major shifts in how we grow, distribute, and consume food.

For example, Oxfam is working closely with workers in poultry-processing facilities throughout the United States who face some of the most dangerous and difficult jobs for extremely low wages. Many of the workers in these plants are people of color, often undocumented immigrants who lack basic workplace protections.

And of course, we all vote when we make choices about what we eat. The more people are willing to adjust their diets—like by eating less meat—and use their voice, the more we can take the growing concern over how our food is produced and create systemic change. The more we can shift incentives for the food industry to produce more plant-based foods and build greater ties with like minds in developing countries to do the same at the local level, the more we can avoid the spread of the worst sins of our current production model.

The simple truth is that we cannot sustain the current model of production and consumption without regard for the effect on resources and our climate. Faced with constrained resources it is always the poorest and most vulnerable who lose out. The more we can do to use our voices to advocate for change and our pocketbooks to support those businesses who are doing the right thing, the better everyone will be.

Ben Grossman-Cohen is campaign manager for Oxfam America. Through its international confederation of organizations working together with partners and local communities in more than ninety countries, Oxfam mobilizes the power of people against poverty.

Caged chickens in India used to support a growing dependence on animal proteins. CREDIT: FRANK LOFTUS/THE HSUS

"When the poison control center official spoke to Julie Jansen, his words were shocking: Ma'am, the only symptoms of hydrogen sulfide poisoning you're not experiencing are seizures, convulsions, and death. Leave the area immediately. Panic-stricken, Jansen grabbed her six children and her friends' two children and drove away from her home. Jansen first thought the 11-year-old, home-based day care center she owned in Olivia, Minnesota had been hit by a flu bug. In the spring of 1995, 17 children ranging in age from newborn to 13 shared a long list of symptoms—diarrhea, nausea, headaches, vomiting, teary eyes, and stuffy noses. She soon noticed that it only happened when the wind blew from the south. Two factory-scale hog farms had recently located not more than a mile and a half away. It turned out the hog operations were poisoning the air with toxic wastes."[115]

—FROM THE NRDC REPORT *CESSPOOLS OF SHAME*

> "The same factory farmers who intensively confine animals and deal them never-ending privation also release massive volumes of untreated animal waste, making life miserable for people and animals."[116]
>
> —WAYNE PACELLE, PRESIDENT AND CEO, THE HUMANE SOCIETY OF THE UNITED STATES

Actually, we *made* them: in 1960, the average American ate only 34.3 pounds of poultry each year. In 2016, that amount had climbed to more than 108 pounds per person, according to the National Chicken Council.[117]

So compared to 1960, today we have nearly twice as many people each eating more than twice as many birds.[118, 119] No wonder production has gotten so intensified, so concentrated, so dangerously out of control.

The good news is that we can each use the power of our plates to fix this problem, simply by cutting back on chicken and other poultry products in our diets.

That's exactly what Lisa Inzerillo has done. "I can't even eat chicken anymore," she told me. "I feel like I've gone through a grieving process and I just can't get past being angry over what they've done to us. They're ruining our lives, disrespecting animals, hurting our neighbors. So yeah, I just can't eat it anymore."

Fortunately for Lisa and countless other people cutting back on poultry, there are protein-packed plant-based foods that can help us live healthier and avoid supporting the types of industrial operations that are polluting our air and making life so difficult for so many communities. There are products like tempeh and seitan. The market for tofu is exploding as more Americans enjoy the product, going from a $1 billion industry to nearly a $5 billion industry.[120] And a huge variety of chicken-like-but-chicken-free meatless products have taken off in the market and are now available virtually everywhere.

Many restaurants now offer plant-based chicken products. Tropical Smoothie Café offers customers the opportunity to replace chicken with a product called Beyond Meat in nearly any item.[121] Beyond Meat, made entirely from plant-based ingredients, has the taste and texture of chicken, yet has 20 grams of protein in each 3-ounce serving, compared to 13 grams for the same portion of chicken.[122]

Besides Beyond Meat, there are brands like Gardein (meat-free chicken tenders, scaloppini, and more), Boca (plant-based chicken patties and nuggets), and Morningstar Farms (Buffalo wings and more)—to name only a few.

Grocery stores now offer entire sections of these products—and not just Whole Foods: at Walmart, Kroger, Safeway, Albertsons, and nearly every other supermarket chain, one can find delicious plant-based "chicken" products. Target has even launched its own brand of vegetarian chicken. The company's Simply Balanced store brand meat-free "meats"—like Korean BBQ Meatless Chicken, Teriyaki Meatless Chicken, Smoky Chipotle Meatless Chicken, and Mushroom Miso Meatless Turkey—are available nationwide.

These products are certainly not zero-footprint foods. But their success is the result of millions more consumers now mixing meat-free meals into their diets. Just as many people are seeking out more humane products from local producers committed to higher animal welfare and environmental standards, countless people are also shifting to more plant-focused diets.

Some do it for their own health, with data clearly showing that diets lower in meat and higher in plant proteins are better for us.[123] Some do it for the animals—perhaps uncomfortable with the way these chickens are warehoused, or with knowing that seventeen thousand of them are slaughtered for our plates every minute of every day.

Others are doing it for people like Bernadine Edwards in Kentucky and Lisa Inzerillo in Maryland—for all the families and communities nationwide who, with each breath, are victimized by our nation's chicken addiction. They're opting, with every dinnertime decision, to use their forks as a force for change—and each of us can, too. 🌿

IN A NUTSHELL

- Air pollution from factory farms takes a toll on local communities.

- Putrid odors can prevent people from going outside or opening their windows.

- Dangerous gases like methane, ammonia, and hydrogen sulfide are emitted as waste breaks down.

- Exposure to these gases can cause illness and neurological problems, including depression.

- Factory farms tend to be concentrated in low-income areas.

- Poor people and people of color are disproportionately impacted by factory farms' air pollution.

- On Maryland's Eastern Shore, the poultry industry is ravaging poor communities and negatively affecting families who've lived on the peninsula for hundreds of years.

Now for the good news! We can all rest—and breathe—a little easier knowing that plant-based foods are easier on the air. Producing, say, chick*peas* instead of chick*en* is less polluting and gentler on local communities. So simply by enjoying more of these types of foods—even if meat is still sometimes on the plate—we can each help play a significant role in cleaning the air.

CREDIT: RODRIGO BALEIA/GREENPEACE

"Climate change is no longer some far-off problem. It is happening here. It is happening now. And it becomes more dramatic with each passing year."[124]

—PRESIDENT BARACK OBAMA

FIRE

For the final stop on our worldwide voyage, we leave the Delmarva and head, this time, not to another place on the planet—but to a spot far above it. Rise straight up: back through the clouds, into the stratosphere. Continue through the thermosphere until you have a clear view of the Earth below. From above, watch the erratic weather patterns—the hurricanes, the tsunamis. Watch the ice caps shrink and coastal areas flood. This is the raging fire that is global warming; this is climate change. Its impacts are devastating—and all around us.

•

One sweltering Sunday in the summer of 2014, my wife and I headed south from our home in New Orleans toward the Gulf of Mexico. We drove down state highway 90, across the Bayou des Allemands and through all the little Creole towns with names like LaRose and Galliano—past Catfish Lake and Little Lake and Lake Jesse and North Lake and South Lake and Lake Palourde and Lake Laurier—peppered with colorful houses built high up on wooden stilts or floating on empty fifty-five-gallon drums.

The region's so awash that on a map, it looks like a bright blue canvas painted, Jackson Pollock–style, with only slight drizzles of intersecting green.

Six thousand years ago, the region was entirely submerged. Melting glaciers eventually created Lake Pontchartrain and carved out Pine Island, near present-day New Orleans. When the Mississippi changed course, heading toward the new island, it dumped sediment into the Gulf—sediment that formed land and eventually connected with Pine Island, creating the land mass that, today, includes everything between the Gulf and the Big Easy.

That all played out at a snail's pace, over millennia.

Then came climate change.

Though Earth's climate has always been a work-in-progress, today's scientific consensus is that human activities are undoubtedly causing dangerous changes to it[125]—like progressively erratic weather patterns and increasing global temperatures.

Sea levels, too, are rising, which has Joann Bourg and her family gravely worried.

Joann—along with her sisters, mother, son, and niece—are the third generation of Bourgs living on the family's land, about eighty miles south of New Orleans, in Isle de Jean Charles, which is essentially a floating town situated precariously between Lake Chien and Wonder Lake.

But it may not be afloat much longer: thanks to climate change, the region is essentially sinking back into the Gulf.

"Yes, this is our grandpa's land," Ms. Bourg told the *New York Times* in a profile on the region's fate. "But it's going under one way or another."[126]

In 2016, a $48 million U.S. Department of Housing and Urban Development grant became the first use of federal funds to relocate an entire community impacted by climate change.

Louisiana is under constant threat of flooding due to the climate change. CREDIT: USDA

"We're going to lose all our heritage, all our culture," grieved Biloxi-Chitimacha-Choctaw Chief Albert Naquin. "It's all going to be history."[127]

Worldwide, families like the Bourgs and people like Chief Naquin are at war with our changing climate—a war for their land and lives.

Tuvalu—a tiny island nation in the South Pacific, north of Fiji and east of Papua New Guinea, whose highest point is merely fifteen feet above sea level—may be among Earth's first national victims of that war.[128]

"Cyclones and tropical storms have been getting much worse since the 1980s," says Hilia Vavae, Tuvalu's chief meteorologist. "We had a big drought starting in 1999. Flooding from extreme high tides is increasing also. In the late 1990s, water started coming out of the ground—first puddles, then a whole sea."[129]

It seems Tuvalu—like southern Louisiana—may soon meet a watery grave.

"If, as predicted, sea levels continue to rise," confirms the International Federation of Red Cross and Red Crescent Societies, "this string of low-lying islands in the southwest Pacific could gradually disappear."[130]

So who's to blame? In the unending finger-pointing that often accompanies climate change discussions—the few remaining deniers left misguidedly point to natural processes, scientists point to human-caused emissions, the solar industry points to coal, the coal industry to transport, and so on—one thing has become inarguably clear: it's not our fingers we ought to be pointing, but our forks.

The consequences of meat overconsumption are undeniable—on our land, in our waters, in our air. The Amazon being deforested for animal agriculture is a travesty in its own right, as is the oceanic devastation wrought by the seafood sector; Lisa Inzerillo on the Delmarva Peninsula certainly doesn't need any reason

Scientists from ICESCAPE—Impacts of Climate Change on the Eco-Systems and Chemistry of the Arctic Pacific Environment—study the region's melting ice. CREDIT: NASA/KATHRYN HANSEN

other than the attack on her own air quality to protest poultry production.

But making matters far worse is the fact that each of these ecological nightmares, as bad as they are individually, also plays into a much broader catastrophe: climate change.

"The livestock sector is a major stressor on many ecosystems and on the planet as a whole," opens *Livestock's Long Shadow*—that same UN Food and Agriculture Organization (FAO) study that reported on animal agriculture's massive land requirements. "Globally, it is one of the largest sources of greenhouse gasses."[131]

Livestock, the FAO reports, contribute a whopping 14.5 percent of *all* greenhouse gas emissions worldwide.[132]

But in its research, the FAO didn't even count fish or shrimp as "livestock," focusing instead on mammals and birds. This is a grave omission of emissions, points out Risto Isomäki in his 2016 book, *Meat, Milk and Climate: Why It Is Absolutely Necessary to Reduce the Consumption of Animal Products*. It means emissions from animal proteins—not just land-based livestock, but *all* animal proteins—in our diet are actually vastly higher than reported.

Think back to all those ocean-trawling vessels. On top of depleting fish stocks and killing marine mammals like dolphins and whales, all those ship fleets scouring the oceans worldwide also burn massive quantities of fossil fuels, emitting huge amounts of greenhouse gases in the process.

Mangrove canopy, Indonesia. Worldwide, millions of hectares of mangrove swamps have been converted to shrimp farms, emitting enormous quantities of carbon dioxide in the process. CREDIT: SIGIT DENI SASMITO/CIFOR

"If every American skipped one meal of chicken per week and substituted vegetables and grains, for example, the carbon dioxide savings would be the same as taking more than half a million cars off of U.S. roads."[133]

—ENVIRONMENTAL DEFENSE FUND

HOW CLIMATE-FRIENDLY IS MY FOOD?

When it comes to climate impact, not
all foods are created equal.

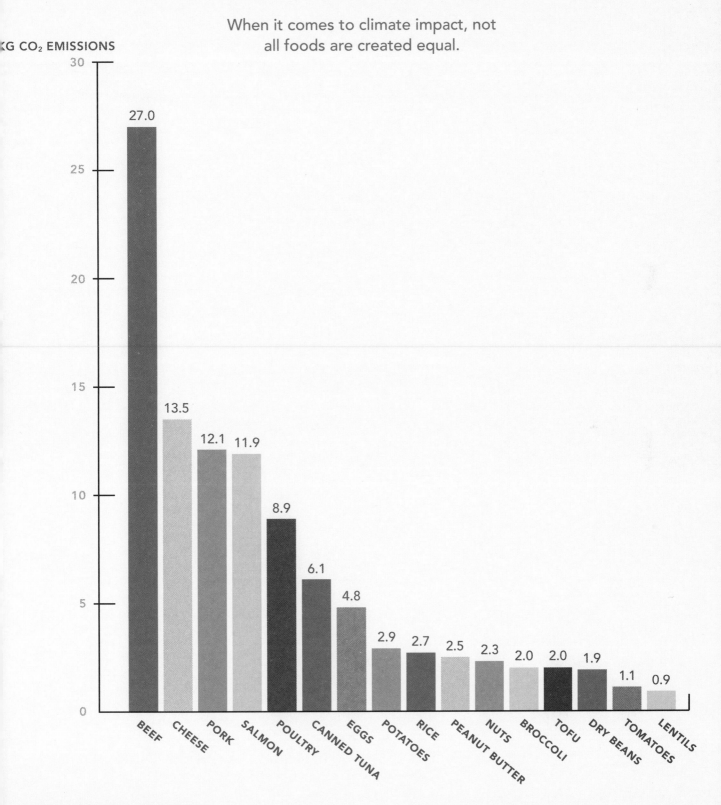

KG CO_2 EMISSIONS

- BEEF: 27.0
- CHEESE: 13.5
- PORK: 12.1
- SALMON: 11.9
- POULTRY: 8.9
- CANNED TUNA: 6.1
- EGGS: 4.8
- POTATOES: 2.9
- RICE: 2.7
- PEANUT BUTTER: 2.5
- NUTS: 2.3
- BROCCOLI: 2.0
- TOFU: 2.0
- DRY BEANS: 1.9
- TOMATOES: 1.1
- LENTILS: 0.9

SOURCE: ENVIRONMENTAL WORKING GROUP

"Did you know that the meat industry is responsible for approximately 20 percent of the world's greenhouse gas emissions? In fact, producing one calorie of meat requires nearly twenty times the amount of energy as one plant calorie! With global meat consumption tripling over the last four decades, the meat industry now emits over 36 billion tons of greenhouse gases annually and is showing no signs of slowing down. If we want to make a real dent in the world's carbon footprint and reduce our own personal footprint, we need to eat less meat."[134]

—EARTH DAY NETWORK

Think back to aquaculture. Fish factory farms are to blame for much more than just localized water pollution. Millions of hectares of mangrove swamps, for example, have been converted to shrimp farms, emitting enormous quantities of carbon dioxide as they're destroyed.[135] In fact, the World Watch Institute points out that *more than half* the world's mangrove forests have been destroyed, with shrimp farming a main perpetrator in their destruction.[136]

And even with these omissions in the FAO's research, the numbers are still staggering.

As the FAO reports, livestock cause "an even larger contribution [to emissions] than the transportation sector worldwide."[137] That's right: our use of animals for food—*not even counting seafood*—contributes more to climate change than all the world's cars, trucks, trains, planes, and ships *combined*.

Much of the livestock sector's emissions are the result of the fact that all these animals we raise for food have to eat food themselves.

Think of the 600 million chickens on the Delmarva, and the billions more throughout the country. Factory farms require massive amounts of feed.

As the *American Journal of Clinical Nutrition* reports, in the United States, farm animals consume more than *700 percent* the amount of grain than is eaten by the *entire* American (human) population.[138]

Where does that feed come from? Remember the Amazon and other tropical forest land being razed for meat production? Though some of that razing is done for *grazing*, much is done to make room for *feed crops*. And during all that deforestation—that converting of forest land to feed land—grave quantities of greenhouse gases are spewed into the atmosphere.

Then, once the land has been converted, managing those feed crops also requires profanely heavy fossil fuel consumption: running all the tractors and processors and cars and trucks and other industrial equipment deals yet another major blow to our climate.

So what about animals who eat grass instead of grain? Though "grass-fed" cows represent only a minuscule percentage of the entire livestock sector, they too are a significant contributor to greenhouse gas emissions.

Cows are very gaseous animals, and especially when they eat grass, their digestive processes emit colossal quantities of methane—a greenhouse gas that's *30 times more potent* than even carbon dioxide.[139] Globally, farm animals are one of the most significant sources of anthropogenic methane, and are responsible for up to 40 percent of all methane emissions worldwide.[140, 141]

This is why "grass-fed meat is more, not less, greenhouse gas intensive," says Dr. Gidon Eshel, a climatologist at Bard College's Center for Environmental Policy.[142]

But people need protein. And while industrial chicken, fish, pig, and cow operations of all kinds are extremely climate *un*friendly, certainly it's true that growing, processing, and transporting food of *any* kind (whether animal- or plant-based) requires resources.

So what would the impact on climate change be if we simply processed more plant foods into protein-packed products of their own, rather than funneling so many through animals? What if we cut out the middle*hen*?

According to the Environmental Defense Fund, if each American replaced chicken with plant-based foods at *just one meal per week*, the carbon dioxide savings would be the same as taking more than half a million cars off U.S. roads.[143]

And that's just chicken—and just carbon dioxide.

On the whole, "the production of animal-based foods," confirms a study published in the journal *Climate*

Grass-fed cows emit huge amounts of methane, making grass-fed beef "more, not less, greenhouse gas intensive," according to climatologist Dr. Gidon Eshel. CREDIT: JO-ANNE MCARTHUR/THE GHOSTS IN OUR MACHINE

SIERRA CLUB DEPUTY EXECUTIVE DIRECTOR BRUCE HAMILTON

As the threat of climate disruption becomes increasingly urgent, it makes sense that every source of greenhouse gas emissions should come under scrutiny. Both the reckless burning of fossil fuels and unsustainable agricultural practices are major contributors to greenhouse gas emissions. However, as the recent documentary film *Cowspiracy* rightly points out, the latter are too often overlooked as a potential source of reductions.

In fact, how we farm and what we eat can make a real difference for our climate future, and that knowledge should inform not only our personal choices but also our public policies.

Eliminating or reducing meat consumption in your diet is one important way to reduce your contribution to climate change, since animal agriculture is the single largest source of global greenhouse gas emissions from food production. At the same time, the Sierra Club continues to support broader reforms in food production that will also help limit climate disruption.

Many current agricultural practices, such as large-scale monocropping (the practice of growing a single crop year after year on the same land) and concentrated animal-feeding operations (CAFOs), consume disproportionate amounts of fossil fuels, pollute our water and air, deplete the soil, and diminish biodiversity. The good news is that we have many opportunities to improve in all of these areas.

We're calling for reform of industrial agricultural and food system practices, to minimize contributions to greenhouse gases and to maximize carbon sequestration in plants and soils. The pollution from concentrated animal-feeding operations in particular is grossly disproportionate to the amount of food produced. Growing heavily subsidized energy-intensive corn to convert to ethanol fuel makes no sense from an energy, food-supply, climate, or pollution standpoint, and it should be opposed.

The single greatest source of agricultural greenhouse gas emissions is livestock, particularly factory-raised animals. Cattle (for both beef and milk, as well as for inedible outputs like manure and draft power) are responsible for about two-thirds of livestock emissions.

Fortunately, we *can* cut livestock emissions significantly not only by reducing personal meat consumption but also by following best practices and ending our reliance on concentrated animal-feeding operations. The Sierra Club continues to strongly oppose the establishment of new CAFOs and believes we should phase out existing operations as soon as possible.

Furthermore, ensuring soil maintains its carbon stock is a highly effective means of carbon sequestration. Yet most agricultural soils have had their carbon stock dramatically reduced by soil loss, excessive tillage, overgrazing, erosion, and overuse of chemical nitrous fertilizers. In fact, the world's cultivated and grazed soils have lost 50 to 70 percent of their original carbon stock. In the process, billions of tons of carbon have been released into the atmosphere. That's why it's critical that we rebuild soil carbon through regenerative agricultural practices.

Massive food production operations are at the root of many of these problems. Converting our natural landscapes into intensive agricultural operations can change land from carbon sinks to carbon sources. Deforestation, plowing up prairies, and filling wetlands destroys existing carbon sinks and releases that carbon into our atmosphere, increasing emissions.

As consumers, we each have a personal role to play as well, through our choices about the foods we eat:

- Whenever possible, we can support locally owned and operated farms, which are generally far less destructive and far more productive. This also reduces the need for long-distance transportation of foods.

- Striving to reduce food waste, through smaller serving sizes, composting, and recycling, will also reduce greenhouse gas emissions.

- Organically grown foods that don't rely on chemicals are better for the soil, climate, and our health.

Addressing climate disruption is important enough that we cannot afford to overlook any strategy for success. Fortunately, just as with transitioning from fossil fuels to clean energy, we can reap important collateral benefits by adopting more responsible and sustainable agricultural practices and by making smarter lifestyle choices.

Bruce Hamilton has worked for the Sierra Club for four decades. He's served on the Environmental Support Center Board of Directors, the U.S. Department of Energy Environmental Advisory Board, and the U.S. Environmental Protection Agency National Advisory Council on Sustainable Economies.

> "There is much the government can do and should do to improve the environment. But even more important is the individual . . . for it is the individual who himself benefits, and also protects a heritage of beauty for his children and future generations."[144]
>
> —LADY BIRD JOHNSON

Change, "is associated with higher greenhouse gas emissions than plant-based foods."[145]

For that study, scientists looked at more than 55,000 individuals' diets—including vegans, vegetarians, and meat-eaters—aged twenty to seventy-nine years old. Their conclusions? Greenhouse gas emissions of those eating meat-heavy diets "are approximately twice as high" as individuals eating a plant-based diet. Thus, concludes the report, reducing our meat consumption would lead to lower greenhouse gas emissions.[146]

Time and again, study after study, leading scientists have urged that in order to curb climate change, we *must* eat more plants and less meat.

"Shifting global demand for meat and dairy produce is central to achieving climate goals," concludes one report from Europe's most reputable think tank, the prestigious Royal Institute of International Affairs—more commonly known as Chatham House.[147]

"Globally we should eat less meat," found another Chatham House study. "We cannot avoid dangerous climate change unless consumption trends change."[148]

The message is clear.

The verdict is in.

The time is now.

At each meal, we make choices. Collectively, all those choices made throughout each day impact individuals and ecosystems across the planet. Pouring cow's milk on our cereal or putting it in our coffee every morning may cause people living next to dairy factory farms to suffer. A ham sandwich for lunch every day may support a pig factory farm. A tuna sandwich may kill whales. And chicken wings for dinner may degrade the lives of people like Lisa Inzerillo on the Delmarva.

Moreover, all told, it's now clear that meat-and-milk-heavy meal plans indisputably and immensely contribute to climate change, putting families like the Bourgs, in Louisiana—and of course, *all* of Earth's inhabitants and ecosystems—at extreme risk.

On the other hand, a diet higher in plant-based proteins can dramatically ease agriculture's planetary pitfalls, creating better outcomes for our neighbors, our waterways, animals, our land, and our climate.

This is certainly one reason why plant-based eating has grown in popularity in recent years, with millions more among us now focusing on plant-forward fare.

And it's part of the reason why entire governments are now starting to try to shift the tides of consumption. In 2016, China announced plans to slash the entire country's meat consumption by 50 percent—a move that was lauded by climate campaigners worldwide. The same year, it was reported that Chiara Appendino—the mayor of Turin, Italy—planned to make the entire city vegetarian by promoting meat-free eating as a matter of public policy.

Meat's impact on our climate has also helped lead major school districts—Los Angeles, Detroit, Houston, and many more—along with countless colleges and universities to now have entirely meat-free days in their cafeterias. And it's also helped pique the interest of

Fishing trawlers in the Western Sahara. As high as the UN figures are for livestock-related greenhouse gas emissions, they don't even include emissions from the countless fishing ships constantly trawling our world's oceans. CREDIT: WESTERN SAHARA RESOURCE WATCH

"The growing meat intensity of diets around the world is one of the issues connected to this global crisis."[149]

—AL GORE

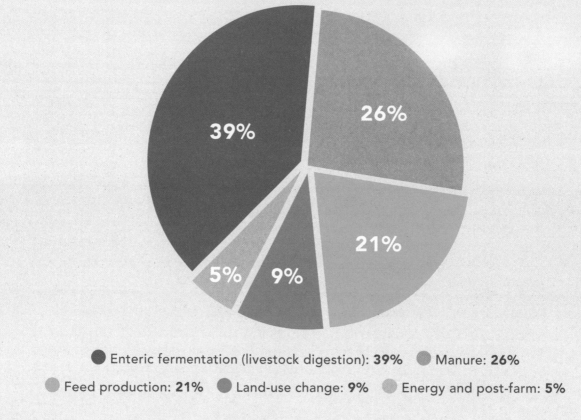

THE MEAT INDUSTRY'S GREENHOUSE GAS EMISSIONS, BY SOURCE

39%

26%

21%

5% 9%

- Enteric fermentation (livestock digestion): **39%**   - Manure: **26%**
- Feed production: **21%**   - Land-use change: **9%**   - Energy and post-farm: **5%**

SOURCE: CHATHAM HOUSE ANALYSIS BASED ON UNITED NATIONS FAO (2013)

Silicon Valley, where venture capital firms are now pouring money into plant-based food startups.

But we don't need to be venture capitalists, school dining directors, or mayors to take part in this shift. Whether adopting a vegan or vegetarian diet, trying Meatless Mondays, drinking almond milk instead of cow's milk, or simply replacing meat with plants more often, there are a myriad of ways for everyone to eat more sustainably.

Indeed, on this spinning ball of green and blue that we all call home, with all its ecological problems, eating more plants and less meat is the most important way—and the tastiest—to turn things around. So to those who've decided to make their tables sustainable by enjoying more food for a better planet, here's to you! 🌿

IN A NUTSHELL

- Erratic weather patterns, the melting of our icecaps, and more—scientists agree we're in a climate catastrophe.

- Island nations are facing threats, like increased storms and flooding, from climate change.

- In the United States, low-lying areas like southern Louisiana are sinking, displacing families and entire communities.

- Scientists are clear that animal agriculture is a major driver of climate change.

- Transforming our land to grow animal feed, raising and processing those crops, then funneling the feed through animals requires huge fossil fuel inputs.

- Even "locally produced" animal proteins can be climate unfriendly, since animals are inefficient at converting natural resources into food.

- All told, industrial animal agriculture contributes more greenhouse gases than the entire transportation sector—than all trains, planes, cars, trucks, and ships combined.

Now for the good news! All the lowest-emitting foods, when it comes to greenhouse gases, are plant-based. Beans emit less than 2 kg of CO_2 per serving while beef emits 27 kg; tofu emits 2 kg while tuna emits 6 kg. This means that by simply enjoying more plant-based foods, we can—in a very concrete, immediate way—help curb climate change.

PART TWO:
OUR PLATES

"Eat food. Not too much.
Mostly plants."[150]

—MICHAEL POLLAN

CAN LENTILS SAVE THE WORLD?

Well, maybe not on their own. But along with other protein-rich legumes and grains, hearty vegetables, wholesome seeds, and even plant-based "meats"—eating more of these foods can play a pivotal role in reversing some of our planet's most serious problems.

Take the humble lentil, for example. It weighs in at less than a single kilogram of carbon emissions per serving, while beef contributes a whopping 27 kilograms. No contest.

But so what? Isn't comparing lentils and beef like comparing apples and oranges? Work your way through these recipes and you'll find out firsthand that isn't the case. Enjoy a Spicy Lentil Burger (page 134) instead of a hamburger, or Spaghetti with Lentil Meatballs (page 176), and you'll see that these protein-packed pulses can offer tastes and textures that are satisfying and delicious, with a much lighter environmental footprint.

Plus, lentils (and other beans and legumes) can help conserve vast quantities of water. Consider Creamy Basil-Chick*pea*—instead of chick*en*—Lettuce Cups (page 148). According to the Water Footprint Network, a pound of chicken requires more than 570 gallons of water to produce, while it takes only 5 gallons to produce chickpeas and other beans. Or try a Spicy Chocolate Milk Shake with Whipped Coconut Cream for dessert (page 248)—instead of cow's milk (one glass of which takes *820 gallons* of water to produce), this tasty treat uses soy milk (20 gallons per glass). That's a 97 percent reduction in water use just from one simple swap!

Concerned not just about our water *use*, but also what we're doing to our world's oceans through overfishing? Try crab-free Crab Cakes (page 172) and Rainbow Veggie Sushi (page 170). These fish-free feasts are easier on our world's oceans, not to mention the aquatic animals that call those oceans home.

"Vegetables are, without a doubt, the most flavorful items on a plate."[151]

—CHEF MARIO BATALI

Enjoy recipes that utilize tree fruits—knowing that trees help purify our air—like Cherry Chia Puff Pastry Breakfast Tarts (page 88) or Oatmeal with Chai-Poached Pears (page 95). And delight in ingredients that can help lower our land footprint—like using rice paper instead of pork to make bacon (page 193) or using tofu instead of eggs to make frittata (page 97).

Of course, no foods have *zero* footprint: living and eating on this earth will always mean consuming *some* amount of resources. But all things considered, plant-based foods—whether whole grains and vegetables, proteins like tofu, or even plant-based meat products—tend to help us tread lighter. They can help us emit fewer greenhouse gases, use less water, save our oceans, reduce air pollution (and even help purify the air), and use less land.

Plus, enjoying more of these delicious foods doesn't have to be a zero-sum endeavor: you needn't go whole hog toward veganism to make a difference. Even simply incorporating *more* of these recipes into your normal repertoire can help you take a big bite out of so many of the problems that plague our planet. And you may discover new foods you love, or new ways to prepare foods you already love.

So eat up and enjoy, knowing you're helping save the planet—one delicious bite after the next. Bon appétit! 🌿

BREAKFAST

SOUPS, STEWS, SALADS, AND SANDWICHES

MAIN DISHES

SIDES AND EXTRAS

DESSERTS

BREAKFAST

Apple Cinnamon Pancakes
78

Biscuits and Gravy
80

Black Bean Breakfast Burritos
82

Blueberry Buckwheat Waffles
85

Breakfast Banana Split
86

Cherry Chia Puff Pastry Breakfast Tarts
88

Classic French Toast
91

Mix 'n' Match Superfood Smoothies
92

Oatmeal with Chai-Poached Pears
95

PB&J Power Smoothies
96

Pea and Potato Frittata
97

Rice Pudding with Coconut
and Cranberries
99

Rise 'n' Shine Breakfast Sandwich
101

Sweet Potato and Parsnip Hash
102

Tofu Scramble 101
105

APPLE CINNAMON PANCAKES

I grew up in New Hampshire, across the street from a maple-sugar shack—where sap is collected from sugar maple trees and boiled down into syrup. On weekends, the Sugar Shack, as we called it, served breakfast, and many people from the neighborhood and town would gather there for pancakes and fresh syrup. My favorite? Apple cinnamon. This recipe offers a healthier, more sustainable twist on those classic pancakes: because they use applesauce instead of eggs, they cut back on water usage and carbon emissions. Eat up!

SERVES 2   PREP AND COOKING TIME: 35 MINUTES

INGREDIENTS

1½ C all-purpose flour

2 Tbsp sugar

1 tsp baking soda

2 tsp ground cinnamon

Pinch of salt

1 C unsweetened applesauce

1 tsp apple cider vinegar

¾ C almond milk

1 Tbsp coconut oil, plus additional as needed

1 apple, peeled, cored, and diced

Fresh fruit, for serving

Pure maple syrup, for serving

METHOD

Combine the flour, sugar, baking soda, cinnamon, and salt in a large bowl. Make a well in the center.

Combine the applesauce, vinegar, and almond milk in a small bowl or measuring cup. Pour the wet ingredients into the well in the dry ingredients, whisking as you go. Continue whisking until the mixture is smooth.

Set a nonstick skillet over medium heat and let it get good and hot. Melt the coconut oil in the pan and swirl it around until the pan is evenly coated.

Pour about 3 tablespoons of the batter into the pan. Once it firms up a bit, sprinkle some of the diced apples on top. Cook until bubbles appear. Using a spatula, flip and cook for another couple minutes on the second side. The pancake will puff up and eventually stop growing. When this happens, it's ready. Transfer the pancake to a plate or serving platter.

Repeat the above steps until all the batter has been used up, adding more coconut oil to the pan as needed.

Pile with whatever fresh fruit you have available and drizzle with maple syrup before devouring.

BISCUITS AND GRAVY

Flaky biscuits topped with rich, creamy gravy will start any morning off right. Because these buttermilk-style biscuits use neither butter nor milk (but rather almond milk mixed with cider vinegar, which creates a similar outcome), they're more environmentally friendly—with almond milk requiring less water and emitting fewer greenhouse gases than cow's milk. The gravy is satisfying, nutritious, and filled with flavor.

SERVES 4   PREP AND COOKING TIME: 40 TO 50 MINUTES

INGREDIENTS

For the Biscuits:

¾ C plain almond milk

2 tsp apple cider vinegar

2 C all-purpose flour, plus more for dusting

2 tsp baking powder

½ tsp baking soda

½ tsp salt

¼ C margarine, chilled

For the Gravy:

¼ C margarine

½ C all-purpose flour

2 C plain almond or soy milk

1 tsp salt

1 tsp freshly ground black pepper

Optional Toppings:

Chopped scallions

Shredded vegan cheese

Fresh or pickled jalapeños, sliced

METHOD

First, make the biscuits:
Preheat the oven to 450°F.

Combine the almond milk and vinegar in a small bowl and set aside.

In a large bowl, combine the flour, baking powder, baking soda, and salt. Using your (clean) hands, work in the margarine until it's evenly distributed but still a bit chunky. Pour in the almond milk–vinegar mixture, stirring gently. Use clean hands to lightly knead the dough, just enough so that everything sticks together and it has a nice, silky consistency.

Transfer the dough to a generously floured work surface. Form it into a rectangle about 1 inch thick. Use a cookie cutter (or drinking glass) to cut biscuits, placing them on a lightly floured baking sheet as you go.

As you cut the biscuits, press the leftover dough together and cut more, until you've used up all the dough. (Avoid waste by pressing the last dough scraps together to create an off-shape biscuit.) Bake for 10 minutes, then remove and set aside.

While the biscuits bake, make the gravy:
Melt the margarine over medium heat in a large skillet or saucepan. Add ¼ cup of the flour and stir continuously for 3 to 4 minutes to make a roux. Add the remaining ¼ cup flour, the milk, salt, and pepper. Increase the heat to medium-high and whisk to combine thoroughly. Heat until the gravy thickens, stirring frequently—about 4 minutes more. If too thick, remove from the heat and whisk in a little water.

To assemble:
Cut open two biscuits and place them in a bowl. Top with as much gravy—and any optional toppings—as you'd like.

"If the factory farming industry does indeed unravel—
and it must—then there is hope that we can,
gradually, reverse the environmental damage it has
caused. . . . None of this will be easy. The hardest
part about returning to a truly healthy environment
may be changing the current totally unsustainable
heavy-meat-eating culture of increasing numbers of
people around the world. But we must try. We must
make a start, one by one."[152]

—DR. JANE GOODALL

BLACK BEAN BREAKFAST BURRITOS

These breakfast burritos are a simple and delicious way to start any day. The black beans and tofu give a boost of planet-friendly protein, while the corn, spices, and toppings add additional flavor and texture. And because the filling is baked—not fried—it's not only better for the planet, but for you as well.

SERVES 2   PREP AND COOKING TIME: 40 MINUTES

INGREDIENTS

2 garlic cloves, finely chopped

3 scallions, finely chopped

½ tsp ground turmeric

½ tsp ground cumin

½ tsp salt

½ tsp paprika

¼ tsp freshly ground black pepper

2½ Tbsp coconut oil

1 C fresh, frozen, or canned corn kernels

1 (15-oz) can black beans, drained

1 (8-oz) block extra-firm tofu

2 Tbsp nutritional yeast

2 (8- or 12-inch) flour tortillas

1 avocado, halved and pitted

¾ C chopped tomatoes (optional)

2 Tbsp vegan sour cream (optional)

Cilantro (optional)

Hot sauce (optional)

METHOD

Preheat the oven to 350°F.

Put the garlic and scallions in a very large bowl. Add the turmeric, cumin, salt, paprika, pepper, coconut oil, and corn. Add the black beans. Stir to combine. Crumble the tofu into the bowl and add the nutritional yeast. Stir to combine everything well.

Transfer the mixture to an 8-inch casserole or baking dish. Bake, uncovered, until the liquid has evaporated and the top is slightly browned, 20 to 25 minutes.

Remove from the oven. Put the tortillas on a baking sheet and place in the oven for 1 minute to warm them up. Remove from the oven. Spread half an avocado onto each wrap. Add as much of the tofu–black bean mixture as you'd like. Add whichever other toppings you're using—chopped tomatoes, sour cream, cilantro, and/or hot sauce—then roll into burritos. Enjoy immediately.

Want to go the extra eco-mile?
Cook the black beans from scratch and cut the corn freshly off the cob to cut down on packaging.

BLUEBERRY BUCKWHEAT WAFFLES

Despite its name, buckwheat is actually not related to wheat, but rather to sorrel and rhubarb. Its seeds are the part we eat, and they're rich in complex carbohydrates—making it a healthier option than white flour, and giving the foods we cook with it an earthier flavor and color. And this recipe for buckwheat waffles uses almond milk instead of cow's milk, which cuts its water footprint down by 97 percent, and uses aquafaba (chickpea juice) instead of eggs, which reduces food waste and the dish's carbon emissions.

MAKES 8 TO 10 WAFFLES   PREP AND COOKING TIME: 30 MINUTES

INGREDIENTS

1½ C buckwheat flour

2 tsp baking powder

1 tsp baking soda

¼ tsp salt

1 tsp ground cinnamon

6 Tbsp aquafaba (chickpea juice; see page 255)

2 Tbsp sugar

1 C almond milk

1 tsp pure vanilla extract

3 Tbsp unsweetened applesauce

1 C plain nondairy yogurt

½ C margarine, melted, plus more for greasing

½ C fresh or frozen blueberries

Pure maple syrup, for serving

Flaked almonds, for serving (optional)

Fresh berries, for serving (optional)

METHOD

In a large bowl, combine the buckwheat flour, baking powder, baking soda, salt, and cinnamon.

In the bowl of a stand mixer fitted with the whisk attachment or in a large bowl using a handheld mixer, beat the aquafaba on medium speed until it holds soft peaks, 5 to 10 minutes. Add the sugar, a little at a time, as you go.

In a separate bowl, whisk together the almond milk, vanilla, applesauce, yogurt, margarine, and ¼ cup water.

Pour the wet mixture into the dry mixture, add the blueberries, and stir to combine.

Carefully fold the beaten aquafaba into the batter—work gently so as to not deflate it too much.

Turn on the waffle iron and let the waffle batter sit for 10 minutes while the waffle iron gets hot.

Lightly grease the waffle iron with margarine and pour in enough batter for one waffle (the amount will depend on your iron). Close and cook for 2 to 5 minutes, until done. Repeat until all the batter has been used up.

Top with warm maple syrup, flaked almonds, berries, and/or any other favorite toppings you have on hand.

> (!) **Equipment Alert:** This recipe requires a waffle iron and stand mixer or some stamina with a handheld one.

BREAKFAST BANANA SPLIT

Who says banana splits are only for dessert? This healthier version of a banana split will start your day off right—with fresh fruit, raw granola, and a jolt of espresso for that morning buzz.

SERVES 2   PREP AND COOKING TIME: 15 MINUTES

INGREDIENTS

Double shot of espresso

¼ C sugar

¼ C dates, pitted and chopped

¼ C shredded coconut

¼ C pecans, chopped

4 Tbsp nondairy yogurt, any flavor

2 bananas

½ C fresh berries

METHOD

In a small saucepan, combine the espresso and sugar and bring to a boil over medium-high heat. Lower the heat to maintain a simmer and cook, stirring continuously, for 5 minutes. Remove from the heat and refrigerate until completely cool.

In a food processor, combine the dates, coconut, and pecans. Pulse to combine well.

Spoon 2 tablespoons of the yogurt onto each plate. Slice the bananas down the middle lengthwise and place on top. Top with the granola, berries, and espresso drizzle. Enjoy immediately.

Tip: Don't own an espresso maker? Order a shot to go from your local coffee shop!

Equipment Alert: This recipe requires a food processor.

"Go vegetable heavy. Reverse the psychology of your plate by making meat the side dish and vegetables the main course."[153]

—CHEF BOBBY FLAY

GREENPEACE USA EXECUTIVE DIRECTOR ANNIE LEONARD

One of the most important shifts we've seen over the past thirty years is that more and more people are realizing that while changing our personal eating habits is critical, we must also recognize the wider impacts of what we put on our plates, and act to change our society's relationship to agriculture and food. From the overfishing of our oceans, to exploited and underage migrant farm workers, to poisonous pesticide intensive farming and more: our food and agriculture system needs an overhaul.

The connection between human consumption of meat and dairy products and damage to our planet is now more widely recognized. Livestock is the most significant contributor to nitrogen and phosphorus pollution of streams, rivers, and coastal waters worldwide. They're also major emitters of greenhouse gas emissions. In fact, the livestock sector is responsible for about 14 percent of global emissions, as much as the transportation sector.

That's not to say that animal agriculture is the only problem; there are also plant-based ingredients that are causing severe environmental destruction. Take palm oil, for instance, which comes from tropical countries like Indonesia, Malaysia, and parts of Africa. As we've tried to ditch trans fats from our diets, demand for palm oil has shot up, and these countries are now chopping down thousands of acres of lush tropical rain forests to clear the way for palm tree plantations. Indonesia has lost over a quarter of its forest—an area the size of Germany—since 1990, which is a tragedy for the indigenous communities and tigers, orangutans, and other endangered species that need the forest to survive.

A lot's changed since I turned vegetarian in the early '80s. Back then, I ate a lot of grilled cheese sandwiches because that was the only thing on the menu. These days,

eating organic, vegetarianism, and trying to live more sustainably have become much more mainstream. If you're used to having meat with every meal, start experimenting with plant proteins like lentils and beans instead. As well as being meat substitutes, they're also a whole new cuisine to explore!

I also recommend trying to eat food that's produced locally, that's in season, and that's organic where possible. If you have access to a CSA or a farmers' market, they're great. I get a box of fresh veggies delivered each week. It often includes things I never saw before. Thank goodness they include recipes.

Another key piece of the puzzle is wasting as little food as possible. Rotting food waste in landfills is a major source of climate-polluting methane. Composting is a great alternative, but if we can be smart about how much we buy and what we do with our leftovers, we can avoid that waste altogether.

Much of the world has become disconnected from the food we eat and lost knowledge about who grows it and how. It's important to remember that our power to change this doesn't just come from dollars we spend. Our voices and votes are essential in helping to fix our broken food system to make sure it's healthy for all eaters, workers, wildlife, and the planet.

Annie Leonard began her career at Greenpeace in 1988 and now serves as Executive Director for Greenpeace USA. She has decades of experience investigating and explaining the environmental and social impacts of our stuff: where it comes from, how it gets to us, and where it goes after we get rid of it. Her book, The Story of Stuff, *is a New York Times bestseller, and her film of the same name blossomed into The Story of Stuff Project, which works to empower people around the globe to fight for a more sustainable and just future.*

CHERRY CHIA PUFF PASTRY BREAKFAST TARTS

Flaky, airy, gooey, sweet—these puff pastry tarts are wonderful for breakfast, parties, dessert, or any time of day. Nutrient-rich chia seeds help thicken the filling in a low-calorie and sustainable way, and cherry trees can have real benefits on our air quality: in addition to trees helping purify our air, a single cherry tree can also perfume the air with more than two hundred thousand flowers.

MAKES 8   PREP AND COOKING TIME: 45 MINUTES

INGREDIENTS

2 (10 x 15-inch) sheets vegan puff pastry

2 C frozen cherries

1 C granulated sugar

2 tsp fresh lemon juice

1 tsp ground cinnamon

1 tsp pure vanilla extract

¼ C chia seeds

2 Tbsp almond milk, plus more for brushing

1 C confectioners' sugar

METHOD

Defrost the puff pastry sheets according to the package directions on the counter in advance.

Preheat the oven to 400°F.

Set two of the cherries aside for the frosting and place the remainder in a small saucepan. Add the granulated sugar, lemon juice, cinnamon, and vanilla. Stir until the sugar is dissolved. Bring to a boil, decrease the heat to low, and simmer for 5 minutes, mashing the cherries as they cook. Stir in the chia seeds and cook to thicken, 5 minutes more. Remove from the heat and let cool for several minutes.

Line a baking sheet with parchment paper. Cut the puff pastry into 16 rectangles (into quarters lengthwise and then in half crosswise) and then gently transfer 8 of them to the parchment-lined baking sheet. These will be the bottoms of the tarts. (You may need to do this in batches depending on the size of the baking sheet.)

Spoon about 1 tablespoon of the filling onto the center of each of the 8 pastry rectangles on the baking sheet. Spread it around, leaving a border of about ½ inch around the edges. Top each with a matching rectangle and then press around the edges with a fork to seal. Pierce three holes in the top of each pastry with the tip of a sharp knife. Brush lightly with almond milk and bake for 20 minutes. Remove from the oven and set aside.

Meanwhile, combine the confectioners' sugar and the almond milk in a small bowl. Stir until smooth. Take those two cherries you set aside earlier and squeeze their juice into the frosting. Stir to combine.

Drizzle the frosting over the pastries while they are still warm.

Tip: Want to save some time? Though not quite as good as making it yourself, you can use store-bought jam of any flavor you'd like as the filling.

CLASSIC FRENCH TOAST

Who doesn't love a nice, hot plate of French toast in the morning? But eggs and milk aren't the most eco-friendly way to make it. For example, it takes 53 gallons of water to produce a single egg and 820 gallons of water to produce just 8 ounces of milk (think of all the feed grown for the chickens and cows, for starters). This recipe uses almond milk, and is thickened with a little tofu and chia seeds instead. It fries up well and is super satisfying— all while being a little lighter on the planet.

SERVES 3   PREP AND COOKING TIME: 20 MINUTES

INGREDIENTS

1½ C almond milk, plus more if needed

½ C firm tofu

1 Tbsp pure maple syrup, plus more for serving

2 Tbsp chia seeds

1½ Tbsp nutritional yeast

1½ tsp ground cinnamon

¼ tsp ground nutmeg

Pinch of salt

6 slices bread, about ¾ inch thick

3 Tbsp margarine, for frying, plus more as needed

Fresh berries, for serving

Confectioners' sugar, for serving

METHOD

Put the almond milk, tofu, maple syrup, chia seeds, nutritional yeast, cinnamon, nutmeg, and salt in a food processor or blender and pulse until mixed and the tofu is almost smooth but a tiny bit crumbly. You want this liquidy enough to coat the bread with; if it's not, add some more almond milk, a little at a time, and pulse.

Place the bread slices neatly inside a large casserole dish and pour the almond milk mixture over the bread. Flip the slices to coat the other side and set aside to soak in the mix.

In a large skillet, melt the margarine over medium heat. Once the pan is hot, about 3 minutes, add a few slices of bread. Cook until golden brown on the first side, about 3 minutes, then flip to cook the other side until golden brown.

Stack on plates and serve topped with maple syrup, fresh berries, and confectioners' sugar.

Want to go the extra eco-mile? Use bread that's on its last leg to avoid food waste! You don't want it stale, but it needn't be totally fresh, either, since it'll soften up once coated in batter.

MIX 'N' MATCH SUPERFOOD SMOOTHIES

Jam-packed with phytonutrients, vitamins, and antioxidants, greens are true superfoods. Combined with other good-for-you-and-the-planet foods—like fresh fruits and vegetables, nut butters, hemp seeds, turmeric, chia seeds, and more—a green smoothie a day may literally help keep the doctor away. Just mix and match, using the options I've listed here as a guide. And don't be afraid to get creative with your smoothies. Drink up!

SERVES 2   PREP AND COOKING TIME: 5 MINUTES

INGREDIENTS

2 C Greens	2 C Liquid	3 C Fruits/Veggies	Optional Boosters
Arugula	Almond milk	Apple	2 Tbsp almond butter
Beet greens	Coconut milk	Apricot	2 Tbsp peanut butter
Bok choy	Coconut water	Banana	2 Tbsp raw cashews
Broccoli	Hemp milk	Blackberries	1 tsp ground cinnamon
Collard greens	Herbal tea (cooled)	Blueberries	2 Tbsp chia seeds
Dandelion greens	Orange juice	Butternut squash	2 Tbsp flax meal
Kale	Soy milk	Carrot	1 tsp fresh ginger
Romaine lettuce	Water	Cherries	2 Tbsp hemp seeds
Spinach		Cucumber	4 Medjool dates
Swiss chard		Mango	1 tsp ground turmeric
		Melon	1 tsp pure vanilla extract
		Peaches	2 Tbps hulled pumpkin seeds
		Pears	2 shots of espresso
		Pineapple	1 tsp spirulina
		Raspberries	
		Sweet Potato	

METHOD

Want to go the extra eco-mile? Use in-season produce (see page 252).

First, pick the combination you want. Start simple if you're new to green smoothies. Spinach, pineapple, raspberries, hemp seeds, and orange juice make a fruity combo if you like sweet smoothies. For something a little lighter on the carbs, try kale, cucumber, spirulina, and almond milk. Feeling adventurous? Swiss chard, banana, pumpkin, vanilla, cinnamon, ginger, coconut milk, and Medjool dates is outrageously good.

Once you're ready to roll, place everything in the blender and blend on high until well combined. (Blending time will depend on how powerful your blender is.) Adjust the liquid amount to reach your desired thickness. Pour into glasses and enjoy immediately. It's really that simple.

OATMEAL WITH CHAI-POACHED PEARS

When I was young, I lived within walking distance of my elementary school. On snowy New Hampshire mornings, my mom would send me off down the road with a stomach full of oatmeal. "It sticks to your ribs," she'd say—and I'd always arrive at school still feeling warm from my breakfast. This recipe uses pears poached in chai tea (yum!) to offer an extra-earthy start to any cold morning.

SERVES 2   PREP AND COOKING TIME: 30 MINUTES

INGREDIENTS

2 small ripe pears

¼ C sugar

1 Tbsp pure vanilla extract

2 chai tea bags

1 C instant oats

1 C almond milk

Pure maple syrup, for serving

METHOD

Peel the pears, leaving the stems intact. Place in a small saucepan with the sugar, vanilla, and tea bags and add enough water so that the pears are just covered. If they're tall pears, lay them down. Bring to a boil, turn the heat down to low, and simmer for 20 minutes. (If your pears aren't ripe yet, add 5 minutes to the cooking time.)

Drain the water and let the pears cool while you make the oatmeal.

Place the oats in a medium saucepan with 2 cups water and bring to a boil, then decrease the heat to low and simmer for 5 minutes or until thick. Remove from the heat and stir in the almond milk.

Spoon the oatmeal into serving bowls. Slice the pears in half and place on top, then drizzle with maple syrup.

"Eating, for me, is how you proclaim your beliefs three times a day."[154]

—NATALIE PORTMAN

PB&J POWER SMOOTHIES

I start almost every day with some variation of this simple smoothie. The chia, pumpkin, and hemp seeds—as well as the peanut butter—give a big ol' boost of protein, flavor, and fiber, while the flax offers a healthy dose of omega-3s.

SERVES 2   PREP TIME: 5 MINUTES

INGREDIENTS

2 ripe bananas, frozen in chunks

2 Tbsp peanut butter

1 C frozen blueberries

2 C almond milk

2 tsp chia seeds

2 tsp flax meal

2 Tbsp hulled pumpkin seeds

2 Tbsp hemp seeds

1 Tbsp pure maple syrup (optional)

METHOD

Blend all the ingredients in a blender until well combined and the seeds are liquefied. In a Vitamix or other high-speed blender on high, that's about 1 minute; in a standard blender, it may take longer. Pour into glasses and enjoy immediately.

SMOOTHIE HACKS GALORE!

Add more almond milk if you prefer a smoother smoothie.

If you'd rather use store-bought protein powder (like Vega brand), you can omit the pumpkin, hemp, and chia seeds. Unless you want to be like Arnold—in which case, go nuts.

Or you can make your own protein powder in advance by blending chia seeds, flax meal, hulled pumpkin seeds, and hemp seeds. Just be sure to refrigerate it if you make it in advance—it'll keep for up to 2 weeks.

If you've forgotten to freeze your bananas in advance, don't fret! They work well fresh, too.

Making this just for one person? Cut the amounts in half (duh).

 Want to go the extra eco-mile? Have bananas that are starting to turn brown? Avoid waste by peeling and freezing them in chunks before they go bad, then add them to your smoothies!

PEA AND POTATO FRITTATA

Frittata is an Italian egg dish—similar to a quiche, but sans crust and filled with savory ingredients. Tasty, yes. Sustainable? Not so much. Enter tofu: it's protein-packed and holds vegetables well—and it's more eco-friendly. (One egg may contribute to rain forests being destroyed for chicken feed, and an egg results in about 140 percent more greenhouse gas emissions than a serving of tofu does.) In this version of the classic Italian dish, arrowroot flour provides a smooth texture, nutritional yeast gives it a slightly sharp taste (like Parmesan might), and green peas add a little color and some extra protein.

SERVES 4   PREP AND COOKING TIME: 1½ HOURS

INGREDIENTS

2 Tbsp olive oil

4 russet potatoes, cut into ½-inch dice

1 tsp black salt

1 C frozen peas

1 (14-oz) package silken tofu

2 heaping Tbsp arrowroot flour

¼ C nutritional yeast

1 tsp onion powder

½ tsp garlic powder

½ tsp ground turmeric

Pinch of freshly ground black pepper

¼ C chopped fresh parsley

1 C shredded vegan cheese (optional)

Fresh spinach, for serving (optional)

Sriracha, for serving (optional)

Ketchup, for serving (optional)

METHOD

Preheat the oven to 375°F. Pour the olive oil into an 8 x 12-inch casserole dish.

Add the potatoes, stirring to coat evenly. Sprinkle with ½ teaspoon of the salt and bake for 30 minutes.

Remove the peas from the freezer and let them defrost while the potatoes cook.

Place the tofu, arrowroot flour, nutritional yeast, onion powder, garlic powder, turmeric, remaining ½ teaspoon salt, and the pepper in a food processor or blender. Puree until smooth.

Once the potatoes are cooked, loosen them from the bottom of the dish using a spatula. Add the peas and parsley. Fold in the tofu mixture. Sprinkle the top with cheese (if using) and return to the oven. Bake for 40 minutes more.

Remove from the oven and let rest for 10 minutes before serving.

Serve the frittata on its own, or with fresh spinach, Sriracha, or ketchup.

Tip: Want to make it even more colorful and healthy? Swap in sweet potatoes for the russet potatoes!

"We can make a commitment to promote vegetables and fruits and whole grains on every part of every menu."[155]

—MICHELLE OBAMA

RICE PUDDING WITH COCONUT AND CRANBERRIES

Rice pudding is a truly global dish, eaten in virtually every corner of the world. In Iraq, they call it *zarda wa haleeb*, and eat it with date syrup. In India, they call it *dudhapak* and prepare the dish with sugar, nuts, and saffron. In Italy, *budino di riso* is made with milk and orange peel. And in Norway, *risengrynsgrøt* is eaten around Christmas, often with cinnamon. This rice pudding is made with tart cranberries and rich coconut milk, sweetened with a bit of sugar, and rounded out with cinnamon and vanilla.

SERVES 2 TO 4   PREP AND COOKING TIME: 50 MINUTES

INGREDIENTS

1½ C short-grain white rice

1 heaping tsp ground cinnamon, plus more for serving

1 tsp pure vanilla extract

¾ C canned coconut milk

⅓ C sugar

1 C fresh cranberries

¼ C unsweetened coconut flakes

METHOD

Place the rice, cinnamon, vanilla, and 3 cups water into a medium saucepan. Cover and bring to a boil over high heat, then lower the heat to low and simmer for 25 minutes, or until almost all the liquid has been absorbed.

Add the coconut milk, sugar, and cranberries. Cover and bring the mixture to a boil, then lower the heat to maintain a simmer and cook, stirring occasionally, until all the coconut milk has been absorbed and the rice is thick and creamy, about 15 minutes. Be careful of the cranberries when you remove the lid to stir the pudding; they will pop as they cook!

Remove from the heat and let rest for 5 minutes, uncovered. Give it another stir and then spoon into bowls and top with flaked coconut and a dusting of cinnamon.

RISE 'N' SHINE BREAKFAST SANDWICH

Go above and beyond with this delightful breakfast sandwich. A vegan sausage patty, an easy homemade egg-free patty using chickpea flour, and a slice of gooey vegan cheese all piled onto a toasted English muffin—what a morning! And because chickpeas emit 60 percent less CO_2 than eggs, this recipe is as environmentally conscious as it is tasty.

SERVES 4   PREP AND COOKING TIME: 45 MINUTES

INGREDIENTS

¾ C chickpea flour

2 Tbsp nutritional yeast

2 Tbsp olive oil

½ tsp black salt

½ tsp ground turmeric

¼ tsp freshly ground black pepper

1 Tbsp vegetable oil, plus more for greasing

4 vegan sausage patties

4 English muffins, toasted

Ketchup

4 slices vegan cheese (optional)

METHOD

Whisk together the chickpea flour, nutritional yeast, olive oil, salt, turmeric, pepper, and ¾ cup water until smooth. Let sit for 30 minutes, giving one final stir at the end. Don't be tempted to taste it yet—chickpea flour tastes weird before it's cooked.

In a large skillet, heat the vegetable oil over medium-high heat. Oil the insides of four egg rings.

Place the egg rings in the pan and fill with the batter. Cook the first side for 3 minutes. Gently remove the egg rings, flip, and cook for 3 minutes more. Remove from the pan and set aside.

Add the vegan sausage patties to the pan and cook until browned, about 3 minutes per side.

Build each sandwich on an English muffin: a sausage patty, an egg patty, ketchup, and cheese!

Want to go the extra eco-mile? Substitute a slice of the Sun-Dried Tomato and Basil Sausage (page 183) for a store-bought patty, and replace the vegan cheese slices with avocado to cut down on packaging.

No egg rings? No problem. Make DIY egg rings using round cookie cutters or the screw-on rings of mason jar lids. Just make sure they're clean and oiled before using. And when you flip the patties, use a spatula to flip the whole thing—DIY ring and all—rather than removing the ring first. When you go to pop the patty out at the end, carefully hold the ring using a fork and push the patty through the wide end.

Shopping Tip: Chickpea flour is sometimes called garbanzo flour, gram flour, or *besan.*

SWEET POTATO AND PARSNIP HASH

Nothing says earthy like root vegetables! Parsnips have cream-colored skin and flesh; left in the ground, they become sweeter after winter frosts. (If unharvested, they produce a stem topped by small yellow flowers.) Mixed with sweet potatoes, they make a wonderful morning hash. Some experts even say eating lots of sweet potatoes, considered a superfood, will help you live longer and healthier. How sweet is that?

SERVES 2 AS A MAIN OR 4 AS A SIDE   PREP AND COOKING TIME: 20 MINUTES

INGREDIENTS

1 Tbsp coconut oil

1½ C ½-inch cubes sweet potato

1¼ C ½-inch cubes parsnip

1 tsp Old Bay seasoning

1 tsp onion powder

½ tsp freshly ground black pepper

½ tsp garlic powder

METHOD

In heavy-bottomed skilled, heat the coconut oil over medium-high heat.

Add the cubed vegetables and sprinkle with the Old Bay, onion powder, pepper, and garlic powder. Stir to coat thoroughly with the oil and seasonings. Cook for about 5 minutes, without stirring. Once the underside starts to brown, use a spatula to turn them all over and cook, stirring every minute or so, until all sides turn golden brown and soft, 5 to 10 minutes.

Remove from the heat and let sit for 5 minutes before serving.

 Want to go the extra eco-mile? Make this recipe when sweet potatoes and parsnips are in season (see page 252).

 Serving Suggestion: I like to serve this with the Apple Cinnamon Pancakes (page 78) or Blueberry Buckwheat Waffles (page 85) to add a little something savory alongside something sweet.

TOFU SCRAMBLE 101

There's nothing quite like waking up on a Sunday morning and spending a couple hours drinking coffee, listening to music, and whipping up a big breakfast. And no full breakfast would be complete without a scrumptious scramble. If you're looking for a zero-cholesterol, filling, planet-friendly recipe, this introductory scramble made with tofu instead of eggs is the perfect place to start.

SERVES 2   PREP AND COOKING TIME: 20 MINUTES

INGREDIENTS

½ tsp ground turmeric

½ tsp black salt

¼ tsp garlic powder

2 Tbsp nutritional yeast

1 Tbsp canola oil

4 scallions, finely chopped

1 (16-oz) block extra-firm tofu

Fresh baby spinach, for serving

Ketchup, for serving

METHOD

Combine the turmeric, salt, garlic powder, and nutritional yeast in a small bowl. Set aside.

In a large skillet, heat the canola oil over medium-high heat. Add the scallions. Cook for about 2 minutes.

Crumble the tofu into the pan, making some chunks small and some larger.

Add the spice mixture, stirring to evenly coat the tofu.

Cook, stirring frequently to ensure it doesn't stick to the pan, until the liquid has evaporated, about 10 minutes.

Enjoy immediately, served atop some fresh baby spinach and topped with ketchup.

Serving Suggestion: Serve with some toast, Sweet Potato and Parsnip Hash (page 102), and Crispy Rice Paper Bacon (page 193) alongside.

Note: This is a basic scramble. Try adding fresh broccoli, kale, mushrooms, or all of the above! Just double the oil and add the vegetables with the scallions, cooking for a few minutes before adding the tofu.

"I don't eat meat, fish, or eggs . . . I eat a lot of tofu."[156]
—SHANIA TWAIN

SOUPS, STEWS, SALADS, AND SANDWICHES

BLT BAGEL SANDWICH

When I was growing up, my small town had one lunch spot where basically everyone would eat. We'd go every weekend, and my favorite was the BLT, which they did perfectly. But industrial pig farms take a toll on the communities where they operate. So here's a tasty, healthy, eco-friendly version using rice paper bacon instead of pork bacon.

SERVES 2   PREP AND COOKING TIME: 15 MINUTES

INGREDIENTS

6 pieces Crispy Rice Paper Bacon (see page 193)

2 bagels, any type

Vegan mayo

A few lettuce leaves

1 tomato, sliced

1 avocado, sliced (optional)

½ medium cucumber, sliced (optional)

2 radishes, thinly sliced (optional)

1 small red onion, thinly sliced (optional)

2 fresh chives, chopped (optional)

2 Tbsp sprouts (optional)

METHOD

Break each piece of the rice paper bacon in half.

Slice and toast the bagels.

Build your sandwiches on the bagels using the mayo, bacon, lettuce, and tomato. If desired, add the avocado, cucumber, radishes, onions, chives, and/or sprouts.

BLOODY BEET BURGERS

Beets are healthy, versatile, and full of iron. With a single (beef-based) burger emitting a whopping 6.8 pounds of carbon, these bloody beet burgers are lighter on the planet and oh-so-tasty to boot!

SERVES 4   PREP AND COOKING TIME: 50 MINUTES

INGREDIENTS

For the patties:

1 (15-oz) can green or black lentils, drained

1 large beet, peeled and shredded (about 2 C)

½ C fresh parsley, finely chopped

½ C walnuts, coarsely chopped

1 tsp onion powder

1 tsp garlic powder

1 tsp ground cumin

1 tsp salt

¼ tsp freshly ground black pepper

½ tsp liquid smoke

½ tsp soy sauce

¼ C tahini

¾ C instant oats

2 Tbsp tomato paste

Squeeze of lemon juice

4 Tbsp canola oil

To assemble:

4 buns

Your favorite burger condiments

A few pickles, sliced (optional)

Finely sliced red onion (optional)

1 tomato, sliced (optional)

METHOD

Put the lentils, shredded beet, parsley, and walnuts in a large bowl. Add all the remaining patty ingredients—except the canola oil—and stir to combine well. Let sit for 30 minutes.

Form the mixture into four large balls. Flatten into patties and set aside on a plate or tray.

In a skillet, heat 2 tablespoons of the canola oil over medium heat. Cook the patties, two at a time, until golden brown, about 4 minutes per side, adding more oil as needed. (If cooking all four patties at once, use all 4 tablespoons oil.) Transfer to a paper towel–lined plate.

Build the burgers on buns with your favorite condiments and any of the optional toppings.

Serving Suggestion: Enjoy with a side of Quick Country Coleslaw (page 207) and topped with the ranch dressing from the Spicy Sweet Potato Fries recipe (page 212).

Want to go the extra eco-mile? Cook the lentils from scratch to cut down on packaging. You'll need 1½ cups cooked lentils.

BUFFALO CAULIFLOWER WRAPS WITH BLUE CHEESE

My mother was only twelve when upstate New York's Anchor Bar invented a new kind of hot wing. News of the dish spread like wildfire, and it quickly became a staple throughout her hometown of Buffalo. My mom is now a vegetarian and has made the switch from Buffalo chicken to Buffalo cauliflower. With low carbon and air footprints, cauliflower is a much more sustainable choice: all the kick without the cluck.

SERVES 2   PREP AND COOKING TIME: 1 HOUR

INGREDIENTS

For the cauliflower:

Vegetable oil, for greasing

1 C rice flour

½ tsp baking powder

½ tsp garlic powder

1 tsp salt

1 medium head cauliflower, sliced

2 Tbsp margarine

⅓ C Frank's Red Hot sauce

For the blue cheese:

⅔ C plain dairy-free yogurt

1 C vegan mayo

2 Tbsp apple cider vinegar

1 Tbsp lemon juice

2 Tbsp nutritional yeast

1 tsp vegan Worcestershire (optional)

1 tsp garlic powder

1 tsp onion powder

½ tsp agave nectar

¼ tsp salt

¼ tsp freshly ground black pepper

About ¼ block firm tofu

For serving:

2 flour wraps

Lettuce

Celery sticks

METHOD

First, make the Buffalo cauliflower:
Preheat the oven to 400°F. Lightly oil a rimmed baking sheet.

In a large bowl, whisk together the rice flour, baking powder, garlic powder, salt, and 1 cup plus 2 tablespoons water. Coat the cauliflower pieces in the batter and place on the prepared baking sheet. Roast for 20 minutes.

Melt the margarine in a saucepan on medium heat. Whisk in the hot sauce and remove from the heat.

While the cauliflower is cooking, make the blue cheese dressing:
Combine all the dressing ingredients except the tofu in a medium bowl and mix well. Crumble in the tofu and stir until combined. Set aside in the fridge.

Remove the cauliflower from the oven and transfer to a bowl. Toss with the hot sauce–margarine mixture and return to the baking sheet. Place back in the oven and roast for 10 minutes more. Remove from the oven and let cool for 5 minutes.

Serve the Buffalo cauliflower in the wraps with lettuce and celery and a liberal dose of blue cheese.

GINGER-SESAME SOBA NOODLE SALAD

I travel a lot for work, so I spend a lot of time in airplanes and hotel rooms. I feel like I'm in a constant war with germs. Enter: ginger. This immune-boosting wonder root can help keep you strong and healthy, and it packs a spicy little bite. Combined with sesame oil for some (good) fat, umami-rich soy sauce, edamame for added protein, and maple syrup for a sweet note, ginger shines in this cold salad.

SERVES 4   PREP AND COOKING TIME: 30 MINUTES

INGREDIENTS

2 Tbsp toasted sesame oil

1 garlic clove, finely minced

1 tsp ginger, finely minced

2 Tbsp rice vinegar

2 Tbsp soy sauce

2 Tbsp pure maple syrup

2 C frozen shelled edamame

2 tsp sea salt

1 (10.5-oz) package buckwheat soba noodles

2 large carrots, julienned

1 red bell pepper, julienned

1 large cucumber, julienned (optional)

2 scallions, thinly sliced

½ C fresh cilantro, finely chopped (optional)

2 Tbsp black sesame seeds

METHOD

Heat the sesame oil in a small saucepan. Add the garlic and ginger and remove from the heat. Let the mixture sit for 5 minutes and then add the vinegar, soy sauce, and maple syrup. Stir until well combined and set aside.

Bring a medium pot of water to a boil. Add the edamame and 1 teaspoon of the salt and cook for 5 minutes. Remove the edamame with a slotted spoon or spider, transfer to a colander, and rinse under cold water. Set aside.

Return the water to a boil and cook the soba noodles according to the package instructions. Drain and rinse (to prevent sticking) and transfer to a large bowl.

Add the carrots, bell pepper, cucumber (if using), and edamame. Add the dressing and lightly toss. Sprinkle the scallions, cilantro (if using), and sesame seeds on top and serve.

Enjoy at room temperature or chilled in the fridge for a few hours.

LOADED BLACK BEAN DOGS

These black bean dogs are protein-packed and so flavorful. The liquid smoke and smoked paprika give them a nice, smoky flavor and the fresh cilantro gives a bit of a bite. Top 'em off with corn, avocado, sour cream, or really any other dog toppings you like. And because these dogs are all pup without the pork, you can enjoy them knowing your franks are easier on your waistline and the planet.

SERVES 4   PREP AND COOKING TIME: 1½ HOURS

INGREDIENTS

For the dogs:

¾ C canned black beans

2 Tbsp chopped fresh cilantro

2 Tbsp olive oil

2 Tbsp tomato paste

1 tsp liquid smoke

1½ C vital wheat gluten

1 heaping tsp onion powder

¾ tsp garlic powder

1 tsp smoked paprika

2 Tbsp nutritional yeast

¾ tsp sea salt

½ tsp freshly cracked black pepper

METHOD

First, make the dogs:

Place a metal steaming basket inside a large pot. Add 2 to 3 inches water, ensuring the water is below the steaming basket. Cut four pieces of aluminum foil, about 7 inches wide.

Combine the black beans, cilantro, olive oil, tomato paste, liquid smoke, and ¾ cup plus 2 tablespoons water in a blender or food processor. Puree until smooth.

Place the vital wheat gluten, onion powder, garlic powder, paprika, nutritional yeast, salt, and pepper in a large bowl and stir with a fork to combine. Pour the black bean mixture into the wheat gluten mixture, stirring with a fork as you go, then use clean hands to knead everything into a ball.

Break the ball into four pieces and form each piece into a sausage shape. Place each sausage in the middle of a piece of foil and then roll it up like a Tootsie Roll—not too tightly, as the dogs expand as they cook.

Place the foil-wrapped hot dogs in the steamer basket, cover, and bring the water to a boil. Steam for 40 minutes. (If the water level gets too low, add more as needed.) Remove from the heat and let cool for at least 10 minutes before unwrapping each hot dog.

RECIPE CONTINUES

For the salsa:

15 cherry tomatoes, quartered

½ C corn kernels, fresh or canned

¼ C finely chopped red onion

¼ tsp salt

½ tsp freshly ground black pepper

½ C finely chopped red bell pepper

1 Tbsp distilled white or apple cider vinegar

To assemble:

4 hot-dog buns

2 Tbsp canola oil

1 large avocado, pitted, peeled, and cut into ¼-inch chunks

½ C vegan sour cream

Chopped fresh cilantro

Microgreens

1 jalapeño, sliced (optional)

While the dogs are cooking, make the salsa:
Combine all the salsa ingredients in a medium bowl. Stir and set aside.

Assemble and enjoy:
Slice and toast the hot-dog buns.

In a large skillet, heat the canola oil over medium-high heat. Add the dogs and cook, turning every 2 to 3 minutes, until golden brown all over.

Place a dog in each toasted bun. Top with the salsa, avocado, sour cream, cilantro, microgreens, and jalapeño (if using). Enjoy immediately.

Serving Suggestion: Serve with a side of Quick Country Coleslaw (page 207) or Spicy Sweet Potato Fries (page 212).

Tips: On a hot summer day, cook the dogs on the grill instead of in a skillet. Also, want a more traditional dog? Skip the toppings and instead enjoy with classic hot-dog condiments—like ketchup, mustard, and relish.

Shopping Tip: You can final vital wheat gluten in the flour aisle of most grocery stores!

"Reduce your red meat intake to help the environment." [157]

—LEONARDO DICAPRIO

MARDI GRAS GUMBEAUX

Gumbo is a hearty stew that originated during the 1700s in southern Louisiana—the same region that's now sinking back into the Gulf of Mexico in large part due to climate change. Gumbo is thickened with a roux (in this case, made from flour and oil) and always includes what Bayou Staters call the "Holy Trinity" of vegetables: celery, peppers, and onions. It usually includes meat or fish, but for those of us who want to get all those Louisiana flavors without contributing to the region's watery fate, this version uses beans, mushrooms, veggie chicken, and vegetables instead. As they say in the Big Easy, *laissez les bons temps rouler*!

SERVES 6   PREP AND COOKING TIME: 1 HOUR

INGREDIENTS

1 C brown rice

1 (9-oz) package Beyond Meat grilled chicken strips

1 (14-oz) can crushed tomatoes

2 vegetable bouillon cubes

½ tsp filé powder (optional)

¾ tsp dried thyme

½ tsp cayenne pepper

½ tsp paprika

3 bay leaves

½ tsp sea salt

1½ tsp vegan Worcestershire sauce

1 green bell pepper, finely diced

2½ C sliced fresh okra

1½ celery stalks, finely diced

4 garlic cloves, minced

1 C canned red kidney beans, drained and rinsed

1 C canned great northern beans, drained and rinsed

¼ C coconut oil

¼ C all-purpose flour

1 large onion, finely diced

2 C mushrooms (any kind), chopped

Crystal hot sauce, for serving (optional)

METHOD

Combine the rice and 2 cups water in a saucepan. Cover and bring to a boil over a high heat. Lower the heat to low and simmer until the water has been absorbed, about 20 minutes. Remove from the heat and set aside.

While the rice is cooking, remove the chicken strips from the freezer and set aside to defrost slightly.

In a large bowl or pitcher, combine the crushed tomatoes, bouillon cubes, filé, thyme, cayenne, paprika, bay leaves, salt, Worcestershire, and 3 cups water. Set the mixture aside.

Combine the bell pepper, okra, celery, and garlic in a bowl and set aside. Combine the beans in a separate bowl and set aside as well.

In a large, wide pot with a lid (I use a 4-quart cast-iron braiser), melt the coconut oil over medium heat. Sprinkle the flour over the oil and stir or whisk continuously until the roux darkens to a caramel-brown color, about 10 minutes. To keep the roux from burning (which will ruin the dish), make sure to stir continuously and don't have the heat too high—it takes a while, but is worth it.

RECIPE CONTINUES

Add the onion to the roux and stir continuously until soft, about 5 minutes. Add the vegetables and cook, stirring frequently, until all the vegetables are soft, about 10 minutes. (During this time, the sliminess of the okra will cook off.)

Add the crushed tomato mixture, mushrooms, and chicken strips and bring to a boil. Lower the heat to maintain a simmer, cover, and cook for about 15 minutes. After 15 minutes, remove the cover, add the beans, and return to a boil. Lower the heat to maintain a simmer and cook, uncovered, for 15 minutes more, until slightly thickened.

Serve the gumbo over brown rice and top with Louisiana's own Crystal hot sauce if you enjoy that extra kick.

 Want to go the extra eco-mile? Replace the Beyond Meat chicken strips with 1½ cups extra beans to cut down on packaging.

 Shopping Tip: Filé powder is ground sassafras leaves and acts as a thickener and a seasoning for gumbo. Find it in the spice aisle.

MASSAGED KALE CAESAR WITH PUMPERNICKEL CROUTONS

Most anchovies are used in the unsustainable practice of turning wild-caught fish into food for farmed fish. That makes this nutty, creamy, anchovy-free Caesar both satisfying and ocean-friendly. Plus, because the recipe doesn't contain eggs, it has less of a water footprint. Vibrant kale, sweet and hearty pumpernickel croutons, creamy cashew dressing, and capers: this salad is an explosion of flavors.

SERVES 2 AS A MAIN OR 4 AS A SIDE   PREP AND COOKING TIME: 20 MINUTES

INGREDIENTS

For the dressing:

1 C cashews, soaked in water to cover for 4 hours

2 Tbsp apple cider vinegar

2 Tbsp olive oil

½ tsp garlic powder

1 tsp Dijon mustard

2 heaping Tbsp capers

1 tsp vegan Worcestershire sauce

2 Tbsp nutritional yeast

Generous pinch of salt

Freshly ground black pepper

For the croutons:

3 or 4 slices pumpernickel bread

3 Tbsp olive oil

½ tsp garlic powder

1 Tbsp nutritional yeast

½ tsp salt

For the salad:

1 (16-oz) bag or bunch of kale

1 tsp salt

1 (14-oz) can chickpeas, drained and rinsed

Nutritional yeast

METHOD

Preheat the oven to 400°F.

Make the dressing:

Drain the cashews and place all the dressing ingredients in a blender along with ½ cup water. Blend until smooth. Add 1 tablespoon more water at a time as needed until the desired consistency is reached. Store in the fridge until ready to use.

Make the croutons:

Cut the bread into small, crouton-size pieces—about ¼ inch each—and place in a container or bowl with the olive oil, garlic powder, nutritional yeast, and salt. Cover and shake so the bread is evenly coated. Spread the croutons out on a baking sheet and bake for 10 minutes or until totally crispy but not burnt. Set aside.

Meanwhile, make the salad:

Rinse the kale in cool water. If not using pre-chopped kale, rip the leaves into bite-size pieces and place in a bowl, discarding the thicker, tougher parts of the stems. Sprinkle the salt over the leaves and massage them until they go limp and are taking up about half the amount of room they were taking up before.

Pour the dressing over the leaves and use clean hands to evenly coat the leaves with the creamy, salty goodness.

Transfer to a serving bowl. Add the chickpeas. Top with the croutons and a generous sprinkle of nutritional yeast.

REUBEN SANDWICH

A Reuben sandwich is typically made with loads of unsustainable (and not the healthiest) ingredients—like corned beef, cheese, and Russian dressing. This recipe uses tempeh instead of corned beef, egg-free Russian dressing, and plant-based cheese to make an eco-friendly Reuben that's meaty and filling and, of course, perfectly messy.

SERVES 2   PREP AND COOKING TIME: 30 MINUTES

INGREDIENTS

For the Russian dressing:

½ C vegan mayo

¼ C ketchup

2 tsp prepared horseradish

½ tsp vegan Worcestershire sauce

2 Tbsp pickle relish

For the tempeh:

2 Tbsp apple cider vinegar

2 Tbsp pure maple syrup

2 Tbsp soy sauce

1 (8-oz) package tempeh, cut into ½-inch-thick slices

To assemble:

4 slices rye bread

4 slices vegan cheese

1 C sauerkraut, excess liquid squeezed out

2 Tbsp margarine

METHOD

Make the Russian dressing:
Combine all the dressing ingredients in a small bowl. Set aside in the fridge.

Prepare the tempeh:
Combine the vinegar, maple syrup, soy sauce, and 1 tablespoon water in a small bowl.

Put the tempeh in a large skillet in a single layer. Add the vinegar mixture and turn the tempeh so it's thoroughly coated in the marinade.

Cook over medium-high heat until the mixture starts to thicken and the tempeh is brown on both sides, 5 to 7 minutes. Remove from the heat and set aside.

Assemble and enjoy:
Build the sandwiches by spreading the Russian dressing on the bread and topping with 2 slices of cheese, some tempeh, and sauerkraut.

Melt the margarine in a clean pan over medium-high heat. Place the sandwiches in the pan and cook until golden on each side and the cheese has softened, about 3 minutes per side.

Remove from the pan, cut in half, and serve immediately.

Serving Suggestion: Serve with a pickle spear and potato chips or a side of Quick Country Coleslaw (page 207).

ROASTED COCONUT–BEET SOUP

Beets have served people well for ages. We turn them into sugar. We've used them as a dye. In the Middle Ages, they were often used to treat digestive illnesses. In the nineteenth century, wine was sometimes colored with them. Earthy and sweet with a vibrant red color, they combine nicely with veggie stock, thyme, and coconut milk in this hearty soup.

SERVES 4   PREP AND COOKING TIME: 1½ HOURS

INGREDIENTS

6 to 8 medium beets

¼ C olive oil

2 yellow onions, finely chopped

4 C vegetable stock

½ tsp freshly ground black pepper

1 C canned coconut milk

4 garlic cloves, finely chopped

Fresh thyme, for garnish

METHOD

Preheat the oven to 400°F.

Trim the greens and root ends off the beets. Place them, whole, in a roasting or cast-iron pan and roast for 1 hour.

Let the beets cool a bit, then hold them under cold running water and rub off their skins. (If they're stubborn skins, you may need the help of a peeler.) Chop into ½-inch cubes.

In a medium saucepan, heat the olive oil over medium-high heat. Add the onions and cook until browned, about 8 minutes. Add the beets and stir for 2 minutes, then add the stock, pepper, coconut milk, and garlic. Simmer for 5 minutes so that the garlic is cooked and all the flavors are combined.

Let cool for 10 minutes and then transfer to a blender and blend until smooth. Pour into bowls and garnish with lots of fresh thyme.

Tips: Roast the beets ahead of time and store in the fridge overnight.

Serving Suggestion: Serve with toasted sourdough, Rosemary Cornbread Mini Muffins (page 211), or Sun-Dried Tomato and Basil Sausages (page 183).

"Most people are eating more vegetables at this point. It's a good way to live and it's a good way to have a healthy, long natural life."[158]

—CHEF MARIO BATALI

ROASTED ROOT VEGETABLE AND QUINOA SALAD

Here's a hearty, healthy salad straight from the earth. Carrots and sweet potatoes give the dish vibrant hues and a sweet taste, balanced out by the creamy parsnip, tahini, and cider vinegar. The whole thing is capped with a Middle Eastern flair thanks to the cumin, coriander, and pomegranate seeds.

SERVES 4   PREP AND COOKING TIME: 50 MINUTES

INGREDIENTS

For the salad:

1 C quinoa

2 C vegetable stock

2 C ½-inch cubes parsnip

2 C ½-inch cubes carrot

2 C ½-inch cubes sweet potato

2 C ½-inch cubes russet potato

2 Tbsp olive oil

1 tsp salt

1 tsp ground coriander

1 tsp ground cumin

1 C raw almonds, chopped

4 C arugula, washed and dried

For the dressing:

½ C tahini

¼ C pure maple syrup

¼ C apple cider vinegar

2 tsp ground turmeric

Generous pinch of salt

Cracked black pepper

½ C pomegranate seeds, for garnish (optional)

METHOD

Preheat the oven to 400°F.

First, make the salad:
Place quinoa and stock in a medium saucepan. Bring to a boil over high heat. Lower the heat to maintain a simmer, cover, and cook until all the stock has been absorbed—about 20 minutes. Remove from the heat, fluff with a fork, and set aside.

Place the parsnip, carrot, sweet potato, and russet potato cubes into a large bowl. Add the olive oil, salt, coriander, and cumin. Stir to coat thoroughly, then spread the cubed vegetables evenly over two baking sheets. Roast for 15 minutes.

Remove the baking sheets, turn the vegetables with a spatula, add the chopped almonds, and return to the oven for another 10 minutes. Remove and let cool slightly.

Place the arugula in a large bowl. Top with half the quinoa, then half the vegetables, then the remaining quinoa and the remaining vegetables. Toss a couple of times to lightly combine.

Make the dressing:
Combine all the dressing ingredients in a small bowl and mix well.

Drizzle the salad with as much of the dressing as you'd like (refrigerate any leftovers) and sprinkle pomegranate seeds over the top, if desired.

Tip: Try this as a macro bowl, with the quinoa, vegetables, greens, and almonds served in "clusters" together in a bowl, rather than tossed as a salad.

"My diet had . . . a gradual trend toward less and less meat, even less and less fish, until now I rely so much on other sorts of protein, on many vegetables, most of them farm raised, and on fruits and pastas. My shift has been the result of many things—books like Jonathan Safran Foer's *Eating Animals*, films such as *Food, Inc.*, and my own observations of factory farms, feedlots, fish farms, and the condition of the meats and fish sold in many of our supermarkets."[159]

—MARTHA STEWART

SESAME SEAWEED SALAD

Seaweed = super food. Wakame (edible seaweed) contains a compound that can help burn fatty tissue, as well as healthy omega-3 fatty acids. When you want that taste of the sea without all the problems associated with fish farming or trawling, this seaweed salad is poised to become your go-to.

SERVES 4   PREP TIME: 5 MINUTES, PLUS 20 MINUTES FOR SOAKING

INGREDIENTS

1 oz (28g) dried seaweed (wakame or dulse)

2 Tbsp sesame seeds

1 Tbsp miso paste

2 Tbsp soy sauce

1 Tbsp toasted sesame oil

2 Tbsp rice vinegar

½ tsp agave nectar

½ tsp grated fresh ginger

1 red chile, finely sliced

METHOD

Place the seaweed in a bowl, add water to cover, and soak for 20 minutes to rehydrate. Drain and squeeze out excess water, then finely chop the seaweed.

While the seaweed is rehydrating, toast the sesame seeds in a dry skillet over a medium heat. Stir continuously until they become fragrant and start to make a popping noise, 3 to 5 minutes. Transfer to a plate and let cool.

Place about three-quarters of the toasted sesame seeds in a mortar (setting the rest aside) and lightly grind with the pestle. (If you don't own a mortar and pestle, you can skip this step.)

Transfer the ground seeds to a small bowl, add the remaining ingredients, and whisk to combine. Pour over the seaweed, tossing lightly with clean hands to distribute.

Cover and refrigerate for at least 10 minutes, or until ready to serve.

Sprinkle with the reserved toasted sesame seeds before serving.

Serving Suggestion: Serve with Rainbow Veggie Sushi (page 170).

SLAWPPY JOES

I grew up eating the worst possible sloppy Joes—courtesy of my grade school cafeteria. I revisited them as an adult and was surprised to learn that when done right, they're actually quite amazing. This grown-up version uses Beyond Meat ground beef—made entirely from plants, and with more protein than beef—and is topped with a big ol' pile of coleslaw to offer a healthy, eco-friendly version of that old cafeteria standby.

SERVES 2   PREP AND COOKING TIME: 30 MINUTES

INGREDIENTS

1 Tbsp olive oil

1 yellow onion, finely chopped

1 (12-oz) bag Beyond Meat beef crumbles

1 C tomato puree

3 garlic cloves, minced

3 Tbsp tomato paste

1 Tbsp vegan Worcestershire sauce

2 soft buns

Quick Country Coleslaw (page 207), for serving

METHOD

In a heavy-bottomed skillet, heat the olive oil over medium-high heat. Add the onion and cook until translucent, about 2 minutes. Add the beef crumbles and cook until lightly browned all over, about 5 minutes.

Add the tomato puree, garlic, tomato paste, and Worcestershire. Simmer for 5 to 10 minutes more.

Once the meat is cooked, remove from the heat.

Toast the buns (or don't, if you prefer them soft). Build the sloppy Joes on the buns with a pile of coleslaw topped with the meat. Enjoy—and don't be afraid to get messy!

"By eating meat, we share the responsibility of climate change."[160]

—THICH NHAT HANH

SOURDOUGH PANZANELLA

Originally from Tuscany, panzanella—or panmolle—is a light, airy salad made from bread and tomatoes. Plus, you can use stale (or going-stale) bread, which can help cut back on food waste and make the dish extra-eco-friendly.

SERVES 2 AS A MAIN OR 4 AS A SIDE   PREP AND COOKING TIME: 20 MINUTES

INGREDIENTS

3 to 5 big slices sourdough bread

3 Tbsp olive oil

2 Tbsp apple cider vinegar

1 tsp whole-grain mustard

½ tsp sea salt

1½ lbs cherry tomatoes, halved

1 small red onion, thinly sliced

½ C baby spinach

2 Tbsp capers

10 to 20 fresh basil leaves

Freshly cracked black pepper

METHOD

Toast the bread (in a toaster or grill pan, or under the broiler) until lightly blackened. Let cool.

Combine the olive oil, vinegar, mustard, and salt in a medium bowl. Add the tomatoes, along with the red onion. Stir until well coated in the dressing.

Place the baby spinach in a serving bowl. Tear the cooled sourdough into bite-size chunks and place on top of the spinach. Spoon the tomatoes and onion over the sourdough, then pour the dressing remaining in the bowl over the entire salad. Top with the capers and fresh basil and then season generously with freshly cracked black pepper.

Serve immediately.

SPICY LENTIL BURGERS

Lentils and beef both pack protein, but one is resource-intensive, requiring copious amounts of land, feed, and water while emitting huge volumes of climate-changing gases like carbon and methane. (Can you guess which one that is?) Try tossing one of these lentil burgers into the mix every once in a while. It'll make your meal more environmentally friendly plus offer some varied taste and texture to spice up that tired old burger routine.

SERVES 4   PREP AND COOKING TIME: 40 MINUTES

INGREDIENTS

For the patties:

1 (15-oz) can green or black lentils, drained and rinsed

5 or 6 sun-dried tomatoes, chopped

¼ C almonds, chopped

¼ C fresh parsley, chopped

½ tsp garlic powder

1 tsp onion powder

½ tsp paprika

½ tsp ground cumin

¼ tsp freshly ground black pepper

¾ tsp salt

¾ C instant oats

1 Tbsp almond butter

1 Tbsp nutritional yeast

1 Tbsp Sriracha (optional)

2 Tbsp canola oil

To assemble:

1 avocado, quartered, pitted, and peeled

4 burger buns

Lettuce

4 slices vegan cheese (optional)

Sliced fresh tomato

Sliced red onion

METHOD

First, make the patties:
Combine all the patty ingredients except the canola oil in a large bowl. Using moist, clean hands, form the mixture into four balls and then flatten them into patties roughly 1-inch thick.

In a large skillet, heat the canola oil over medium-high heat. Gently place the patties in the oil and cook until golden brown on the underside, about 3 minutes. Flip and cook for 3 minutes more.

Assemble and enjoy:
Cut the avocado into quarters and spread each quarter over the bottom of a burger bun. Add lettuce, vegan cheese (if using), a burger patty, a slice of tomato, red onion, and any other condiments you'd like.

Want to go the extra eco-mile? Cook the lentils from scratch in advance to cut down on packaging. You'll need 1½ cup cooked lentils for 4 burgers.

Serving Suggestion: Try the ranch dressing from the Spicy Sweet Potato Fries recipe (page 212) on these.

"Beef, barbecue, and chicken wreak havoc on the air, water, soil, and on the health and well-being of communities."[161]

—RACHEL CARSON COUNCIL

VIETNAMESE BÁNH MÌ WITH SRIRACHA CHICKEN

Báhn mìs use a single-serving airy baguette that's light and airy on the inside and crunchy on the outside. Less heavy than other breads, this lets all the fillings inside shine. Note that you'll need to make the pickles ahead of time, so plan accordingly.

SERVES 1   PREP AND COOKING TIME: 30 MINUTES

INGREDIENTS

4 Gardein Seven Grain Crispy Tenders

1 baguette or French bread loaf, cut into roughly 6-inch pieces

Vegan mayo

1 small handful of homemade pickles (recipe follows)

2 sprigs cilantro, coarsely chopped

Fresh jalapeño slices

Sriracha

1 wedge of lime

Cracked black pepper

METHOD

Cook the tenders according to the instructions on the package.

Halve the baguette lengthwise and spread a good slathering of mayo on the cut side of each half.

Place the cooked tenders inside and top with pickles, cilantro, some jalapeño slices, and Sriracha. Squeeze some lime over everything, crack a little black pepper on top, and enjoy immediately.

Want to go the extra eco-mile? Replace the Gardein with slabs of broiled tofu, cut into 1-inch-thick rectangles (see page 251 for instructions) or the seitan "meat" from the Kebab recipe on page 175, to cut down on packaging.

PICKLES

This recipe makes enough pickles for 10 to 15 sandwiches.

MAKES ABOUT 6 CUPS PREP TIME: 15 MINUTES, PLUS OVERNIGHT CHILLING

INGREDIENTS

½ large daikon radish, peeled and julienned

3 medium carrots, julienned

1 large cucumber, peeled, seeded, and julienned

2 C boiling water, plus more as needed

2 Tbsp salt

3 Tbsp sugar

1 Tbsp Sriracha

½ C rice vinegar

METHOD

Divide the daikon, carrots, and cucumber evenly between two clean 1-quart jars with lids.

Combine the boiling water, salt, and sugar in a bowl and stir until the salt and sugar have dissolved. Add the Sriracha and vinegar and stir to combine. Pour into the jar and top with extra boiling water if needed, so that all the vegetables are covered.

Loosely place the lid over the top and let cool to room temperature. Once cool, seal and refrigerate overnight before serving. The pickles will keep in the refrigerator for up to 2 weeks.

WILD MUSHROOM CHILI

I like to make this recipe when I know I'll be spending a cozy fall Sunday at home—just so I can be immersed in its smell for as long as possible. The black beans offer a hearty protein that's far more eco-friendly than beef (who wants all the deforestation that goes along with industrial cattle ranching?), and the mushrooms add a nice earthy flavor with an additional meaty texture.

SERVES: 2 TO 4   PREP AND COOKING TIME: 1½ TO 3 HOURS, DEPENDING ON THE BEANS' AGE

INGREDIENTS

1 C dried black beans

1 tsp salt

18 oz assorted wild mushrooms, coarsely chopped

2 medium yellow onions, finely chopped

1 bunch cilantro, finely chopped

4 garlic cloves, finely chopped

1 (14-oz) can chopped tomatoes

1 Tbsp soy sauce

2 Tbsp tomato paste

1 tsp crushed red pepper

1 (10.75-oz) can condensed tomato soup

Vegan sour cream, for garnish (optional)

METHOD

Place the beans in a large pot with 5 cups water and the salt. Cover and bring to a boil, then lower the heat to maintain a simmer. Cook, half covered, until you can easily squish a few beans on the side of the pot and most but not all the water has been absorbed, 60 to 90 minutes, depending on the beans' age.

Once the beans are soft, add the mushrooms, onions, cilantro, garlic, chopped tomatoes, soy sauce, tomato paste, and crushed red pepper. Increase the heat a little and cook until the vegetables are soft, 15 to 30 minutes more. At the end, stir in the tomato soup and let warm through, 2 to 3 minutes.

Enjoy immediately or remove from the heat and cover with a lid until ready to serve. Garnish with vegan sour cream, if desired.

Want to go the extra eco-mile? Swap the sour cream for homemade cashew cream! Just combine ¼ cup raw cashews, water to cover, a squeeze of lemon juice, and a pinch of salt in a high-speed blender and blend until very smooth.

Serving Suggestion: Serve with a side of Rosemary Cornbread Mini Muffins (page 211).

MAIN DISHES

Cashew Cream Mac 'n' Cheese
143

Chicken and Cabbage Wontons
144

Coconut-Lemongrass Curry with Rice Noodles
147

Creamy Basil-Chickpea Lettuce Cups
148

Grilled Veggie Pizza with BBQ Sauce
150

Jerked Jackfruit Tacos with Grilled Pineapple
153

Meat-Free Meat Loaf with Tomato-Maple Glaze
154

Mushroom and Kale Galette
158

No-Frills Cheese Pizza
160

Oyster Mushrooms à la Marinière
162

Pittsburgh Pierogis
165

Protein-Packed Burrito Bowl
169

Rainbow Veggie Sushi
170

Save-the-Bay Crab Cakes
172

Smoky Seitan Kebabs with Peanut Sauce
175

Spaghetti and Lentil Meatballs
176

Steamed Buns with Tofu and Mushrooms
180

Sun-Dried Tomato and Basil Sausages
183

Wild Rice Risotto with Peas and Asparagus
184

CASHEW CREAM MAC 'N' CHEESE

Why rely on boxed mac 'n' cheese when you can get a bit crafty with your mac 'n' cheese? This dish uses cashews for that rich, fatty flavor—combined with nutritional yeast for a cheesy taste. It's quick, easy, healthy, and better for the planet than using cow's cheese: cashew trees are lighter on the land than cows, providing wildlife habitat and preventing erosion. So give two big, creamy thumbs up for planet-friendly pasta!

SERVES 4   PREP AND COOKING TIME: 30 MINUTES, PLUS SOAKING TIME FOR CASHEWS

INGREDIENTS

1 C raw cashews, soaked in water to cover for 4 hours

2 Tbsp lemon juice

½ tsp soy sauce

¾ tsp mustard

2 tsp onion powder

½ tsp garlic powder

1 tsp salt

¼ C nutritional yeast

2 Tbsp margarine

1 (16-oz) box pasta (shells or macaroni)

Freshly ground black pepper

Smoked paprika, for garnish (optional)

Fresh basil, for garnish (optional)

METHOD

Rinse the soaked cashews. Put them in a blender. Add enough fresh water so that they are just covered, then blend until very smooth, about 1 minute. Add the lemon juice, soy sauce, mustard, onion powder, garlic powder, salt, nutritional yeast, and margarine. Blend until well combined. Add a little more water, 1 tablespoon at a time, until you have a smooth and creamy sauce.

Bring a large pot of water to a boil. Cook the pasta according to the package instructions. Drain in a colander and rinse thoroughly. Return the pasta to the pot and add the cashew cheese sauce.

Spoon into bowls and garnish with pepper, paprika (if using), and basil (if using), or whatever other toppings you love (sautéed onions, garlic, and cherry tomatoes work well!).

Tip: Like baked mac? Put the mac 'n' cheese in a baking dish and bake for 10 to 15 minutes at 350°F, or until slightly browned.

"If you're driving a Prius or you're shopping green or looking for organic, you should probably be a semi-vegetarian."[162]

—MARK BITTMAN

CHICKEN AND CABBAGE WONTONS

Travel to almost any corner of the world and you'll find a dumpling, or some variation of it: ravioli (Italy), pierogis (Poland), samosas (India), empanadas (Latin America), kibbeh (the Middle East), and of course wontons (China). These little fried wontons use meat-free chicken and fresh vegetables instead of meat to cut back on air pollution in an oh-so-delicious way.

SERVES 2   PREP AND COOKING TIME: 30 TO 40 MINUTES

INGREDIENTS

For the dipping sauce:

1 Tbsp toasted sesame oil

3 Tbsp soy sauce

2 Tbsp rice vinegar

½ Tbsp sugar

1 Tbsp Sriracha (optional)

For the wonton filling:

2 C chopped Beyond Meat chicken strips

1½ C shredded cabbage

½ C chopped scallions

1 garlic clove, chopped

1 Tbsp chopped fresh cilantro

1 Tbsp grated fresh ginger

1 Tbsp toasted sesame oil

1 Tbsp soy sauce

1 Tbsp rice vinegar

1 Tbsp sesame seeds

To assemble and garnish:

30 wonton wrappers, defrosted if frozen

Sesame oil

Chili oil

Sesame seeds

Chopped, fresh cilantro

METHOD

Make the dipping sauce:
Combine all the dipping sauce ingredients, including the Sriracha (if using), in a small bowl. Set aside in the refrigerator.

Make the filling:
Place all the filling ingredients in a food processor. Pulse until the chicken and cabbage are finely minced and everything is well combined.

Assemble the wontons:
Fill a small bowl with water and set it to the side. You'll use this to wet the edges of the wrappers.

Lay out a few wrappers, keeping the rest covered with a damp paper towel so they don't dry out. Place roughly 1 to 2 teaspoons of the filling in the center of each wrapper. Make sure the filling is just in the middle (not on the edges) or it will prevent the ends from sticking together. Gently wet the edges of one wrapper with your fingertips and fold it in half, squeezing out the air and squeezing the edges together to ensure they stick together. Place the finished wonton on a plate or platter. Repeat until you have used up all the filling.

Place a heavy-bottomed skillet over a medium-high heat and lightly coat the bottom with sesame oil. Fill the pan with wontons, leaving room to flip them, and cook until the bottoms turn golden, about 3 minutes. Add about ¼ cup water and then cover. (If you don't have a lid for your pan, you can use another pan, the lid from a large saucepan, a large plate, or aluminum foil as a cover.) Cook until all the water has evaporated, 2 to 3 minutes.

Remove from the heat and garnish with chili oil, sesame seeds, and cilantro. Serve with the dipping sauce alongside.

 Want to go the extra eco-mile? Replace the meatless chicken with 1½ cups crumbled pressed extra-firm tofu (see page 251 for instructions on pressing tofu). Just add it to the other filling ingredients after you've processed them.

Equipment Alert: This recipe requires a food processor.

COCONUT–LEMONGRASS CURRY WITH RICE NOODLES

Lemongrass is a tropical plant in the grass family. It's widely used as a culinary herb in Asian cooking and as a medicinal herb in India. Its oil is sometimes used as a "lure" to attract honeybees. And it's commonly used in teas, soups, and curries for its subtle, delicious, citrusy flavor. This dish combines lemongrass with meaty shiitake mushrooms, rich coconut milk, tofu, vermicelli rice noodles, and other deliciousness to create an aromatic, flavorful curry that'll leave you full and happy. Just watch out for bees!

SERVES 2   PREP AND COOKING TIME: 30 MINUTES

INGREDIENTS

½ (14-oz) package extra-firm tofu

3 stalks lemongrass

1 Tbsp coconut oil

1 Tbsp red curry paste

2 C canned coconut milk

¼ tsp salt

1 C vegetable stock

1 C thinly sliced shiitake mushrooms

1 C ½-inch pieces carrot

1 C ½-inch pieces broccoli

About 6 oz rice vermicelli noodles

Fresh lime wedges, for garnish

Chopped fresh cilantro, for garnish

Sliced scallions, for garnish

METHOD

Cut the tofu block in half crosswise. Cut into triangles and set aside.

Cut the lemongrass stalks down the middle, remove the outer layer, and set aside.

In a large saucepan, melt the coconut oil over medium-high heat. Add the curry paste and lemongrass. Stir until fragrant, about 2 minutes.

Add the coconut milk, salt, stock, mushrooms, and carrots. Increase the heat to high and bring to a boil, then lower the heat to maintain a simmer. Cook for about 7 minutes and then add the tofu and broccoli. Cook for 5 minutes more.

Divide the vermicelli noodles in half and place into two large serving bowls—the bowls you're going to serve or eat this dish from. Remove any large pieces of lemongrass from the curry and then pour the curry over the noodles. Cover by at least an inch, or more (depending on how soupy you want it at the end). Let sit for a few minutes so the noodles soften, and then gently stir to soften the noodles even more. (You don't need to cook the rice noodles first. By the time the curry is the right temperature to eat, they will be cooked.)

Top with a squeeze of fresh lime, chopped cilantro, and scallions and enjoy immediately.

 Want to go the extra eco-mile? Save the broccoli stems and use them in the Quick Country Coleslaw (page 207) to cut down on food waste.

CREAMY BASIL–CHICKPEA LETTUCE CUPS

The chickpea is a rain-fed crop with a low water footprint. It also improves soil structure, enriching it by fixing nitrogen. This favors crop rotation, contributing to a more sustainable model of agriculture. So we celebrate the humble chickpea for its earth-saving properties in this creamy, nutty lettuce cup recipe.

SERVES 2   PREP AND COOKING TIME: 15 MINUTES, PLUS SOAKING TIME FOR CASHEWS

INGREDIENTS

1 C raw cashews, soaked in water to cover for 4 hours, plus more (unsoaked) for serving

¼ C fresh basil leaves, plus more for serving

1 Tbsp rice vinegar or distilled white vinegar

1 garlic clove

Juice of ½ lemon

½ tsp salt

1 (14-oz) can chickpeas, drained and rinsed

1 Tbsp capers

1 medium cucumber, cut into ½-inch cubes

2 celery stalks, chopped

½ C chopped red onion

10 romaine lettuce leaves

2 Tbsp hulled pumpkin seeds

1 Tbsp black sesame seeds

Freshly cracked black pepper

Raisins, for garnish (optional)

METHOD

Rinse the soaked cashews. Place them in a blender with 1 cup water. Add the basil leaves, vinegar, garlic, lemon juice, and salt. Blend until totally smooth (about 1 minute in a Vitamix or other high-speed blender, or a bit longer in a normal blender).

Place the chickpeas and capers in a large bowl. With a potato masher or a large fork, mash them a little bit. Add the cucumber, celery, and red onion. Add the sauce and stir to combine.

Lay the lettuce leaves out like cups or taco shells. Spoon 2 heaping tablespoons of the creamy chickpea mix into each cup. Sprinkle with pumpkin seeds, black sesame seeds, a few additional cashews, and basil leaves, season with some freshly cracked black pepper, and garnish with a few raisins, if you like. Enjoy immediately.

Tip: Try toasting the pumpkin seeds first in a hot, dry pan until lightly browned.

Want to go the extra eco-mile? Save the aquafaba (chickpea juice; see page 255) for Chocolate Brownies (page 225) or Lemon Meringue Pie (page 232)—to cut down on waste.

"If more people had vegetarian or vegan diets, especially in the developed world, the environmental impact would be significant."[163]

—MARK TERCEK, NATURE CONSERVANCY CEO

GRILLED VEGGIE PIZZA WITH BBQ SAUCE

Homemade pizza is one of my all-time favorite things to make. I recommend inviting people over and making multiple pizzas. (Who says adults can't have pizza parties?) This pizza uses grilled eggplant, zucchini, and mushrooms along with BBQ sauce and dollops of vegan cream cheese (I like the Tofutti and Kite Hill brands) to create a smoky, fiery pie that's sure to please.

SERVES 2   PREP AND COOKING TIME: 2 HOURS

INGREDIENTS

For the grilled vegetables:

1 medium eggplant, cut into ¼-inch-thick rounds

1 medium zucchini, cut into ¼-inch-thick rounds

3 large button mushrooms, cut into ¼-inch pieces

¼ C balsamic vinegar

¼ C canola oil

½ tsp salt

1½ tsp liquid smoke

For the crust:

1½ C all-purpose flour, plus more for dusting

1 tsp salt

1 tsp active dry yeast

½ C plain almond milk

2 Tbsp olive oil

Cornmeal, for dusting (optional)

To assemble:

½ C BBQ sauce

½ C plus 1 Tbsp vegan cream cheese

Fresh basil leaves

METHOD

First, prep the vegetables:

Put the eggplant, zucchini, and mushrooms in a large casserole dish or container.

Whisk together the vinegar, canola oil, salt, and liquid smoke in a small bowl. Pour over the vegetables and turn to coat evenly. Let sit for at least 30 minutes.

Cook the vegetables in a hot grill pan for about 3 minutes per side. Alternatively, lay them flat on a baking sheet and place them under the broiler for 6 to 8 minutes on one side, then flip them and broil for 4 minutes on the other. Return them to the dish they were marinating in and let cool while you prepare the rest of the pizza.

Next, make the crust:

Place the flour, salt, and yeast in a large bowl and stir to combine. Make a well in the center.

Warm the almond milk by microwaving it in a microwave-safe mug for 40 seconds. Add 1 tablespoon of the olive oil and stir to combine. Slowly pour the almond milk mixture into the well in the dry ingredients, gently stirring as you go. It'll start out as a liquidy paste, and then get more solid. Once the mixture is solid enough to handle, use your hand to form the dough into a ball.

Place the dough on a lightly floured surface and knead for about 3 minutes, until you have a nice, silky-smooth ball of dough. Wipe out the bowl and place a little bit of olive oil in the bottom of it. Return the dough to the bowl, turning to coat it with oil. Cover with a clean dish towel and place it somewhere warm until the dough has doubled in size. This usually takes an hour but can take up to two depending on where you live.

Once the dough has doubled, punch it to deflate it, then return it to the floured counter. Roll it into a football shape, cover with the dish towel, and let sit for 20 minutes more.

At this point, preheat the oven to 400°F while the dough rests.

After 20 minutes, press the dough football flat and then sprinkle the top with a little flour and roll it into a pizza crust roughly 12 x 20 inches. (I find it helps to sprinkle a little cornmeal on my rolling surface, too.) Carefully transfer the dough to a large baking sheet.

Finish the pizza:

Spoon the BBQ sauce over the pizza dough and spread it around with the back of a tablespoon, leaving a 1-inch border along the edges.

Pile the grilled veggies onto the pizza and bake for 20 minutes.

Remove from the oven and add the cream cheese in roughly 1-tablespoon dollops. Return the pizza to the oven for a final 5 minutes.

Remove from the oven and let cool for 3 to 5 minutes. Top with fresh basil leaves and cut into 6 to 8 slices. Enjoy alone or with a side salad.

JERKED JACKFRUIT TACOS WITH GRILLED PINEAPPLE

Jerk is a style of Jamaican cooking that involves a super-hot spice mixture and (usually) meat. But what's a guy or gal to do if you want that same fiery flavor without the environmental problems that often accompany meat production? Well, bring on the jackfruits! This fruit, when marinated and shredded, mimics the taste and texture of pulled pork. So this recipe offers a real culinary mashup of ingredients—tropical fruit with Caribbean meat spices in a Mexican tortilla. You'll never think of fruit the same way again!

SERVES 2   PREP AND COOKING TIME: 30 MINUTES

INGREDIENTS

3 Tbsp agave nectar

3 Tbsp apple cider vinegar

2 Tbsp olive oil

1½ Tbsp ground cinnamon

2 Tbsp freshly ground black pepper

1 Tbsp dried thyme

2 tsp ground allspice

1½ tsp cayenne pepper

½ tsp ground nutmeg

½ tsp garlic powder

½ tsp onion powder

½ tsp salt

1 (20-oz) can jackfruit, drained

3 pineapple rings, fresh or canned

6 soft corn or flour tortillas

1½ C sliced red cabbage

12 cherry tomatoes, quartered

Vegan sour cream, for serving

Chopped fresh cilantro, for serving

Fresh lime, for serving

METHOD

In a small bowl, combine the agave nectar, vinegar, olive oil and ¼ cup water. Set aside.

Combine the cinnamon, black pepper, thyme, allspice, cayenne, nutmeg, garlic powder, onion powder, and salt in a small bowl. Place a large, flat-bottomed skillet over a medium-high heat. Once hot, add the spice mixture and stir for about 2 minutes, or until fragrant. Pour the agave mixture into the skillet and heat for 30 seconds. Add the jackfruit and stir to break up the jackfruit as it softens. Heat through, about 3 minutes, and set aside.

Heat a grill pan over high heat and grill the pineapple rings until lightly blackened, about 3 minutes per side. (If you don't have a grill pan, just use a regular heavy-bottomed skillet and sear them for a couple of minutes on each side.)

Warm the tortillas on the stove or in the microwave. Build your tacos using the jackfruit, grilled pineapple, cabbage, cherry tomatoes, sour cream, and cilantro. Serve with wedges of lime.

MEAT-FREE MEAT LOAF
WITH TOMATO-MAPLE GLAZE

Mom's meat loaf was always one of my absolute favorites. But a single beef serving dishes out almost 30 kg of climate-change-causing CO_2, so this recipe uses chickpeas instead. Coming in at less than 2 kg of CO_2 per serving, they're a much eco-friendlier choice. And combined with carrots, celery, panko bread crumbs, and delicious flavorings, they cook up into a robust, hearty loaf that'll leave you wanting seconds.

SERVES 4   PREP AND COOKING TIME: 1 HOUR 10 MINUTES

INGREDIENTS

For the loaf:

2 Tbsp olive oil, plus more for greasing

2 (14-oz) cans chickpeas, drained and rinsed

1 large yellow onion, diced

2 celery stalks, finely diced

2 carrots, finely diced

2 garlic cloves, minced

3 Tbsp chopped walnuts

2 C panko bread crumbs

½ C plain almond milk

2½ Tbsp soy sauce

3 Tbsp vegan Worcestershire sauce

2 Tbsp nutritional yeast

2 Tbsp flax meal

2½ Tbsp tomato paste

1 tsp liquid smoke

¼ tsp freshly ground black pepper

½ tsp ground sage

½ tsp dried thyme

For the glaze:

¼ C tomato paste

2 Tbsp pure maple syrup

2 Tbsp apple cider vinegar

1 Tbsp soy sauce

1 tsp paprika (preferably smoked paprika)

½ tsp freshly ground black pepper

Dash of crushed red pepper

2 Tbsp sesame seeds

METHOD

(!) **Equipment Alert:** This recipe requires a food processor.

🍴 **Serving Suggestion:** Serve with a side of Massaged Kale Caesar salad (page 123).

First, make the loaf:

Preheat the oven to 375°F. Lightly oil a 9 x 5-inch loaf pan.

Place all the meat loaf ingredients in a large bowl and mix together.

In ¾-cup batches, place the loaf mixture into a food processor and process until most of the chickpeas are broken up (you want it smooth, but still a little chunky in the end). Place each batch into the oiled loaf pan as you go.

Pack the mixture into the pan and smooth out the top. Bake, uncovered, for 30 minutes.

Meanwhile, make the glaze:

Whisk together all the glaze ingredients, except the sesame seeds, in a bowl and set aside.

After 30 minutes of baking, remove the loaf and top it with the glaze, smoothing it over. Sprinkle the sesame seeds on top and bake for 25 minutes more.

Remove from the oven, let cool for at least 15 minutes, slice, and serve.

PHOTO ON FOLLOWING SPREAD

"Reducing meat consumption is a growing trend, driven by health and environmental considerations . . . I feel healthier, more active, and by making my diet more varied, I never feel like I'm missing out on anything."[164]

—SIR RICHARD BRANSON

MUSHROOM AND KALE GALETTE

In French cooking, galette can refer to several types of round or free-form crusty cakes or pies. (In New Orleans, where I used to live, they eat a sweet version called galette des rois—or King Cake—around Mardi Gras each year.) This galette is savory, made with mushrooms, kale, eggplant, and capers, plus some soy yogurt for creaminess. It's perfect for dinner parties, when you want a pretty centerpiece meal that'll be sure to please.

SERVES 4   PREP AND COOKING TIME: 1½ HOURS

INGREDIENTS

2 Tbsp olive oil

1 red onion, finely chopped

1 small eggplant, cut into ½-inch cubes

6 baby bella or button mushrooms, sliced

1½ C chopped tomatoes

6 kale leaves, stemmed and chopped

2 Tbsp capers

¼ C nondairy yogurt

1 tsp dried oregano

2 tsp sea salt

2 C whole wheat flour, plus more for dusting

½ C instant oats

¼ C chilled margarine

¼ to ½ C cold water

Almond milk, for brushing

Pine nuts, for garnish

METHOD

In a large skillet, heat the olive oil over medium-high heat.

Add the onion and stir so that it is coated in the oil. Add the eggplant and cook for about 5 minutes. Add the mushrooms and tomatoes and cook for 2 minutes more. (If sticking, add a splash of water as you go.) Add the kale and stir until the leaves are limp, about 2 minutes. Add the capers, yogurt, oregano, and 1 teaspoon of the salt. Sprinkle 1 tablespoon of the flour on top, then stir to combine. Remove from the heat and let sit while you prepare the crust.

Preheat the oven to 375°F.

Place the remaining flour, the oats, and the remaining 1 teaspoon salt in a large bowl. Stir to combine. Add the margarine and work it through with clean fingers until the mixture is crumbly. Add the water, 2 tablespoons at a time, kneading between additions, until the mixture forms a ball.

Lightly dust a clean work surface with flour. Knead the dough a few times until it forms a nice, compact ball. Flatten with the palm of your clean hands and then sprinkle with a little bit of flour and roll into a circle with a rolling pin. Roll back and forth a few times and then flip, sprinkle with some more flour, roll, flip, and repeat until you have a circle about 15 inches in diameter.

Transfer the dough to a baking sheet and spoon the filling into the middle. Fold the edges up, pressing the dough together where the edges touch to encourage sticking. Brush the dough with almond milk and sprinkle the pine nuts over the exposed part of the filling.

Bake for 45 minutes. Remove and let cool for 5 minutes before cutting and serving.

"I'm eating a far more plant-based diet."[165]

—OPRAH WINFREY

NO-FRILLS CHEESE PIZZA

Who doesn't love a classic cheese pie once in a while? But cow's-milk mozzarella comes with all kinds of devastation—like runoff from factory farms into local waterways and using copious amounts of water to grow cattle feed. So once in a while, try your pie with Daiya mozzarella instead—it uses a blend of tapioca flour (for meltability) and pea protein instead of cow's milk. *Molto delizioso!*

SERVES 2   PREP AND COOKING TIME: 45 MINUTES

INGREDIENTS

2½ C all-purpose flour, plus more for dusting

2½ tsp baking powder

1 tsp salt

3 Tbsp olive oil

1 (6-oz) can tomato paste

½ tsp garlic powder

1 tsp dried oregano

1 (8-oz) packet Daiya mozzarella shreds

METHOD

Preheat the oven to 400°F.

Place the flour, baking powder, and salt in a large bowl and stir to combine. Make a well in the center.

Combine ¾ cup water and 1 tablespoon of the olive oil in a small dish. Slowly pour this into the well in the dry ingredients, stirring as you go. It'll start out as a liquidy paste. Once firm enough to handle, use clean hands to form the dough into a ball inside the bowl. If the dough isn't coming together, add up to another ¼ cup water, a little at a time, until it forms a nice ball. (If it's too wet, add some more flour.)

Place the dough on a lightly floured work surface and knead for about 3 minutes. Divide it into two balls and roll each out into a 10-inch circle. Carefully transfer each dough round to its own baking sheet.

Place the tomato paste, remaining 2 tablespoons olive oil, the garlic powder, and the oregano in a small dish and stir to combine. Spoon the sauce onto the crusts and spread it evenly with the back of a tablespoon, leaving a 1-inch border along the edges. Top the pizzas evenly with the mozzarella.

Bake the pizzas until the crusts are crispy but not burnt, 10 to 12 minutes. (If your oven is too small to fit both, cook one and then the other.) Enjoy immediately.

 Serving Suggestion: Try dipping your pizza in the ranch dressing from the Spicy Sweet Potato Fries recipe (page 212).

Note: Want some frills on your no-frills pizza? Plant-Based Parmesan (page 206), fresh basil leaves, olives, capers, sun-dried tomatoes, artichokes, mushrooms, and red onion all make tasty additions.

WHOLE FOODS MARKET FOUNDER AND CEO JOHN MACKEY

In my early twenties, I became vegetarian, back before anyone had even heard of vegans. I thought it was just a healthier way to live and was aware it did less harm to animals. I moved into a vegetarian co-op and fell in with that lifestyle. My friends were vegetarian, and so I was a vegetarian. You might say it was the good kind of peer pressure. Then, much later in life, when I was already running Whole Foods, I was challenged by an animal protection advocate to learn more about factory farming and some of the products we were selling. That process led me to become vegan, and I haven't looked back since.

In my opinion, you can't be an environmentalist—not a true environmentalist—unless you're eating a plant-based diet. The environmental impact of eating so much animal-based food is terrible for our planet in so many ways. From animal-waste disposal and polluting ground waters to devastating the rain forests and increasing our carbon footprint—there's no question that a plant-based diet is gentler and more environmentally sustainable.

And yet there's so much confusion out there about what healthy, sustainable eating is. That's no accident. There are big, vested interests—the egg industry, the dairy industry, the meat industry—that put out a lot of dummy studies to purposely cause that confusion.

But there's a strong consensus in the legitimate science. The really *good* science increasingly shows that there are certain things everyone agrees about. Whatever you're eating—vegan or omnivore or paleo or whatever else—everyone agrees we should eat more fresh fruits and veggies. And the science is clear that we should be eating, as Michael Pollan says, "real food, mostly plants, not too much." The science is clear that eating too many animal-based foods correlates very closely with heart disease, obesity, cancer, diabetes, and environmental harm. Anyone who says anything to the contrary will have no legitimate studies to support their point of view.

Do we all have to be vegan? I certainly am, but there's a place at the table for everyone when it comes to eating a healthier, more plant-forward, eco-friendlier diet.

John Mackey has led Whole Foods Market as it has grown from a single store, founded in 1978, to an $11 billion Fortune 300 company and a top U.S. supermarket. For fifteen consecutive years, Fortune magazine has included Whole Foods Market on its "100 Best Companies to Work For" list. Mackey has been recognized for his work over the years by being named Ernst & Young's "United States Entrepreneur of the Year," Institutional Investor's "Best CEO in America," Barron's "World's Best CEO," MarketWatch's "CEO of the Year," Fortune's "Businessperson of the Year," and Esquire's "Most Inspiring CEO."

OYSTER MUSHROOMS Á LA MARINIÈRE

À la marinière is a French style of cooking mussels in butter and wine. This version is more sea- (and sea creature–) friendly, using oyster mushrooms instead of mussels. The French lentils add protein, and the dish is served in a pool of broth with a chunk of rustic bread. It's perfect for a cool fall evening.

SERVES 2   PREP AND COOKING TIME: 1 HOUR

INGREDIENTS

½ C dried French lentils

2 vegetable bouillon cubes

2 Tbsp raw cashews, soaked in water to cover for at least 4 hours

3 Tbsp olive oil

2 garlic cloves, minced

¾ C chopped shallots

¼ C fresh parsley, chopped

6 dried bay leaves

1½ Tbsp fresh thyme

1 tsp chopped fresh rosemary

¼ tsp salt

¼ tsp freshly ground black pepper

2 C oyster mushrooms, chopped

1 C Pinot Grigio or other dry white wine

A baguette or other rustic bread, for serving

METHOD

Place the lentils in a pot with 1½ cups water and the bouillon cubes. Cover and bring to a boil. Lower the heat to maintain a simmer and cook until soft, about 30 minutes.

Meanwhile, drain and rinse the soaked cashews. Place them in a blender. Add enough water to just cover them and blend until smooth, about 1 minute. Pour the cashew cream into a small bowl and set it aside.

After 30 minutes, remove the lentils from the heat. Drain, reserving ½ cup of the cooking liquid. Set aside.

In a skillet, heat the olive oil over medium-high heat. Add the garlic and shallots and cook, stirring, until soft, 3 to 4 minutes. Add the parsley, bay leaves, thyme, rosemary, salt, and pepper and cook for 1 minute more.

Add the oyster mushrooms. As they cook, they'll release liquid. Cook until that liquid has evaporated, 5 to 8 minutes. Add the wine and cook for 3 to 4 minutes to let some of the alcohol burn off. Remove and discard the bay leaves. Add the cashew cream you made earlier and the reserved ½ cup lentil cooking liquid. Stir to combine. Add the cooked lentils and cook for about 1 minute more.

When finished, you'll have a hearty dish in a light broth. Spoon this onto a plate and top it off with some of the broth, so the broth pools on the plate. Serve with a chunk of baguette or other type of rustic bread.

Tips: If oyster mushrooms are too pricey, any kind of mushrooms will work. Also, enjoy the leftover white wine with your dinner—the best kind of zero-waste dining!

PITTSBURGH PIEROGIS

My wife is from Pittsburgh, where pierogis are basically the city's official food (and a way of life). Every time the Steelers are in a big game, she makes a massive plate of these delicious Polish dumplings for our friends and family. Here's her recipe for straight-out-of-Pittsburgh vegan pierogis.

MAKES 30 TO 40 SMALL PIEROGIS   PREP AND COOKING TIME: 2 HOURS

INGREDIENTS

For the dough:

1¼ C all-purpose flour

¼ tsp salt

1 Tbsp olive oil

¼ C lukewarm water

¼ C vegan sour cream

2 Tbsp margarine, at room temperature

For the filling:

⅓ tsp sea salt, plus more for the cooking water

1¼ lb Yukon Gold potatoes, peeled and cut into ½-inch pieces

1 Tbsp margarine

¼ C plain soy milk

1 tsp onion powder

½ tsp garlic powder

¼ tsp freshly ground black pepper

For frying and serving:

All-purpose flour, for dusting

Salt

1 Tbsp canola oil

½ C vegan sour cream

½ C sauerkraut, squeezed

METHOD

First, make the dough:
Combine the flour and salt in a large bowl.

Whisk the olive oil into the water and then slowly pour that into the flour, mixing as you go. Add the sour cream and margarine.

With clean hands, work the dough until it loses most of its stickiness, about 5 minutes, kneading it into a loose ball. Wrap the dough ball in plastic wrap and refrigerate for 30 minutes or up to 2 days.

Meanwhile, make the filling:
Bring a large pot of salted water to a boil. Add the potatoes and cook until soft, about 15 minutes.

Remove from the heat and drain. Rinse with cold water to cool them slightly. Return them to the pot and add the rest of the ingredients for the filling. Mash with a potato masher until smooth. Set aside.

RECIPE CONTINUES

Flour a clean work surface. Unwrap the dough and transfer it to the work surface. Knead for about 5 minutes, adding more flour as you go, until the dough is smooth but not sticky.

Roll the dough into a large, very thin rectangle. Using a cookie cutter or thin-rimmed drinking glass roughly 3 inches in diameter, cut as many circles as possible into the rectangle of dough.

Lift away the remaining dough, knead it into a ball, roll that out again, and cut more circles. Repeat these steps until all the dough has been used up. You should have 30 to 40 small dough circles at the end.

Take the mashed potato filling and roll it into roughly 30 to 40 small balls (one for each dough circle).

Bring a very large pot of salted water to a low boil. Set up a workstation with the dough circles, potato balls, a lightly floured baking sheet, and a small bowl of cold water (to wet your fingers when forming the pierogis).

Place a potato ball in the center of a dough circle, and then flatten the filling slightly. Using your clean finger, wet the edges of the dough circle. Fold the dough together to make a half circle and pinch the edges shut. Place the pierogi on the floured baking sheet and use a fork to seal the edges. Repeat with the remaining dough and filling. Your first few might be a bit weird, but you'll quickly get the hang of it.

Place about 6 pierogis into the pot of boiling water. Once they float to the surface, about 3 minutes, scoop them out with a slotted spoon and place them on a plate. Repeat until all the pierogis are boiled.

In a large nonstick skillet, heat the canola oil over medium-high heat. Add a few pierogis and fry until browned, 1 to 2 minutes per side. Repeat to fry the entire batch.

Transfer the cooked pierogis to a serving plate. Top with vegan sour cream and sauerkraut. Enjoy!

"I'm eating less meat these days myself, and I'm proud of it . . . Twenty-eight percent of greenhouse gases come from livestock farming, so cutting back on meat consumption even slightly can have a big, positive impact."[166]

—ARNOLD SCHWARZENEGGER

PROTEIN-PACKED BURRITO BOWL

This is one hearty bowl of deliciousness! Gardein's plant-based chicken tenders are meaty and have a much greener footprint than real-meat chicken fingers (just think of all those Delmarva Peninsula residents dealing with poultry farm air pollution). Add quinoa and black beans, and this bowl is a protein-packed meal.

SERVES 2   PREP AND COOKING TIME: 40 MINUTES

INGREDIENTS

For the vinaigrette:

2 Tbsp fresh lime juice

1 garlic clove, minced

½ tsp agave nectar

½ tsp sea salt

⅛ tsp ground cumin

2 Tbsp olive oil

1 Tbsp chopped fresh cilantro

For the bowl:

1 (9.5-oz) packet Gardein Chipotle Lime Chicken Fingers

1 C quinoa

Sea salt

2 ears corn, husked

1 Tbsp coconut oil

¼ head purple cabbage, thinly sliced

1 (15-oz) can black beans, drained and rinsed

1 ripe avocado, halved and pitted, then diced, if desired

10 cherry tomatoes, halved

½ red onion, finely sliced

Fresh cilantro, for garnish

Lime wedges, for garnish

Sesame seeds, for garnish

METHOD

Preheat the oven to 450°F.

First, make the vinaigrette:
Mix the vinaigrette ingredients together in a small bowl. Set aside in the fridge.

Assemble the bowl:
Bake the Gardein according to the package instructions. Set aside once done.

Put the quinoa in a saucepan with 1½ cups water and a pinch of salt. Cover, bring to a boil, and lower the heat to maintain a simmer. Cook until the liquid has been absorbed, 15 to 20 minutes. Remove from the heat and fluff with a fork. Set aside.

Heat a skillet over medium-high heat. Brush the corn with coconut oil, sprinkle with salt, and place in the hot pan. Cook, turning every few minutes, until lightly charred and cooked all over. Set aside.

Cut the corncobs into thirds and slice the chicken fingers. Assemble each bowl with half the corn, chicken fingers, cabbage, black beans, avocado, tomatoes, and onion. Sprinkle garnishes on top, add the dressing, and enjoy!

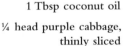 **Want to go the extra eco-mile?** Replace the Gardein with tofu. Just broil a few strips (see page 251).

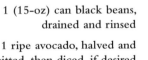 **Serving Suggestion:** This also pairs well with a side of Roasted Red Pepper Hummus (page 208).

RAINBOW VEGGIE SUSHI

You know what they say: give a man a fish and he'll eat for a day; teach a man to fish and all the world's fish will be gone by 2050. This no-fish dish uses red pepper, yellow mango, purple cabbage, green cucumber and avocado, and orange carrot to create flavorful, colorful sushi that's easy on our oceans and their inhabitants.

SERVES 2   PREP AND COOKING TIME: 1 HOUR

INGREDIENTS

2½ C short-grain brown rice

⅓ C vegan mayo

8 sheets roasted nori

1 red bell pepper, thinly sliced

1 carrot, julienned

1 mango, pitted, peeled, and julienned

1 cucumber, julienned

1 avocado, pitted, peeled, and thinly sliced

2 C thinly sliced cabbage

Soy sauce, for dipping

Wasabi paste (optional)

Pickled ginger (optional)

METHOD

Place the rice and 5 cups water in a medium saucepan. Cover and bring to a boil over high heat. Turn the heat down to low and simmer for 30 minutes. Remove from the heat and let sit, covered, for 10 minutes. Remove the lid, fluff with a fork, and let cool. Once fully cool, stir in the mayo.

While rice is cooking, if you've never made homemade sushi before, now would be a good time to watch a video of it online so you can see the rolling technique.

Once you're ready to roll (literally!), wet a sushi mat and place a nori sheet on top of it, shiny-side down. Place one-eighth of the cooked rice on the bottom two-thirds of the nori sheet and press it out into a flat, even layer.

Place one-eighth of each ingredient (or any combination thereof that you'd like!) along the middle of the rice. Roll the bottom end of the sushi mat over the ingredients to enclose them in the rice and then continue to roll, using quite firm pressure to ensure that everything holds together. Set aside and repeat with the remaining ingredients to make a total of 8 rolls.

Use a slightly wet serrated knife to cut each roll crosswise into 8 equal-size pieces.

Enjoy immediately with soy sauce for dipping and wasabi and pickled ginger alongside, if you like.

Tip: Make the rice in the morning or even the night before so it's fully cooled by the time you use it. If you try to roll rice that's too warm, you'll end up with soggy sushi—and no one likes soggy sushi.

Serving Suggestion: Serve with Sesame Seaweed Salad (page 129).

SAVE-THE-BAY CRAB CAKES

I've spent much of my life near the Chesapeake Bay, where crab cakes are a local favorite. But rather than pulling crabs from the bay to make the dish, this recipe instead uses hearts of palm—which are soft and hearty and pull apart like crabmeat does. It's an eco-friendlier twist on a regional favorite.

SERVES 4   PREP AND COOKING TIME: 1 HOUR

INGREDIENTS

For the tartar sauce:

¼ C vegan mayo

2 tsp sweet relish

1 tsp yellow mustard

½ tsp fresh lemon juice

Dash of salt

Freshly cracked black pepper

For the crab cakes:

1 (14-oz) can hearts of palm, drained

1 Tbsp olive oil

½ C minced onion

2 tsp minced garlic

¼ C minced bell pepper

1¼ C fresh, frozen, or canned corn kernels

1 C bread crumbs

2½ Tbsp finely chopped fresh parsley

2 tsp yellow mustard

1½ Tbsp Old Bay seasoning

¼ C vegan mayo

¼ C vegetable oil

METHOD

First, make the tartar sauce:

Mix all the sauce ingredients together in a small bowl and refrigerate.

Make the crab cakes:

Drain the hearts of palm and lay them out on a cutting board. Thinly slice them lengthwise and then chop them. Into a large bowl, squeeze the chopped pieces between clean fingers until they break apart. Set aside.

In a large skillet, heat the olive oil over medium-high heat. Add the onion, garlic, and bell pepper. Sauté until tender, about 4 minutes. Add the corn and sauté for 1 minute more. Remove from the heat.

Place the vegetable mixture into the bowl with the hearts of palm, setting the skillet aside for later. Mix well to combine. Add ⅓ cup of the bread crumbs, the parsley, mustard, 1 tablespoon of the Old Bay, and the mayo. Mix well.

Fill the bottom of a shallow bowl or pie plate with the remaining ⅔ cup bread crumbs. Add the remaining ½ tablespoon Old Bay and mix.

Take about ¼ cup of the vegetable mixture and drop it into the bread crumbs. Roll it around until it's well coated and form into a small patty with clean hands. Transfer to a large plate or baking sheet. Repeat until all the vegetable mixture has been used. (You should have about 7 large crab cakes; if you want them a bit smaller, you could form 8 to 10 smaller patties instead.)

Gently wipe out the skillet. Add the vegetable oil and heat over medium-high heat. Once the oil is hot (about 1 minute), place the patties in the skillet, carefully—so as not to splatter the oil—and cook until golden brown on each side, about 2 minutes per side. Transfer to a paper towel–lined plate to drain excess oil. Repeat until all the crab cakes have been fried.

Top with tartar sauce and enjoy immediately, either on their own or with a side of Quick Country Coleslaw (page 207).

Tip: As you fry all the crab cakes, the bread crumbs left over in the oil may burn. If this happens, drain the oil between batches, wipe out the pan, and heat up fresh oil.

SMOKY SEITAN KEBABS WITH PEANUT SAUCE

Kebab is a general term that can apply to various types of Middle Eastern grilled meats. In America, we're most familiar with shish kebab: small pieces of meat that are skewered and grilled. But beef and lamb come with a high eco-footprint (especially when the animals eat grass, resulting in higher methane emissions). This smoky kebab recipe uses easy homemade seitan instead, to cut down on emissions. Topped with peanut sauce and served with fresh lime and herbs, it's a deliciously smoky and more sustainable way to enjoy this tasty dish.

SERVES 2   PREP AND COOKING TIME: 30 MINUTES

INGREDIENTS

2 Tbsp creamy peanut butter

4 Tbsp soy sauce

2 Tbsp pure maple syrup

1 tsp Sriracha (optional)

1 C vital wheat gluten

1 tsp garlic powder

1 tsp onion powder

1 tsp smoked paprika

1 tsp dried thyme

2 Tbsp nutritional yeast

½ tsp liquid smoke

1 tsp vegan Worcestershire sauce

1 Tbsp olive oil

1 Tbsp tomato paste

Fresh cilantro, for garnish

Lime wedges, for serving

METHOD

Preheat the oven to 375°F. Line a baking sheet with parchment paper and set aside.

Combine the peanut butter, 2 tablespoons of the soy sauce, maple syrup, and Sriracha, if using, in a small bowl. Stir until well combined. Set the peanut sauce aside until ready to serve.

Place the vital wheat gluten, garlic powder, onion powder, paprika, thyme, and nutritional yeast in a large bowl and stir to combine.

In another bowl, place the liquid smoke, Worcestershire, olive oil, tomato paste, remaining 2 tablespoons soy sauce, and ½ cup water. Stir to combine.

Pour the wet mixture into the dry mixture. Stir gently as you pour, until it vaguely resembles ground beef. Knead the dough in the bowl for 2 minutes. It shouldn't stick to your hands at all.

Once you have a loose ball, break it into 18 small chunks. Press 3 chunks together to form one larger piece, then flatten it out. That'll be one kebab. Repeat this until you have 6 kebabs.

Place the kebabs on the prepared baking sheet. Flatten them out and bake for 10 minutes. Remove and let cool slightly. Turn the oven to broil.

Wet your skewers with water, and skewer each kebab. Place them back on the baking sheet and return to the oven, broiling each side for 2 minutes. Remove and serve topped with fresh herbs, with the peanut sauce and lime wedges alongside.

Serving Suggestion: These are also great as the meat inside a Vietnamese Bánh Mì (page 137).

"Please eat less meat."[167]

—DR. RAJENDRA PACHAURI, FORMER CHAIR OF THE UN INTERGOVERNMENTAL PANEL ON CLIMATE CHANGE (IPCC)

SPAGHETTI AND LENTIL MEATBALLS

What could be more classic than spaghetti and meatballs? But alas, one serving of beef creates about 27 kg of CO_2 emissions. A serving of lentils? Only 0.9 kg. That's a 96.6 percent reduction. With lentils, walnuts, oats, and—yes—even peanut butter (trust me), this dish will win over the hearts and stomachs of even the hungriest carnivore.

SERVES 4   PREP AND COOKING TIME: 1 HOUR

INGREDIENTS

For the meatballs:

3 Tbsp olive oil

½ C minced onion

4 garlic cloves, minced

1 tsp peanut butter

2 Tbsp rolled (not instant) oats

5 sun-dried tomatoes

½ tsp dried oregano

½ tsp dried rosemary

½ tsp dried thyme

¼ tsp crushed red pepper

½ tsp dried sage

¼ tsp freshly ground black pepper

½ tsp sea salt

¼ C fresh parsley

1½ Tbsp tomato paste

1 Tbsp flax meal

1 (15-oz) can green or black lentils, drained

6 Tbsp Plant-Based Parmesan (page 206)

5 Tbsp bread crumbs

For the sauce:

½ tsp salt, plus more for the pasta water

1 Tbsp olive oil

1 yellow onion, finely chopped

3 to 5 garlic cloves, finely chopped

2 (14-oz) cans chopped tomatoes

¼ C tomato paste

½ tsp freshly ground black pepper

½ tsp dried oregano

½ tsp dried thyme

1 tsp agave nectar or sugar

Small handful of fresh basil leaves

To assemble:

1 (16-oz) box spaghetti

Olive oil

Fresh basil leaves, for garnish

Fresh parsley leaves, for garnish

Plant-Based Parmesan (page 206)

METHOD

(!) **Equipment Alert:** This recipe requires a food processor.

First, make the meatballs:

Preheat the oven to 375°F. Line a baking sheet with parchment paper.

Heat a large skillet (I use cast iron) over medium-high heat. Once hot, add 2 tablespoons of the olive oil, and all of the onion and the garlic. Cook for about 3 minutes, then remove from the heat.

Transfer the garlic and onions to a food processor (set the skillet aside) and add the rest of the meatball ingredients and 2 tablespoons water. Pulse to combine well, but avoid pureeing entirely. (You're going to roll this into balls next, so if it's too wet, add more bread crumbs, a little at a time, and pulse to combine.)

Scrape the mixture into a large bowl and stir once more to combine.

RECIPE CONTINUES

Form the meatball mixture into about 12 small balls, gently rolling them in the palm of your hand with your fingertips and arranging them on the prepared baking sheet as you go.

Set the skillet over medium-high heat. Add the remaining 1 tablespoon olive oil and as many meatballs as you can fit, leaving room to turn them. Cook until browned on most sides, about 2 minutes per side, turning or rolling them as you go. (Don't worry—you bake them next, so they don't need to be fully cooked yet.)

Rearrange all the cooked meatballs on the baking sheet and bake for 20 minutes. Remove from the heat and set aside.

Meanwhile, make the sauce:
In a saucepan, heat the olive oil over medium heat. Add the onion and garlic and cook for about 4 minutes. Add the remaining sauce ingredients and mix well. (Be careful of splatter when you add the chopped tomatoes.) Bring to a boil, then lower the heat to maintain a simmer and cook, uncovered, for about 10 minutes while you make the pasta.

Assemble and enjoy:
Bring a large pot of salted water to a boil. Cook the pasta in the boiling water according to the directions on the package. Drain and mix some olive oil through to keep the pasta from sticking.

Serve the pasta in deep bowls topped with meatballs, sauce, fresh basil and parsley, and Plant-Based Parmesan. Mangia!

 Serving Suggestion: Serve with a side of Easy Cheesy Garlic Bread (page 195).

 Want to go the extra eco-mile? Cook the lentils from scratch to cut down on packaging. You'll want 1½ cups cooked lentils, and may want to make them in advance to save time.

NATURAL RESOURCES DEFENSE COUNCIL PRESIDENT RHEA SUH

I grew up in Boulder, Colorado, which is surrounded by the magnificent Rocky Mountains and spectacular landscapes. When I was a kid, I kind of assumed that everyone had a backyard like mine, overlooking the Rockies. I was privileged to regularly hike, and camp, and ski, and fish, and to relax in the great outdoors. This experience was a critical part of my early years, and really influenced my vision of myself and of the world around me. That environmentalism was sort of "baked into" me from childhood.

Today, climate change is the central environmental challenge of our time. It threatens our people, our oceans, our forests, our lands. It has the potential to cause a catastrophic collapse of species worldwide. It is a threat to the natural systems that support all life.

Directly connected to that is the growing scarcity of fresh water. Glaciers are melting worldwide, and that is already causing water shortages in Andean countries, parts of China, and elsewhere. We're seeing tens of thousands of Rocky Mountain whitefish dying in the Yellowstone River, for heaven's sake, because a microscopic parasite is thriving and fish are being stressed in water levels that are lower and temperatures that are higher than they should be.

And finally, there is environmental injustice, with low-income communities and people of color bearing a disproportionate burden of dirty air, polluted water, and other environmental ills. We have a lot of work to do to get this right.

And food touches on all of this—air, water, wildlife, lands—and impacts everything we're working to change—energy, transportation, conservation. It's all wrapped up in how we produce, process, distribute, and consume our food. We won't get the equation right unless we get the food piece right.

We can eat more plants, for starters. Pound for pound, plants have a vastly smaller carbon and environmental "food-print" compared to animal products. Beef is the SUV of food, resulting in more than thirty times more climate-changing emissions, pound for pound, than lentils, for example.

Going vegetarian or vegan is great, but even changing your diet a little bit can make a big difference. But reducing the amount of red meat we eat—even by a small amount—can improve our health, save us money, and reduce our contribution to the planet's environmental burden. And don't forget that eating is an act of pleasure. Make some healthy, environmentally friendly changes to your diet that you truly enjoy, and chances are you'll want to repeat them and share with friends and family. That's making a difference.

Rhea Suh is president of the Natural Resources Defense Council, leading nearly five hundred scientists, attorneys, and policy experts at one of the country's most effective environmental-action organizations. Before joining NRDC, Suh was nominated by President Barack Obama and served as the Assistant Secretary for Policy, Management, and Budget at the U.S. Department of the Interior.

STEAMED BUNS WITH TOFU AND MUSHROOMS

Legend says that thousands of years ago, Chinese military leader Zhuge Liang encountered a river his troops couldn't cross. He was told to sacrifice his men and toss their heads into the river, to appease the gods for safe crossing. Instead, he ordered that head-shaped buns stuffed with meat be thrown into the river. Thus was born the steamed bun. This version takes Liang's compassion further: rather than being meat-filled, they're filled with hearty tofu, mushrooms, and vegetables. You can toss them into a river, though I recommend eating them.

SERVES 2 (MAKES 6 SMALL BUNS)   PREP AND COOKING TIME: 1 HOUR, PLUS 1 HOUR RISING TIME

INGREDIENTS

1 heaping Tbsp sugar

1 C lukewarm water

2 tsp instant yeast

2¼ C all-purpose flour

Tiny pinch of salt

2 Tbsp soy sauce

2 Tbsp rice vinegar

1 Tbsp toasted sesame oil

1 Tbsp agave nectar

1 tsp Sriracha

½ (16-ounce) block extra-firm tofu, cut into 12 slices

Vegetable oil, for brushing

1 tsp black sesame seeds

2 large brown mushrooms, thinly sliced

¼ large cucumber, thinly sliced

Chopped scallions

Chopped fresh cilantro

METHOD

In a measuring cup or small bowl, dissolve the sugar in the warm water. Add the yeast. Stir and let sit until it gets foamy, about 5 minutes.

Place the flour and salt in a large bowl. Once the yeast mixture has some bubbles, add it to the flour. Stir gently and knead until it's smooth and soft.

Return the dough to the bowl, cover with a dish towel, and leave in a warm place until the dough has doubled in size, about 1 hour. (If you live in a cold climate, place the bowl in a 95°F oven to rise.)

While the dough is rising, combine the soy sauce, vinegar, sesame oil, agave, and Sriracha in a small dish. Add the tofu and turn to coat in the marinade.

When the dough has doubled in size, punch the air out and split the dough into 6 pieces. Roll them into balls and lightly brush the bottoms with vegetable oil. Sprinkle with the sesame seeds and let sit for 10 minutes.

While the buns are sitting, arrange bamboo steaming baskets so they are sitting in a wok or saucepan with just enough water in the bottom of the pan to not get the baskets wet.

Place the buns in the steamer baskets with enough room for them to expand a little. Bring to a boil, cover, and steam for 20 minutes. Remove from the heat and let sit for 5 minutes. Remove the lids, being careful not to drip water onto the buns.

Set a skillet over medium heat. Add the mushrooms, 1 tablespoon water, and 2 tablespoons of the tofu marinade (reserving the rest). Cook until brown, about 5 minutes.

Move the mushrooms to one side of the pan and add the tofu to the other side. Cook for 2 minutes per side to heat the tofu through.

Remove the buns from their baskets and carefully split them down the middle. Fill with the tofu, mushrooms, cucumber slices, scallions, and cilantro. Pour the remaining marinade into a small dish to spoon over the buns as you eat them.

SUN-DRIED TOMATO AND BASIL SAUSAGES

Sausage's environmental footprint can be high. Think about that mega pig farm the people of Arrow Rock, Missouri, fought against—or all the pollution caused by pig factories in North Carolina. These sausages use vital wheat gluten: all protein, no pork. Mixed with white beans, sun-dried tomatoes, and basil for Italian flair, they're perfect for any occasion.

SERVES 2 TO 4   PREP AND COOKING TIME: 1 HOUR

INGREDIENTS

4 sun-dried tomatoes, chopped

2 garlic cloves, minced

½ C canned white beans, drained and rinsed

10 fresh basil leaves

2 Tbsp olive oil

1 Tbsp apple cider vinegar

1 tsp seeded mustard

1½ C vital wheat gluten

1 tsp onion powder

¾ tsp sea salt

½ tsp freshly ground black pepper

2 Tbsp nutritional yeast

METHOD

Place a metal steaming basket inside a large pot. Add 2 to 3 inches of water, ensuring the water is below the basket. Cut eight pieces of aluminum foil about 7 inches wide.

Place the sun-dried tomatoes, garlic, and white beans in a blender or food processor. Add the basil leaves, olive oil, vinegar, mustard, and 1 cup water. Puree until smooth.

Place the vital wheat gluten, onion powder, salt, pepper, and nutritional yeast in a large bowl and stir with a fork to combine. Pour the puree into the dry ingredients, stirring with a fork as you go, then use clean hands to knead everything into a ball.

Break the ball into 8 pieces and form each into a sausage shape. Roll each sausage in a piece of foil and twist at either end (like a Tootsie Roll)—not too tight, as the sausages will expand as they cook.

Place the sausages in the steamer basket. Cover and bring to a boil. Steam for 40 minutes. (If the water gets too low, add more.) Once done, remove from the heat and let cool for at least 10 minutes before unwrapping each sausage.

You now have sausages that you can use as you please—fry them in a pan, serve with mashed potatoes, take them to a BBQ and grill them, put them in a sandwich. The sky's the limit! Use immediately or store in an airtight container in the fridge for up to 3 days.

Serving Suggestion: Serve with a side of grilled veggies drizzled with balsamic vinegar, or a simple salad.

Shopping Tip: You can find vital wheat gluten in the flour aisle of most grocery stores.

WILD RICE RISOTTO
WITH PEAS AND ASPARAGUS

Risotto is a northern Italian rice dish slowly cooked in stock. The stock is added a little at a time and continually topped off as the rice cooks and absorbs it. This releases starches from the rice that give the final product a creamy finish. The stock can be derived from meat, but for this version, we use veggie stock. The addition of wild rice—which grows in water—gives a nice earthy feel, and the peas help pack a little extra protein into the dish.

SERVES 4 TO 6   PREP AND COOKING TIME: 1 HOUR

INGREDIENTS

10 C vegetable stock (see Note)

2 Tbsp olive oil

3 shallots, finely chopped

3 garlic cloves, minced

2 C Arborio rice

1 C wild rice

½ C dry white wine

2 C frozen peas

1 (16-oz) bunch asparagus, cut into 1-inch pieces

Salt and freshly ground black pepper

½ C fresh mint leaves, chopped, plus more for serving

½ C fresh basil leaves, chopped, plus more for serving

½ C pine nuts

Fresh lemon wedges, for serving

METHOD

Bring the stock to a boil in a large saucepan, then lower the heat to maintain a simmer or very low boil.

Meanwhile, in a large saucepan, heat the olive oil over medium heat. Add the shallots and garlic and cook for about 3 minutes. Add the rices and stir until coated in oil and slightly translucent. Add the wine.

You now want to add just enough hot stock to cover the rice by about 1 inch. Bring it to a boil, then lower the heat to maintain a simmer and cook until the liquid has been mostly absorbed by the rice.

Once the first round of liquid has absorbed by the rice, add more hot stock—about ½ cup—and repeat until that liquid has been absorbed, too. Repeat as many times as you need to until the rice is fully cooked and very soft. (The amount of stock you need and the number of times you'll need to do this depends on how dry the rice is, how hot your kitchen is, etc. Generally, it takes about 30 minutes.)

Once the rice is cooked, stir in the frozen peas and cook for 3 minutes.

Add the asparagus to the pot and cook for 2 minutes more.

Remove the risotto from the heat, cover, and let sit for 5 minutes. Season with salt and pepper. Stir the mint and basil leaves into the risotto.

Serve immediately, garnished with pine nuts, additional mint and basil, and a squeeze of lemon juice.

Note: If you don't have stock, bring 10 cups water to a boil and add 5 cubes of vegetarian bouillon.

SIDES AND EXTRAS

Blackened Brussels Sprouts with
Capers and Raisins
188

Creamy Herbed Mashed Potatoes
190

Crispy Rice Paper Bacon
193

Easy Cheesy Garlic Bread
195

Green Bean Casserole
196

Lonestar BBQ Beans
199

Mint and Tofu Summer Rolls
201

Minted Green Pea Guacamole
202

Pistachio and Sunflower Seed Dukkah
205

Plant-Based Parmesan
206

Quick Country Coleslaw
207

Roasted Red Pepper Hummus
208

Rosemary Cornbread Mini Muffins
211

Spicy Sweet Potato Fries with Ranch
212

Sweet-and-Salty Curried Popcorn
215

BLACKENED BRUSSELS SPROUTS WITH CAPERS AND RAISINS

This recipe combines Brussels sprouts with vinegar and agave for a sweet-and-sour taste. Add walnuts, capers, raisins, garlic, and more, and you've got a flavorful, aromatic dish that's crave-worthy on its own, as a snack, or as a side dish.

SERVES 4 TO 6   PREP AND COOKING TIME: 1 HOUR

INGREDIENTS

2 lb Brussels sprouts

¼ tsp sea salt

½ C olive oil

¼ C red wine vinegar

1½ Tbsp agave nectar

¾ C walnuts, chopped

⅓ C capers

3 Tbsp golden raisins

2 garlic cloves, minced

¼ tsp ground cumin

1 shallot, minced

Pinch of freshly ground black pepper

METHOD

Preheat the oven to 425°F.

Peel any bad leaves from the outsides of the sprouts and cut any larger sprouts in half. Place them in a large bowl as you go. Add the salt and ¼ cup of the olive oil. Stir to coat well.

Pour the coated sprouts into a large cast-iron skillet and roast for 20 minutes, turning several times so the sprouts cook evenly.

While the sprouts are in the oven, put the remaining ¼ cup olive oil, the vinegar, and the agave in a blender and blend until emulsified, about 20 seconds. (You can also whisk this instead of blending, but you need to whisk well to emulsify the oil.) Pour into a small bowl and add the walnuts, capers, raisins, garlic, cumin, shallot, and pepper.

Remove the sprouts from the oven and evenly pour the dressing over them. Mix to coat and bake for 15 minutes more.

Turn the oven to broil and let the tops of the sprouts blacken, 3 to 10 minutes, depending on your oven and how blackened you want them.

Remove from the oven (carefully, as the skillet will be hot!) and enjoy immediately on their own or as a side dish.

Serving Suggestion: Serve alongside Meat-Free Meat Loaf (page 154).

CREAMY HERBED MASHED POTATOES

It's hard to go wrong with a big, piping hot plate of mashed potatoes. This vegan version uses almond milk instead of cow's milk, margarine instead of butter, nutritional yeast for a little cheesy flavor, and chopped chives for . . . well, just so we can say there's something green in there!

SERVES 4   PREP AND COOKING TIME: 30 MINUTES

INGREDIENTS

2 lb Yukon Gold potatoes, peeled and cubed

1½ tsp salt

1 C plain almond milk

2 Tbsp margarine

2 Tbsp nutritional yeast

¼ tsp freshly ground black pepper, plus more to taste

1 tsp dried rosemary

½ tsp dried thyme

2 Tbsp chopped fresh chives

METHOD

Put the potatoes and 1 teaspoon of the salt in a large pot with enough cold water to cover them by 3 to 4 inches. Bring to a boil over high heat. Lower the heat to maintain a simmer and cook for 15 to 20 minutes, or until soft.

Drain the water from the cooked potatoes and return them to the pot. Add the almond milk, margarine, nutritional yeast, remaining ½ teaspoon salt, the pepper, rosemary, and thyme. Mash until smooth using a potato masher. Serve, topped with chives and additional pepper.

Tip: You can use any unsweetened, unflavored, creamy plant-based milk, such as soy, hemp, or coconut, in place of the almond milk.

"Eliminating or reducing meat consumption in our diets is one important way to reduce our contribution to climate change . . . So enjoy Meatless Mondays, Tofu Tuesdays, Salad Sundays and everything in between. Because a locally sourced plant-heavy diet is not only good for you, but good for our planet too."[168]

—THE SIERRA CLUB

CRISPY RICE PAPER BACON

Crispy, salty, smoky—this bacon hits the spot, without all the eco-woes that accompany industrial pig farming. It crisps and bubbles, and is marbled with shades of brown and red and white.

SERVES 4   PREP AND COOKING TIME: 30 MINUTES

INGREDIENTS

2 Tbsp olive oil

3 Tbsp soy sauce

½ tsp pure maple syrup

½ tsp liquid smoke

2 Tbsp nutritional yeast

1 tsp smoked paprika

½ tsp garlic powder

¼ tsp onion powder

Pinch of freshly ground black pepper

10 sheets rice paper

METHOD

Preheat the oven to 400°F.

In a small bowl, combine all the ingredients except the rice paper and whisk together.

Now you're going to cut the rice paper sheets into strips. It's tricky. Lay out one sheet of rice paper and, using a sharp knife, cut it into roughly 1-inch-wide strips. It'll crack apart (especially if your knife isn't sharp). Set the intact strips aside and repeat for all 10 sheets. At the end, you should have a nice pile of cut strips. (And it doesn't matter if they aren't perfect-looking!)

Next, set up a large workspace with a parchment-covered baking sheet, a wide bowl or pie dish of water, and a dish of the marinade.

Take two strips of roughly the same shape and hold them together. Dip them in the water. They'll stick together. Squeegee some of the water off with your fingers.

Dip the doubled strip in the marinade, gently, to coat both sides. Place on the parchment-lined baking sheet. Repeat until all the strips have been dipped and you have a bunch of double-thick bacon strips.

Bake until crispy, about 8 minutes. Careful: They'll go from crispy to burnt quickly.

Enjoy immediately, or transfer to a wire rack and let cool before transferring to an airtight container and storing in the fridge. They're great on sandwiches, as a breakfast side, and more!

Tip: Like your bacon a little chewier? Just bake it for a minute less.

Serving Suggestion: Serve alongside the Tofu Scramble (page 105) or any other breakfast dish.

"Like most people, I don't think I can be easily fooled. But that's just what happened when I was asked to taste a chicken taco and tell whether the meat inside was real or fake. The meat certainly had the look and the smell of chicken. I took a bite and it had the taste and texture of real chicken, too. But I was surprised to learn that there wasn't an ounce of real chicken it. The 'meat' was made entirely of plants. And yet, I couldn't tell the difference. What I was experiencing was more than a clever meat substitute. It was a taste of the future of food."[169]

—BILL GATES

EASY CHEESY GARLIC BREAD

When I was young, I worked in a pizzeria. I became obsessed with the cheesy garlic bread that was one of their specialties. This is my reinvention of that recipe using plant-based, planet-friendly ingredients.

SERVES 2 TO 4   PREP AND COOKING TIME: 10 MINUTES

INGREDIENTS

2 soft sub rolls

1 Tbsp margarine

½ tsp salt

1½ tsp garlic powder

1 Tbsp nutritional yeast

1 tsp dried oregano

½ tsp freshly ground black pepper

Daiya mozzarella shreds

METHOD

Preheat the oven to 400°F.

Slice each sub roll in half lengthwise. Lay them sliced-side up on a baking sheet.

On each half, spread about half the margarine. (If it's too cold to spread, warm it in the microwave for a few seconds to soften.)

In a small bowl, mix together the salt, garlic powder, nutritional yeast, oregano, and pepper. Sprinkle this across all four roll halves equally and use a butter knife to push it into the margarine a little bit.

Sprinkle each half with as much or as little mozzarella as you'd like.

Bake until toasted and the cheese has melted, 5 to 7 minutes.

 Want to go the extra eco-mile? Cut down on packaging by replacing the vegan mozzarella shreds with an extra 1 tablespoon nutritional yeast.

Serving Suggestion: Enjoy with Spaghetti and Lentil Meatballs (page 176) or Massaged Kale Caesar salad (page 123).

GREEN BEAN CASSEROLE

This was always a Thanksgiving must-have in the Prescott household. And a Christmas must-have. And a Hanukkah must-have. Creamy mushroom soup, fresh green beans, and indulgent French-fried onions: You can't go wrong. This recipe is a new take on our family's classic, using shiitakes instead of button mushrooms and almond milk instead of cow's milk. Perfect any time of year—especially holidays.

SERVES 4 TO 6   PREP AND COOKING TIME: 30 MINUTES, PLUS SOAKING TIME FOR THE MUSHROOMS

INGREDIENTS

¾ C dried shiitakes

1 C boiling water

4 C halved green beans

¼ tsp salt, plus a pinch

1 C almond milk

1 vegetable bouillon cube, crushed into powder

2 Tbsp nutritional yeast

¼ tsp freshly ground black pepper

¼ tsp dried sage

1½ C French-fried onions

METHOD

Place the dried mushrooms in a heatproof bowl. Add the boiling water and let sit for 1 hour.

Preheat the oven to 375°F.

Meanwhile, place the beans in a pot of cold water with a pinch of salt. Cover and bring to a boil. Cook for 3 to 4 minutes. Remove from the heat, drain immediately, and rinse under cold water.

Pour the liquid from the mushrooms into a medium bowl. Add the almond milk, crushed bouillon cube, nutritional yeast, ¼ teaspoon salt, pepper, and sage. Whisk to combine. Finely chop the rehydrated mushrooms and add these to the liquid, along with half the French-fried onions.

Place the beans in a casserole dish, pour the liquid over, and then toss a couple of times to make sure the onions and mushrooms are nicely distributed throughout the beans and not sitting on top. Sprinkle the remaining onions over the top of the beans and bake for 15 minutes.

Remove from the heat and let sit for 5 minutes before serving.

Serving Suggestion: Serve with Meat-Free Meat Loaf (page 154) and Creamy Herbed Mashed Potatoes (page 190).

Want to go the extra eco-mile? Make this recipe when green beans are in season (see page 252).

THE CENTER FOR BIOLOGICAL DIVERSITY'S STEPHANIE FELDSTEIN

If you're looking for an easy and enjoyable way to conserve water; protect our oceans, lakes, and rivers; and save an amazing array of wild animal species, it's simple: eat less meat.

There are more than 7.4 billion people on the planet. It took about two hundred thousand years for the human population to reach 1 billion, then only two hundred years for that to increase sevenfold. There's never been another large, vertebrate animal that's grown as much, as quickly, or with such devastating consequences. In the past fifty years alone, our population has doubled, while wildlife populations—including animals living in our oceans—have plummeted by about half.

And it's not just our sheer numbers that are crowding out other species—it's our reckless overconsumption, relying on polluting, destructive industries. And at the top of that list is factory farming, the planet's single most environmentally destructive industry.

Thirty-five thousand miles of U.S. rivers, which provide habitat to countless fish, amphibians, and birds, are polluted by factory farms. Orange clownfish (like the star of *Finding Nemo*) and many other unique, beautiful species are losing their coral reef habitat to ocean acidification caused by greenhouse gas pollution—caused in large part by the meat industry.

Every time we eat, we can make a wildlife-friendly choice. Fortunately, there are abundant plant-forward foods out there to help us do this. We can choose veggie sushi over fish sushi, bean burgers over hamburgers. Almond milk is easier on the planet than cow's milk. There's a whole rainbow of produce available at local grocers nationwide that offers delicious and vibrant ways to help save the planet. It's one of the best—and tastiest—ways to protect the environment.

Stephanie Feldstein is Population and Sustainability Director for the Center for Biological Diversity—a national nonprofit conservation organization dedicated to the protection of endangered species and wild places. Using science, law, and creative media, the Center works to secure a future for all species great and small, with a focus on protecting the lands, waters, and climate that species need to survive.

LONESTAR BBQ BEANS

I make these beans whenever I've got visitors—when I want an easy and filling meal with some Welcome-to-Texas flair. And because beans have remarkably low carbon and water footprints, my visitors and I can rest easy (and full) knowing we're eating something that's healthy, great tasting, and sustainable.

SERVES 4 TO 6   PREP AND COOKING TIME: 1½ TO 2 HOURS

INGREDIENTS

2 C dried pinto beans

1 vegetable bouillon cube

½ tsp paprika

½ tsp liquid smoke

1 Tbsp vegan Worcestershire sauce (optional)

1 Tbsp agave nectar or molasses

¼ C ketchup

1 tsp mustard

¼ tsp cayenne pepper

2 Tbsp olive oil

½ C chopped onion

½ C finely chopped celery

¼ C finely chopped carrots

2 garlic cloves, minced

METHOD

Place the beans, 4 cups water, and the bouillon cube in a medium saucepan. Cover and bring to a boil. Lower the heat to maintain somewhere between a simmer and a very low boil and cook until the beans are soft, 60 to 90 minutes.

While the beans cook, in a small bowl, whisk together the paprika, liquid smoke, Worcestershire (if using), agave, ketchup, mustard, cayenne, and 1 tablespoon water. Set aside.

Once the beans are done, remove them from the heat and set aside—but don't drain them. Also, you want the water level to be just below the beans when they're done; if it's too high, remove the cover and boil for 2 minutes or so to let some of the excess water evaporate before removing from the heat.

In a large, deep skillet, heat the olive oil over medium-high heat for 2 to 3 minutes. Add the onion, celery, carrots, and garlic. Cook, stirring occasionally, until the vegetables soften, 5 to 8 minutes.

Pour the beans—plus their cooking liquid—into the skillet. Be careful! The water hitting the hot skillet will cause splatter. The beans will kind of pile up in the center of the skillet and the water will push to the sides. Go with that (no need to stir). Cook over medium heat until most of the liquid has evaporated, about 10 minutes. Add the BBQ sauce, stir to combine, and cook to heat through, about another 1 minute. Enjoy!

Serving Suggestions: Top with vegan sour cream and serve over rice, or alongside the Jerked Jackfruit Tacos (page 153) or Sun-Dried Tomato and Basil Sausages (page 183).

MINT AND TOFU SUMMER ROLLS

Unlike their spring counterparts, summer rolls aren't fried, but rather eaten cold and fresh. These Vietnamese rolls often contain pork and shrimp. But if you want a meat-free version that avoids all the troubles wrought by industrial pig and shrimp farming (air pollution, mangrove forest destruction, and so on), try using fresh vegetables and tofu instead. It's lighter on the planet and makes this already-fresh dish even fresher tasting.

SERVES 2   PREP AND COOKING TIME: 30 MINUTES

INGREDIENTS

½ (8.8-oz) package rice vermicelli noodles

2 Tbsp creamy peanut butter

2 Tbsp soy sauce

2 Tbsp pure maple syrup

2 tsp Sriracha

1 tsp rice vinegar

1 tsp ground ginger

1 medium cucumber, seeded and julienned

½ (16-oz) block extra-firm tofu, cut into matchsticks

½ head iceberg lettuce, chopped

½ green bell pepper, sliced (optional)

½ C enoki mushrooms (optional)

About 24 fresh mint leaves

About 24 fresh Thai basil leaves

8 (10-inch) sheets rice paper

2 tsp sesame seeds

METHOD

Cook the rice noodles according to the directions on the package. Rinse in cold water, drain, and set side.

Combine the peanut butter, soy sauce, maple syrup, Sriracha, vinegar, and ginger in a small bowl. Stir to combine. Thin with water if too thick. Set the peanut sauce aside in the fridge.

Set the cucumber, tofu, lettuce, bell pepper (if using), mushrooms (if using), mint leaves, and basil leaves in individual piles.

Fill a large bowl or saucepan—something a little bigger than 10 inches in diameter—with lukewarm water. Set up a station with a plate to make the summer rolls on, a plate to put finished rolls on, and all the ingredients within arm's reach.

Immerse a rice paper sheet in the water for about 10 seconds and then place on the rolling plate. It will still be a little hard. This is okay—it will soften on the plate and be perfect for rolling once all the ingredients are on it. Leaving it in the water until completely soft makes it incredibly difficult to work with.

Sprinkle some of the sesame seeds onto the rice paper sheet, near one of the edges. Add a few pieces of cucumber, mint leaves, basil leaves, a piece of tofu, a smidge of the noodles, and a piece of lettuce. Add bell pepper and enoki mushrooms, if using. (For your first few, go light on the fillings, as it'll be easier to get the technique down.) Fold the sides over the fillings and then fold the bottom flap up and over the fillings, tuck, and roll like you're rolling a burrito. Repeat until all the rolls are done and enjoy immediately, with the dipping sauce.

 Want to go the extra eco-mile? To avoid food waste, if you have leftover fillings, make them into a small salad and top with the peanut sauce or even just a splash of rice vinegar.

Tip: Never made summer rolls before? Watch a video online of the technique first!

MINTED GREEN PEA GUACAMOLE

Living in Texas, my guac bar is set pretty high. I'm not gonna lie, when traveling outside the Lone Star state, I find most guacamole is simply not up to snuff. But as good as the classic avocado-tomato-onion recipe is, sometimes I just want a little somethin' extra in my guac. Enter: minted green pea guacamole. It's like your classic guac, but with mint for a little added freshness and green peas for a little added protein.

SERVES 4 TO 6   PREP AND COOKING TIME: 25 MINUTES

INGREDIENTS

1 Tbsp pine nuts

Handful of fresh cilantro, chopped

Handful of fresh mint leaves, chopped

1 garlic clove, minced

1 C frozen peas

⅓ C finely chopped red onion

2 large ripe avocados

Juice of 1 lime

½ tsp salt

Freshly ground black pepper

Tortilla chips or crudités, for serving

METHOD

In a dry pan, toast the pine nuts over medium heat until browned but not burnt.

Place the toasted pine nuts in a mortar and add the cilantro, mint, and garlic. Mash together with the pestle to make a pesto, then transfer to a large bowl.

Place the peas in a small bowl and microwave for 60 seconds. Add them to the pesto.

Add the onion to the bowl, along with the avocado flesh, lime juice, and salt. Mash until somewhere between smooth and chunky, according to your preference.

Season with the pepper and stir to combine.

Garnish with additional fresh mint and serve immediately, with tortilla chips or crudités.

Note: No mortar and pestle? Just mix all the pesto ingredients together, finely chopping the cilantro, mint, and garlic first—or process in a food processor.

PISTACHIO AND SUNFLOWER SEED DUKKAH

Dukkah is an Egyptian condiment made using nuts, seeds, herbs, and spices. Blended into a crumbly powder, dukkah is used for dipping bread into, or for sprinkling atop vegetables. This version uses toasted pistachios and sunflower seeds, along with sesame seeds and spices, to create an aromatic, delicious blend that's great for parties, or just to keep on hand as a tasty addition to any meal.

SERVES 6 TO 8   PREP AND COOKING TIME: 20 MINUTES

INGREDIENTS

½ C shelled pistachios

½ C shelled sunflower seeds

½ C sesame seeds

1 Tbsp coriander seeds

1 Tbsp cumin seeds

1 tsp sea salt

1 tsp black peppercorns

METHOD

Place all the ingredients in a dry skillet over medium heat and toast, turning continuously with a spatula until fragrant and the seeds start to make a popping sound, about 5 minutes.

Remove from the heat and let cool for 10 minutes.

Transfer to a food processor or blender. Process in 3- to 5-second intervals, until you have a chunky powder. (Stop and check every few seconds to ensure you don't accidentally turn it into nut butter by overprocessing!)

Serve with bread and olive oil (dip the bread in the oil, then the dukkah), or sprinkle on roasted vegetables, salads, pizza, and more. Store leftovers in an airtight container at room temperature.

Serving Suggestion: Along with bread and oil, Roasted Red Pepper Hummus (page 208) makes a great addition.

PLANT-BASED PARMESAN

No pasta would be complete without parm. I'm a fiend for the stuff, and like to really heap on big piles of it. Fortunately, you can use nuts and nutritional yeast to replace the fatty, tangy flavors that parmesan lends to Italian cuisine. I dare you not to eat it out of the jar by the spoonful.

MAKES 1¼ CUPS   PREP AND COOKING TIME: 15 MINUTES

INGREDIENTS

½ C pine nuts

¼ C chopped Brazil nuts

¼ C shelled sunflower seeds

¼ C nutritional yeast

½ tsp garlic powder

1 tsp salt

METHOD

Place the pine nuts, Brazil nuts, and sunflower seeds in a dry skillet over medium heat and stir until lightly toasted. Keep an eye on them, as pine nuts can burn quickly. Once golden brown, remove from the heat and let cool.

Place all the ingredients in a food processor or blender and pulse until the mixture resembles bread crumbs. Spoon into an airtight jar and store in the fridge until ready to use (up to 2 weeks).

Tip: Don't have Brazil nuts? Just double the sunflower seeds.

Equipment Alert: This recipe requires a food processor or blender.

Serving Suggestion: This shines atop pizza (see pages 150 and 160), the Spaghetti and Lentil Meatballs (page 176), the Massaged Kale Caesar salad (page 123), and so many other foods.

"A plant-based diet can and will change your life."[170]

—RYAN SEACREST

QUICK COUNTRY COLESLAW

This slaw is perfect for any BBQ, picnic, or potluck! The tangy cider vinegar with creamy mayo and sweet agave combine for a balanced slaw just like Mama used to make. And because it uses nondairy milk and egg-free mayo, it's easier on the earth—conserving water and land, and emitting fewer greenhouse gases.

SERVES 8 TO 10   PREP AND COOKING TIME: 15 MINUTES

INGREDIENTS

1¼ C vegan mayo

3 Tbsp apple cider vinegar

2 Tbsp plain almond milk

1 tsp sea salt

1 Tbsp sugar

1 tsp celery seed

½ tsp freshly ground black pepper

¼ tsp garlic powder

¼ tsp onion powder

2 medium carrots

½ head green cabbage

½ head red cabbage

METHOD

In a small bowl, whisk or stir together the mayo, vinegar, almond milk, salt, sugar, celery seed, pepper, garlic powder, and onion powder. Set aside.

Shred the carrots and cabbages using a grater. Place in a large bowl and mix with clean hands.

Pour the dressing on top and mix well to combine.

Cover and refrigerate. Enjoy chilled as a side, especially with a Spicy Lentil Burger (page 134) or any other sandwich.

Note: Check out the Slawppy Joe recipe (page 131) for another tasty way to enjoy this dish!

Want to go the extra eco-mile? Next time you make broccoli, save the stems. Shred them in a food processor and then replace the cabbage with them (or add them to the cabbage). It'll cut down on food waste and is delicious!

"I am a firm believer in eating a full plant-based, whole-food diet."[171]

ROASTED RED PEPPER HUMMUS

Hummus has become so popular that some farmers in the South have begun switching from tobacco to chickpeas in order to accommodate the demand. In this recipe, roasted red peppers offer a fiery addition, making it ideal as a dip, a spread, or added to any salad.

SERVES 2 TO 4   PREP TIME: 10 MINUTES

INGREDIENTS

1 (14-oz) can chickpeas, drained and rinsed

½ C roasted red peppers

2 garlic cloves, minced

2 Tbsp tahini

Juice of ½ lemon

1 Tbsp olive oil, plus more for garnish

½ tsp ground cumin

½ tsp salt

Sesame seeds, for garnish

1 Tbsp chopped fresh parsley, for serving

METHOD

Combine the chickpeas, roasted peppers, garlic, tahini, lemon juice, olive oil, cumin, salt, and a splash of water in a blender or food processor and blend until well combined. Continue blending, adding water a little at a time until the desired consistency is achieved (water is what will make your hummus creamy).

Garnish with sesame seeds, some more olive oil, and the parsley. Store in an airtight container in the fridge for up to 5 days.

Tip: If you like your hummus tangier, double the lemon juice.

Want to go the extra eco-mile? Save the aquafaba (chickpea juice) for the Chocolate Brownies (page 225) or the Lemon Meringue Pie (page 232)—to cut down on food waste.

ROSEMARY CORNBREAD MINI MUFFINS

These go wonderfully with the Wild Mushroom Chili (page 138). Moist and filling, with aromatic rosemary, they'll make the whole house smell great. Bet you can't eat just one!

MAKES 12 MUFFINS   PREP AND COOKING TIME: 45 MINUTES

INGREDIENTS

1 C canned coconut milk

1 tsp apple cider vinegar

1 C cornmeal

½ C all-purpose flour

½ tsp baking powder

½ tsp baking soda

¼ tsp salt

½ C plus 1 Tbsp olive oil

1 small yellow onion, finely chopped

2 red bell peppers, finely chopped

6 cherry tomatoes, halved

Fresh rosemary, for garnish

METHOD

Preheat the oven to 350°F. Lightly grease a 12-cup muffin pan with vegetable oil or cooking spray.

In a small bowl, combine the coconut milk and vinegar and set aside.

Combine the cornmeal, flour, baking powder, baking soda, and salt in a large bowl and set aside.

In a heavy-bottomed skillet, heat 1 tablespoon of the olive oil over medium heat. Add the onion. Cook for 2 minutes and then add the bell peppers and cook until soft, about 5 minutes more. Remove from the heat and set aside.

Add the remaining ½ cup olive oil to the coconut milk–vinegar mixture. Whisk the wet ingredients into the bowl of dry ingredients. Add the cooked onion–bell pepper mixture, and then stir slightly, to combine.

Spoon into muffin cups. Gently press half a cherry tomato into each top and top with fresh rosemary. Bake for 15 minutes or until a toothpick inserted into the center comes out clean. Let cool for 10 minutes and then enjoy, preferably smothered with margarine.

SPICY SWEET POTATO FRIES WITH RANCH

Sweet potatoes offer all kinds of health benefits over their more common cousins. For this recipe, we take a usually-not-so-healthy favorite and offer a new spin to pack in some extra flavor (and spice) along with better health. So break out the ketchup and eat up.

SERVES 2   PREP AND COOKING TIME: 45 MINUTES

INGREDIENTS

2 medium sweet potatoes

2 Tbsp olive oil

1 tsp salt

½ tsp crushed red pepper

½ C vegan mayo

¼ tsp onion powder

¼ tsp garlic powder

Pinch of freshly ground black pepper

¼ C plain almond milk

1 Tbsp nutritional yeast

3 tsp dried parsley

METHOD

Preheat the oven to 400°F.

Scrub the sweet potatoes. With a sharp knife, cut them into ¼-inch-thick fries. Place in a large bowl and coat well with olive oil, salt, and crushed red pepper.

Spread the fries onto a rimless baking sheet. The trick to getting crispy fries is to place them far enough apart, on a baking sheet with no edges so that as they cook all the steam they are releasing can evaporate, rather than being absorbed by surrounding fries. You may need to use two baking sheets, depending on the size of your oven. Bake the fries for 15 minutes.

Meanwhile, combine the mayo, onion powder, garlic powder, black pepper, almond milk, nutritional yeast, and 1½ teaspoons of the dried parsley in a bowl. Stir to combine well and set aside in the fridge.

Once the fries have baked for 15 minutes, turn them all with a spatula. Return to the oven for another 15 to 20 minutes, depending on how well done you want them.

Sprinkle with the remaining 1½ teaspoons dried parsley and serve with the ranch dressing for dipping. Enjoy alone as a snack, or with the Buffalo Cauliflower Wrap (page 112) or any other sandwich or burger.

 Want to go the extra eco-mile? Make this when sweet potatoes are in season (see page 252).

SWEET-AND-SALTY CURRIED POPCORN

There's nothing quite like plopping down on the couch with a movie (or three) and a huge bowl of homemade popcorn. This is one of our favorites—salty, sweet, and aromatic, it's perfect for a cozy night in.

SERVES 2 TO 4   PREP AND COOKING TIME: 10 MINUTES

INGREDIENTS

6 Tbsp coconut oil

1 Tbsp curry powder

3½ Tbsp pure maple syrup

1 tsp salt

1 C popcorn kernels

METHOD

Melt 4 tablespoons of the coconut oil in a small saucepan. Add the curry powder and stir for 1 minute, or until fragrant. Remove from the heat, stir in the maple syrup and salt, and set aside.

In a large pot with a lid, melt the remaining 2 tablespoons coconut oil over medium-high heat. Add 3 kernels of popcorn and cover. Once those three kernels pop, add all the unpopped kernels and cover. Shake vigorously, using a dish towel to hold the lid in place with your thumbs as you hold the pot by its handles. Place the pot back on the heat and wait for the popping to begin. It will start out slowly and get more and more intense, then slowly die down again. Once you haven't heard a pop for a few seconds, remove from the heat and carefully remove the lid to let the steam escape.

If you're nervous or unsure about the heat on your stove, you can hold the pot just above the burner, shaking it intermittently, to give it a break from being on the heat. It will take a little longer for all the kernels to pop, but is a good way to prevent burning.

Pour the topping over the popcorn, cover, and shake vigorously (or mix in a very large bowl) to combine. Enjoy!

Alternative Topping: Not a sweet curry fan? No worries. Instead of curry powder and maple syrup, use 1 tablespoon Old Bay seasoning and 2 tablespoons nutritional yeast in the first stage instead, and use that as your topping.

DESSERTS

All-the-Nut-Butters Cups
219

Apple-Pecan Crisp
220

Avocado Chocolate Mousse with
Vanilla Bean Whip
222

Chocolate Brownies with Puffed Quinoa
225

Classic Pumpkin Pie
226

Coconut Basbousa
229

Lemon-Ginger Blueberry Cake
with Cream Cheese Frosting
230

Lemon Meringue Pie
232

Minted Lemon-Cucumber Sorbet
234

Mom's Noodle Kugel
237

Peanut Butter Chocolate Chip Cookie
Ice Cream Sandwiches
238

Peanut Butter Trail Mix Cookies
241

Raw Chocolate-Hazelnut Truffles
243

Raw Lemon Vanilla Raspberry Slab
244

Smoky Maple-Pecan Cheesecake
246

Spicy Chocolate Milk Shake
with Whipped Coconut Cream
248

ALL-THE-NUT-BUTTERS CUPS

Why stick with plain peanut butter cups when you could use other nut butters? Almond, cashew, hazelnut—even sunflower butter! And why use milk chocolate when you could make your own super-easy dark chocolate? Mix 'em, match 'em—you can't go wrong!

MAKES TEN 1-INCH CUPS   PREP AND COOKING TIME: 30 MINUTES

INGREDIENTS

3 oz cocoa butter

¼ C pure maple syrup

¾ C unsweetened cocoa powder

Pinch of salt

2 Tbsp confectioners' sugar, plus more if needed

3½ Tbsp nut butter (hazelnut, almond, or peanut)

METHOD

Place ten small paper muffin cup liners or chocolate molds on a dinner plate.

Make a DIY double boiler: bring 1 cup water to a boil in a small saucepan. Place a small metal bowl on top (making sure the bottom of the bowl does not touch the water).

Put the cocoa butter in the hot bowl and stir with a silicone spatula; it will melt quickly. Add the maple syrup and stir to combine. Add the cocoa powder and salt and stir until smooth and well combined. Turn the heat off.

Spoon 1 tablespoon of the mixture into each muffin cup or mold. (You'll have leftover chocolate; save it for later to top the cups.) Place the entire plate of muffin cups in the freezer until the chocolate is firm, about 15 minutes.

While that's firming up in the freezer, sift the confectioners' sugar into a bowl. Add the nut butter. Roll the mixture into 10 small balls. If they're too wet to roll, add more sugar.

Remove the plate from the freezer and place a nut butter ball in the center of each mold, on top of the chocolate. Press down ever so slightly, being careful not to push it all the way to the edges.

Spoon 1 tablespoon of the remaining chocolate mixture on top of each, and then place back in the freezer until firm, about 15 minutes more. Once set, transfer to an airtight container and store in the fridge until ready to eat (up to 1 week).

APPLE-PECAN CRISP

Nothing says fall like spending the day picking apples and then enjoying the fruits of your labor with a warm bowl of comforting crisp. And because trees, including fruit trees, soak up CO_2 and produce oxygen, they can help offset climate-changing emissions. In fact, even a single-acre apple orchard will extract about fifteen tons of CO_2 from the air each year. You know what they say: an apple a day keeps global warming away!

SERVES 4   PREP AND COOKING TIME: 1 HOUR

INGREDIENTS

4 heaping Tbsp margarine, chilled, plus more for the baking dish

10 medium apples (about 3 lb)

2 heaping tsp ground cinnamon

7 heaping Tbsp sugar

1 C all-purpose flour

1 C rolled oats

½ C pecans, coarsely chopped

½ tsp vanilla extract

½ tsp baking powder

Pinch of salt

METHOD

Preheat the oven to 350°F. Lightly coat a 9 x 13-inch casserole dish with a tiny bit of margarine.

Peel, core, and slice each apple, placing them in a large bowl as you go.

Sprinkle the cinnamon and 3 tablespoons of the sugar over the apples. Add 1 tablespoon of the flour and mix well to combine. Pour the apple mixture into the prepared casserole dish.

In the same bowl, combine the remaining 4 tablespoons sugar, remaining flour, the oats, pecans, vanilla, baking powder, and salt. Stir to combine. Add the chilled margarine. Using clean hands, work the margarine into the mixture until it's evenly distributed. Sprinkle the topping over the apples and bake, uncovered, until the apples are soft, 45 to 55 minutes.

Remove from the oven and let cool for 5 minutes before serving.

Serving Suggestion: Top with the Whipped Coconut Cream from page 248.

Want to go the extra eco-mile? Make this when apples are in season—and even try hand picking them yourself at an orchard!

AVOCADO CHOCOLATE MOUSSE WITH VANILLA BEAN WHIP

Avocado makes a creamy, decadent replacement for heavy cream and eggs in this dish. Combined with maple syrup, vanilla, and cocoa powder, you can't taste the avocado at all—and the texture is spot-on. Plus, it's more sustainable! Pound for pound, eggs take almost four hundred gallons of water to produce and cow's milk takes more than eight hundred gallons—while avocados take only about 140 gallons per pound to grow. That's a huge reduction in water use from just one simple swap. How sweet is that?

SERVES 4   PREP TIME: 15 MINUTES, PLUS TIME TO CHILL

INGREDIENTS

2 ripe avocados

¼ C pure maple syrup

3 Tbsp unsweetened cocoa powder, plus more for dusting

½ tsp pure vanilla extract

Pinch of salt

1 (5.4-oz) can coconut cream, chilled

2 Tbsp confectioners' sugar

1 whole vanilla bean

Fresh raspberries, for garnish (optional)

METHOD

Scoop the flesh out of the avocado and place it in a blender. Add the maple syrup, cocoa powder, vanilla extract, and salt. Puree until thick and smooth. It should be sweet and rich and not taste at all like avocado. If it's too avocado-tasting for you, try adding a little more maple syrup and cocoa.

Transfer to an airtight container and refrigerate for several hours, until cold.

Meanwhile, place the coconut cream in a bowl. Add the confectioners' sugar. Cut the vanilla bean down the middle lengthwise and scrape the seeds into the bowl. Using a handheld mixer, whip until thick.

Spoon the mousse into bowls. Top with whip and garnish with fresh raspberries (if using) and a dusting of cocoa.

(!) **Equipment Alert:** This recipe requires a handheld mixer.

PRO RACE CAR DRIVER AND ECO-CHAMPION LEILANI MÜNTER

I became vegetarian (and then vegan) because I love animals and didn't want to see them harmed. It turns out that was also one of the most eco-friendly moves I could have made.

We know, for example, that communities across the country are suffering through the air pollution caused by mega factory farms. We also know that air pollution is causing global warming. Most people associate their eco-footprint with the kind of car they drive or fuel they burn; when they think of our planet's air and the problems it faces, they may just think of industrial smokestacks and smog.

At home, I drive a 100-percent electric car that I power from the solar panels on the roof of my house. But it is likely that I am making a more positive impact on our planet and air through eating plant-based foods.

And no matter where you fall on the spectrum—vegan, vegetarian, or something else entirely—it's easier than ever to make sustainable choices! Look around at the grocery store and you'll see all kinds of amazing veg-forward foods. Check out menus at your local restaurants and I bet you'll see some great veggie options you'd never even noticed.

As someone who's gone through the life- (and planet-) transforming decision to focus my diet on plants rather than animals, I promise you'll be better for it! Whether you go all in on plant-based eating or just make an effort to eat plant-based foods more often, you'll discover a great variety of new foods that are satisfying, delicious, easy to prepare, and eco-friendly! That's something that you, the animals, and the planet can all feel good about.

Leilani Münter—a professional race car driver and environmental activist—has been named Discovery Planet's Green number one eco-athlete in the world and was awarded an ELLE magazine Genius Award. She's an outspoken advocate for solar power, electric cars, plant-based diets, and animal protection. An active lobbyist on these issues, Leilani has been a guest at the White House and the United Nations in Geneva. She also uses her race car to get environmental messages in front of America's 75 million race fans: her cars have carried messages about renewable energy, clean energy legislation, and animal protection.

CHOCOLATE BROWNIES WITH PUFFED QUINOA

Peanut butter and chocolate is my favorite flavor combo. And because this rich brownie recipe uses aquafaba instead of eggs, it's more eco-friendly than your typical brownie. (Aquafaba, after all, is a zero-waste product!) The puffed quinoa on top gives the brownie an extra airy crunch and a little zap of protein.

SERVES 8   PREP AND COOKING TIME: 1 HOUR PLUS COOLING TIME

INGREDIENTS

7 oz dark bittersweet chocolate

2 Tbsp coconut oil

½ tsp pure vanilla extract

3 Tbsp creamy peanut butter

½ C plus 2 Tbsp aquafaba (chickpea juice)

1 C sugar

1 C all-purpose flour

2 Tbsp unsweetened cocoa powder

1 tsp baking powder

½ tsp salt

2 Tbsp puffed quinoa (optional)

METHOD

Preheat the oven to 350°F.

Make a DIY double boiler: Bring 1 cup water to a boil in a small saucepan. Place a small metal bowl on top (be sure the bottom of the bowl does not touch the water).

Break the chocolate into smaller pieces and put them in the bowl, along with the coconut oil, vanilla, and peanut butter. Stir until everything is melted and well combined.

In the bowl of a stand mixer fitted with the whisk attachment or in a large bowl using a handheld mixer, beat the aquafaba and sugar until thick and creamy and doubled in size, about 5 minutes.

Add the melted chocolate mixture to the bowl, scraping all the goodness out with a silicone spatula. Beat until just combined, about 30 seconds. Sift the flour, cocoa powder, baking powder, and salt into the bowl. Use a sieve, as cocoa can be very lumpy. Beat again until it's nicely combined, about 30 seconds.

Line a 7 x 11-inch baking pan with parchment paper. Pour the brownie batter in. It will be quite thick. Use a silicone spatula to scrape everything from the bowl into the pan and then smooth it out.

Sprinkle the puffed quinoa over the brownies and bake for 30 minutes. Remove and let cool before cutting into 8 squares.

 Tip: If you don't have puffed quinoa, you can sprinkle some chopped pistachios (or other kind of nuts) on top.

(!) **Equipment Alert:** This recipe requires a stand mixer or handheld mixer.

CLASSIC PUMPKIN PIE

With no big slice of pumpkin pie to end the feast, my first Thanksgiving as a vegan was a bit rough. Whether you're fully vegan and want to make sure to end your holidays right or you're simply looking for a healthier, eco-friendlier version of this classic dessert to try out, this recipe is sure to please.

SERVES 6 TO 8   PREP AND COOKING TIME: 2 HOURS PLUS OVERNIGHT COOLING TIME

INGREDIENTS

2 C all-purpose flour, plus more for dusting

2 Tbsp sugar, plus more for sprinkling

½ tsp salt

¼ cup very cold margarine

½ C very cold water

1 (15-oz) can pure pumpkin puree

1 C coconut cream

½ C pure maple syrup

3 Tbsp arrowroot powder

2 heaping tsp ground cinnamon

2 heaping tsp ground ginger

½ tsp ground nutmeg

1 tsp pure vanilla extract

METHOD

Place the flour, sugar, and ¼ tsp of the salt in a large bowl. Stir to combine. Add the cold margarine and work it through with clean fingers until the dough resembles bread crumbs. Add the water, 1 tablespoon at a time, kneading after each addition, until the mixture forms into a ball.

Lightly dust a clean work surface with flour. Press the dough into a flat, round disk. Cover with an inverted bowl and let sit for 10 minutes.

Uncover the dough, sprinkle the top with a little flour, and then roll over it with a rolling pin about four times. Flip it over, sprinkle with more flour, and roll over it again. Repeat until the dough is roughly 12 inches in diameter—large enough to cover the bottom and up the sides of a pie dish.

Carefully transfer the rolled-out dough to a pie dish and press it up the sides. Any overhang can be folded down and any broken bits can be easily pressed back together with your fingers. Prick holes in the bottom with a fork and set aside.

Once the dough is made, preheat the oven to 375°F.

Place the remaining ¼ teaspoon salt, the pumpkin, coconut cream, maple syrup, arrowroot powder, cinnamon, ginger, nutmeg, and vanilla in a blender or food processor and blend until smooth. Pour into the pie dish and smooth the top. Sprinkle a little sugar on top.

Bake for 1 hour.

Remove from the oven and let cool fully on the counter. Cover and refrigerate overnight before slicing and serving.

 Equipment Alert: This recipe requires a blender or food processor.

COCONUT BASBOUSA

Basbousa is a super-sweet Middle Eastern cake made from semolina or farina and soaked in simple syrup. It's so moist, you almost need to eat it with a spoon. Semolina is a by-product of wheat milling, making this sweet treat both tasty and more sustainable. And because this particular recipe uses nondairy ingredients, it cuts down on the cake's water and climate footprints too.

SERVES 8 TO 10   PREP AND COOKING TIME: 1 HOUR

INGREDIENTS

1 C vanilla nondairy yogurt

½ C almond milk

2 C coarse semolina or farina

1 tsp baking powder

2½ C sugar

½ C margarine, melted

⅓ C shredded coconut, plus more for garnish

1 tsp ground cinnamon

METHOD

Preheat the oven to 350°F. Lightly grease a baking dish (9 x 13 inches works well) with margarine.

In a large bowl, mix together the yogurt, almond milk, semolina, baking powder, and 1 cup of the sugar. Melt the margarine in the microwave in a mug or small bowl and add it to the mixture, stirring to combine. Let sit for 1 minute. Add the coconut and stir until well mixed.

Pour the mixture into the prepared baking dish, spreading it evenly. Bake for 30 to 45 minutes. (Check at 30 minutes—it should be yellowish with golden brown edges when done.)

While the cake is baking, combine 1½ cup water, the cinnamon, and the remaining 1½ cups sugar in a saucepan. Bring to a boil, stirring until the sugar has dissolved. Once boiling, turn down the heat and simmer until the syrup thickens slightly, 1 to 2 minutes. Set aside to cool.

When the cake is done, remove it from the oven and cut it into pieces (leaving it in the dish). Pour the cooled syrup over the top, making sure to cover all parts. Let the syrup-coated cake rest for 20 minutes, allowing the cake to fully absorb the syrup.

To serve, scoop out the pieces, roughly, with a spatula and stack on a plate, sprinkling with extra coconut as you go. It'll crumble and the pieces will not be uniform (since it's sooooo moist)—don't worry, it's supposed to be like that. Finish it off with some more coconut and eat immediately or chilled.

LEMON-GINGER BLUEBERRY CAKE WITH CREAM CHEESE FROSTING

The tartness of fresh lemons, the zing of ginger, and the sweetness of blueberries all shine in this cake. The vegan cream cheese frosting adds a nice creaminess to the cake, without the planetary pitfalls associated with dairy production. It all comes together to form a more sustainable—and highly delectable—dessert.

SERVES 6 TO 8   PREP AND COOKING TIME: 1 HOUR, PLUS COOLING TIME

INGREDIENTS

1 C almond milk

8 Tbsp fresh lemon juice

6½ Tbsp coconut oil, melted

1 C sugar

2½ C all-purpose flour

1 tsp baking powder

1 tsp baking soda

1 tsp ground ginger

1 tsp ground cinnamon

½ tsp salt

1 C fresh or frozen blueberries

1 (8-oz) package vegan cream cheese

⅓ C margarine, at room temperature

3½ C confectioners' sugar

1 tsp lemon zest

½ tsp pure vanilla extract

¼ tsp pure almond extract (optional)

Additional blueberries, lemon zest, and/or edible flowers, for garnish (optional)

METHOD

Preheat the oven to 350°F. Line a round 12-inch cake pan with parchment paper.

Combine the almond milk and 7 tablespoons of the lemon juice in a medium bowl and set aside for 5 minutes. After 5 minutes, add the melted coconut oil and stir to combine.

In a large bowl, combine the sugar, flour, baking powder, baking soda, ginger, cinnamon, and salt. Stir to combine. Add the wet mixture, whisking or beating with a handheld mixer as you go. Add the blueberries and fold them into the cake batter with a spatula.

Pour the cake batter into the prepared pan. Bake until the top is lightly golden, 45 to 55 minutes. The cake is done when you can stick a toothpick or skewer into the center and it comes out clean. Remove from the oven and let cool.

While the cake is baking, place the cream cheese and margarine in a bowl and beat with a handheld mixer until thick and smooth. Add the remaining 1 tablespoon lemon juice, the confectioners' sugar, lemon zest, vanilla, and almond extract (if using). Beat on high until you have a thick and creamy frosting, 3 to 5 minutes. Set aside.

Once cake is entirely cool, top it with the frosting and additional blueberries, lemon zest, and/or edible flowers.

If not eating within a few hours, store in the fridge and bring to room temperature before serving.

LEMON MERINGUE PIE

This pie brims with fresh lemon taste. Sweet and tart, it's just like Grandma used to make—almost. Instead of using egg whites, it uses aquafaba—the "juice" from canned chickpeas. In 2014, French chef Joël Roessel discovered that this can be whipped into foams that are functionally equivalent to egg whites but healthier. It's also more sustainable: in addition to being a zero-waste food that would otherwise end up down the drain, aquafaba helps us avoid eggs, which means avoiding all the air pollution associated with chicken farming and the climate-changing greenhouse gas emissions associated with feed production. So just like Grandma used to make? Maybe not. Better than Grandma used to make? Definitely. (Sorry, Grandma.)

SERVES 6 TO 8   PREP AND COOKING TIME: 1½ HOURS, PLUS COOLING TIME

INGREDIENTS

For the crust:

2 C all-purpose flour, plus more for dusting

2 Tbsp sugar

⅛ tsp salt

½ C very cold margarine

½ C ice-cold water

For the filling:

½ C sugar

Zest of 1 lemon

⅔ C fresh lemon juice

⅓ C coconut cream

1 Tbsp agar-agar (powder, not flakes)

2 Tbsp arrowroot powder

1 (14-oz) packet silken tofu

½ tsp ground turmeric

For the meringue topping:

¾ C aquafaba (chickpea canning liquid)

½ tsp cream of tartar

½ tsp pure vanilla extract

1 C sugar

METHOD

First, make the crust:
Preheat the oven to 350°F.

Place the flour, sugar, and salt in a large bowl and stir to combine. Add the cold margarine and work it through with clean fingers until the dough resembles bread crumbs. Add the water, 1 tablespoon at a time, kneading after each addition, until the mixture forms into a ball.

Lightly dust a clean work surface with flour. Place the ball of dough on top and press it into a flat, round disk. Cover with an inverted bowl and let sit for 10 minutes.

Uncover the dough, sprinkle the top of the disk with a little flour, and then roll it with a rolling pin about four times. Flip the dough over, sprinkle with more flour, and roll over it again. Repeat until the dough is roughly 12 inches in diameter—large enough to cover the bottom of a pie dish and go up the sides.

Carefully transfer to a pie dish and press it up the sides. Remove or fold down any overhang. Prick holes in the bottom with a fork. If you have dried beans or pie weights on hand, line the dough with aluminum foil and fill with a layer of beans or weights about ½ inch thick, to prevent it from rising while it bakes. (If you don't have this, no problem.) Bake for 30 minutes. Remove from the oven and let cool.

Timesaver: Make the crust and filling the night before and refrigerate, covered, overnight. Then, the next day, make the meringue, bake, cool, and eat.

Meanwhile, make the lemon curd filling:
Place all the filling ingredients in a food processor or blender and puree until totally smooth. Transfer to a saucepan, place over medium-high heat, and whisk continuously until the mixture has thickened, about 5 minutes. Once thick, pour the filling into the cooled piecrust and let set, at least 15 minutes.

Make the meringue:

If you've made meringue using eggs, then this is much the same—except you're using aquafaba (the juice from a can of beans) instead of the whites of a chicken egg. Chick*pea* protein instead of chick*en* protein.

Pour the aquafaba into a large bowl or the bowl of a stand mixer fitted with the whisk attachment. Add the cream of tartar and vanilla and beat on medium-high speed until the mixture holds soft peaks, 5 to 10 minutes. Add the sugar, a little at a time, and beat until the mixture holds stiff peaks. It will take another 10 to 20 minutes of beating, but the end result is well worth your time. If you think you have stiff enough peaks but you aren't sure, hold the bowl upside down; if the meringue stays put, it's ready.

And for the grand finale:

Spoon the meringue on top of the pie. Make it about 2 inches thick and ensure it touches all the edges. Make little peaks as you go. You can also pipe the meringue on instead, if you want something fancier.

Bake for 5 minutes. Remove and let fully cool, at least 2 hours. Enjoy!

 Tip: Want the peaks of your meringue a little darker? Increase the oven temperature to 400°F and place the pie under the broiler for the final minute. Or you can (safely!) blast it with a kitchen blowtorch.

Equipment Alert: This recipe requires a stand mixer.

MINTED LEMON–CUCUMBER SORBET

I scream, you scream, we all scream for . . . sorbet! In this recipe, fresh mint, tart lemon juice, and that oh-so-subtle cucumber flavor join forces to create a dairy-free dessert that's refreshing and eco-friendly. Add a dash of liquor before freezing for an adult-friendly summer treat.

SERVES 2   PREP TIME: 10 MINUTES, PLUS FREEZING TIME

INGREDIENTS

½ C sugar

1½ Tbsp fresh lemon juice

10 fresh mint leaves

1 small cucumber, peeled and cut into ¼-inch chunks

Zest of ½ lemon

1 tsp white rum or vodka (optional)

METHOD

Put the sugar and lemon juice in a small saucepan and place over high heat. Cook until the lemon juice is bubbling, then remove from the heat and stir until the sugar has dissolved to create syrup. Add the mint leaves. Stir, then set aside to fully cool.

Place the cucumber, cooled syrup, lemon zest, and rum (if using) in a food processor or high-speed blender. Pulse until smooth and then pour into a freezer-safe container.

Freeze for at least 4 hours or overnight, stirring once after 2 hours. When it's ready, the sorbet will easily hold its form while being scooped but will never freeze rock-hard, due to the sugar. You can therefore enjoy it as soon as it is ready, or leave it in the freezer for up to 2 weeks.

Serve alone, or garnished with slices of cucumber and lemon.

 Want to go the extra eco-mile? Try growing mint on your windowsill or in your yard to cut down on food miles and packaging.

"I changed my diet to a vegan diet, really just to experiment to see what it was like. And I felt better, so . . . I'm likely to continue it for the rest of my life."[172]

—AL GORE

MOM'S NOODLE KUGEL

Growing up in a mildly Jewish household, we only ate traditional Jewish foods around Passover or Hanukkah. Noodle kugel was always a must-have. Sweet, filling, and creamy, this dessert is one of my favorites. But normally, kugel is made with a laundry list of planet-unfriendly ingredients—like eggs, butter, and cheese. These ingredients require large amounts of water and land, and emit huge quantities of greenhouse gases. (Just the cheese alone emits about 13.5 kg of CO_2 per serving!) So this recipe uses tofu instead—a much gentler choice, emitting only 2 kg of CO_2 per serving—along with plant-based sour cream and margarine. The first time I tried it out on my mother, you can imagine I was nervous. But she loved it, our guests loved it, and the whole dish was gobbled up. Not one person was able to pass over this tasty, eco-friendly kugel.

SERVES 8 TO 10   PREP AND COOKING TIME: 1 HOUR

INGREDIENTS

8 oz pasta (rotini or spelt ribbons)

1 apple or pear

½ (16-oz) package soft tofu

¼ C pure maple syrup

2 tsp pure vanilla extract

1 C vegan sour cream

¼ C margarine, melted

½ C sugar

1 tsp ground cinnamon

Pinch of ground nutmeg

¼ tsp salt

1 C raisins

INSTRUCTIONS

Preheat the oven to 350°F. Lightly grease an 11 x 8-inch casserole dish with margarine.

Bring a large pot of salted water to a boil. Cook the pasta in the boiling water according to the directions on the package. Drain, rinse, and set aside.

Thinly slice the apple or pear and put it in a large bowl. Finely crumble the tofu into the bowl. Stir in all the remaining ingredients, in the order listed, and mix. The tofu should be mashed and fine by the end. Add the cooked pasta and mix thoroughly to combine.

Transfer the mixture to the prepared baking dish. Bake until the kugel is firm on the inside and the top turns golden brown and begins to crisp, 40 to 45 minutes.

Remove from the oven, let sit for at least 10 minutes, and serve.

Serving Suggestion: Kugel is great served cold or at room temperature!

PEANUT BUTTER CHOCOLATE CHIP COOKIE ICE CREAM SANDWICHES

When I first became vegan in the late '90s, these peanut butter chocolate chip cookies were one of the first desserts I learned how to bake. They're rich and creamy, soft and sweet, and total people-pleasers. This recipe combines them with delicious nondairy ice cream for a decadent dessert.

SERVES 3   PREP AND COOKING TIME: 35 MINUTES, PLUS 5 HOURS FREEZING TIME

INGREDIENTS

1½ C all-purpose flour

½ C granulated sugar

½ C brown sugar

¾ tsp baking soda

1 tsp arrowroot powder

¼ tsp salt

1 C peanut butter

½ tsp pure vanilla extract

¼ C margarine, room temperature

½ C almond milk

½ (12-oz) bag dark chocolate chips

Nondairy ice cream (any flavor you'd like)

METHOD

Once you're ready, preheat the oven to 350°F.

In a large bowl, mix the flour, granulated sugar, brown sugar, baking soda, arrowroot powder, and salt. Add the peanut butter, vanilla, and margarine. Using clean hands, mix thoroughly. It's worth the mess (using your hands gives it the right consistency). Add the almond milk, a little at a time, until it's not too wet but not too dry. Continue with your hands. Add the chocolate chips and mix some more.

Roll the dough into 1-inch balls and place on a baking sheet with enough space between them so they can spread to be about 3-inch cookies. Flatten them slightly, first with the palm of your hand and then with your fingers.

Bake for 15 minutes, being careful to not let the bottoms burn. Remove from the oven and let cool. (They'll still be soft when removed—they'll harden as they cool.)

Sandwich as much ice cream between two cookies as you'd like and enjoy immediately.

GOOD FOOD INSTITUTE EXECUTIVE DIRECTOR BRUCE FRIEDRICH

Humans have the unique ability to improve our world and lives through blending imagination with design. Smartphones allow farmers and textile workers in the developing world to start small businesses and move out of desperate poverty. Modern air travel and the Internet have made travel and information more accessible than before.

Today, each of us can bring that same spirit of innovation and improvement to our dinner plates. And we should. After all, what we choose to eat affects everything—the earth, our water and air, our climate, animals. Just as modern automobiles replaced the horse and buggy, better alternatives can now replace industrial animal agriculture.

We now have plant-based meats and milks that have the taste and texture of their animal-based counterparts but that are more environmentally sustainable. These products can help us avoid antibiotics, growth hormones, and Salmonella. They can reduce our land and water costs and slash greenhouse gas emissions. They're healthier for us. They're safer. And most important, they taste fantastic.

Add these types of innovative foods to an abundance of whole grains and legumes, produce, and simple plant-based proteins like tofu and tempeh and the opportunities for better, more sustainable eating are virtually endless. In a world where we all need to eat—and where we all want *what we eat* to be good—the more we capitalize on those opportunities, the better off we and our planet will be.

Bruce Friedrich is Executive Director of the Good Food Institute, and has been a leading food and agriculture reformer for over two decades. He holds degrees from Grinnell College, Johns Hopkins University, and the London School of Economics.

PEANUT BUTTER TRAIL MIX COOKIES

These cookies have all the things. Rolled oats, sunflower seeds, raisins, and peanut butter make for a filling and fun cookie. They are missing one thing, though: eggs. That means they're better for the earth (and, of course, the animals) and have zero cholesterol. Talk about a win-win!

MAKES 10 COOKIES   PREP AND COOKING TIME: 30 MINUTES

INGREDIENTS

2 C rolled oats

½ C all-purpose flour, plus more if needed

1 tsp baking powder

1 tsp ground cinnamon

⅔ C raisins

¼ C shelled sunflower seeds

Pinch of salt

2 Tbsp coconut oil

5 heaping Tbsp peanut butter

½ C sugar

1 tsp pure vanilla extract

½ C almond milk, plus more if needed

METHOD

Preheat the oven to 350°F. Lightly grease a baking sheet with margarine.

Combine oats, flour, baking powder, cinnamon, raisins, sunflower seeds, and salt in a large bowl and mix thoroughly.

Place the coconut oil, peanut butter, sugar, and vanilla in a medium saucepan and and set over medium heat. Stir until all the ingredients are combined and the sugar has completely dissolved.

Pour the warm peanut butter mixture into the bowl of dry ingredients and stir until well combined. Add the almond milk and mix thoroughly. You want it somewhere between wet and dry, and it should hold together. Add about ¼ cup more almond milk if not wet enough, or more flour if too wet.

Using wet hands, roll 10 golf ball–size balls of cookie dough, placing them on the prepared baking sheet as you go. Once you have rolled all the cookie dough into balls, press them flat, first with the palm of your hand and then with a fork, so they're about ½ inch thick.

Bake for 15 minutes. Remove from the oven and let cool completely on the baking sheet.

Enjoy immediately or store in an airtight container.

Tip: Chocolate lovers can substitute chocolate chips for half the raisins. Just be sure the mixture has cooled before adding the chocolate, and add them last (after the almond milk).

RAW CHOCOLATE-HAZELNUT TRUFFLES

Easy, decadent, and the perfect quick chocolate fix—these raw truffles make a great snack.

MAKES 10 TO 20   PREP TIME: 20 MINUTES

INGREDIENTS

10 Medjool dates, pitted

¾ C hazelnut meal, plus more for rolling

⅓ C hazelnut butter

¼ C unsweetened cocoa powder, plus more for rolling

½ tsp pure vanilla extract

Pinch of sea salt

Coconut meal

METHOD

Place the dates, hazelnut meal, hazelnut butter, cocoa powder, vanilla, salt, and 1 tablespoon water in a food processor and pulse until the dates are broken down. Process until everything is sticky and you can easily form a ball from the mixture. If your dates were a little dry and things aren't coming together so easily, add an extra tablespoon of water and process some more.

Using wet hands, roll the mixture into balls. You can go as big or as small as you like, but I find that 12 balls of about 1 ounce each are the perfect size. Roll the truffles in coconut meal, cocoa powder, or hazelnut meal (or mix and match). Store in an airtight container in the fridge until ready to enjoy (up to 1 week).

Tips: Bob's Red Mill hazelnut meal is sold in the baking section of many grocery stores. Can't find hazelnut butter or meal? Almond butter and almond meal work well as replacements.

RAW LEMON VANILLA RASPBERRY SLAB

This delicious dessert is made by layering flavorful cashew cream and berries on top of an almond–date base. It uses coconut milk and nuts instead of cow's milk for a lighter eco-footprint, and lemon zest and juice for a little tartness. It's creamy and sweet, tart and tasty.

SERVES 8   PREP TIME: 20 MINUTES, PLUS TIME TO SET

INGREDIENTS

15 Medjool dates, pitted

1 C raw almonds

1 C shredded coconut

Zest of 1 lemon

2 pinches of salt

4 C fresh raspberries

3 C raw cashews, soaked in water to cover for 4 hours

1 C canned coconut milk

½ C agave nectar

¼ C fresh lemon juice

1½ tsp pure vanilla extract

½ C coconut flakes, for garnish

METHOD

Line an 8-inch square baking pan with parchment paper. (This will make it easier to remove the slab later.) The best way is to cut the paper to 10 inches wide, so it goes up and over two sides of the pan and you can use the excess parchment hanging over to lift the slab out once it's set.

Place the dates, almonds, shredded coconut, lemon zest, and a pinch of salt in a food processor. Pulse until the almonds are finely ground and the mixture holds together. Press the mixture into the bottom of the prepared pan and smooth the top. Place 1½ cups of the raspberries on top of the base.

Drain and rinse the cashews and place them in a food processor or blender, along with the coconut milk, agave, lemon juice, vanilla, and remaining pinch of salt. Process until smooth, 2 to 4 minutes.

Pour half the vanilla–cashew filling on top of the raspberries in the baking pan. Add 1½ cups of the berries to the remaining filling in the food processor and process until well combined. Pour this over the vanilla layer. Top with the remaining berries and the coconut flakes. Freeze until set, at least 4 hours, though overnight is preferable.

Remove from the freezer 10 minutes before serving. To remove from the dish, run a warm, wet knife along the sides that are in direct contact with the dish and then lift it out using the paper overhang on the other edges.

Heat up a sharp knife by running hot water over it and cut the slab into 8 pieces. Enjoy immediately and keep leftovers refrigerated.

(!) **Equipment Alert:** This recipe requires a food processor.

SMOKY MAPLE-PECAN CHEESECAKE

This sultry pecan cheesecake recipe combines the richness of coconut milk and the sweet-ness of maple syrup along with smoked pecans to deliver a creamy, unique, lip-smacking dessert. Because it uses tofu (instead of eggs), it's lighter on our waistlines and the planet.

SERVES 6 TO 8   PREP AND COOKING TIME: 1½ HOURS

INGREDIENTS

1 C plus 1 Tbsp pure maple syrup

1 (13.5-oz) can coconut milk

¾ box of graham crackers (about 18 cracker sheets)

¼ C sugar

¾ C margarine, melted

1 (14-oz) package silken tofu

C all-purpose flour

1 tsp pure vanilla extract

Pinch of salt

2 C chopped pecans

¼ tsp liquid smoke

METHOD

Preheat the oven to 425°F.

Place 1 cup of the maple syrup and the coconut milk in a saucepan. Bring to a boil, lower the heat to maintain a simmer, and cook, whisking occasionally, for 15 minutes. Remove from the heat and place in the fridge to cool a bit.

Using a food processor, turn the graham crackers into fine crumbs. Place them in a bowl. Add the sugar and melted margarine. Stir until the ingredients are well combined and the cracker crumbs are soaked. Press into a 9-inch round cake pan or glass pie dish, working the mixture up the sides. Set aside in the fridge.

Rinse the food processor. Place the slightly cooled coconut milk–maple syrup mixture into it. Add the tofu, flour, vanilla, and salt. Blend until smooth and well combined. Add 1 cup of the pecans and pulse to combine.

Pour that mixture into the chilled piecrust and bake for 10 minutes.

Remove the cheesecake after 10 minutes and lower the oven temperature to 350°F.

Place the remaining 1 cup pecans in a bowl. Add the remaining 1 tablespoon maple syrup and the liquid smoke. Stir to coat, then sprinkle over the cheesecake. Bake for 40 minutes more.

Remove from the oven and let cool. Cover and refrigerate for a few hours or up to overnight before serving.

Note: Don't want this smoky? Just leave the liquid smoke out of the recipe.

SPICY CHOCOLATE MILK SHAKE WITH WHIPPED COCONUT CREAM

Spice up your chocolate with a little kick of cayenne. This spicy milk shake with whipped coconut cream is a decadent dessert that bites back. And since the recipe uses almond milk and nondairy ice cream for the shake, and coconut cream instead of dairy cream for the whipped topping, it has less of a water and climate footprint than a standard milk shake. Moo-ve over dairy, there's a new shake in town!

SERVES 2   PREP TIME: 10 MINUTES

INGREDIENTS

For the whipped cream:

1 (5.4-oz) can coconut cream, chilled

¼ C confectioners' sugar

¼ tsp pure vanilla extract

For the milk shake:

¾ C almond milk

2 C vegan chocolate ice cream

2 Tbsp unsweetened cocoa powder

⅛ tsp ground nutmeg

Tiny pinch of salt

Pinch of cayenne pepper (optional)

Pinch of ground cinnamon, for garnish (optional)

METHOD

First, make the whipped cream:

Scoop the chilled coconut cream into a bowl, discarding the little bit of liquid left in the can. Add the confectioners' sugar and vanilla. Using a handheld mixer, whip until thick. Set aside in the fridge.

Now for the shake:

Place all the milk shake ingredients in a blender and blend until smooth.

Pour the milk shake into glasses and top with the whipped cream and a pinch of cinnamon (if using). Enjoy!

"We should all be . . . focusing on enjoying more plant-based delights."[173]

—JAMIE OLIVER

CHEF JOSÉ ANDRÉS

On January 12, 2010, a massive 7.0-magnitude earthquake hit Haiti, just sixteen miles west of the country's capital city of Port-au-Prince. Over the next two weeks, fifty-two major aftershocks had been recorded, with an estimated three million people affected by the quake.

Shortly after, I traveled to Haiti to assist in relief efforts. I was struck to see that the grinding poverty Haitians live with day-to-day had been exacerbated by dirty cooking conditions in overcrowded and unsafe tent cities. And I was also struck to learn that the problem extends far beyond Haiti.

Every day, all across the world, nearly three billion people eat food prepared using crude cookstoves or open fires in homes with poor or no ventilation. Exposure to this smoke can cause illnesses including pneumonia, lung disease, and cancer—killing an estimated two million people annually. This problem has been categorized by the World Health Organization as the fifth biggest health risk in developing countries.

The fact is that how we cook and eat food can have major social implications—on our own health, the health of our communities, and the health of the planet. Whether it's illness caused by unsafe cooking methods, or heart disease and climate change caused by diets that focus too little on plant-based foods, we owe it to ourselves to make sure that everyone the world over has access to healthy, safely prepared, sustainably produced food—along with a knowledge about how their food choices impact the world.

In 2013, I was honored to join The United Nations Foundation's Global Alliance for Clean Cookstoves as Culinary Ambassador, helping to raise awareness about the death, sickness, and injury caused by toxic smoke from cooking stoves in developing countries. I formed World Central Kitchen to provide innovative solutions to alleviate hunger throughout the developing world, including the deployment of clean and innovative cooking solutions, because for too many women and children in Haiti and elsewhere, the danger and difficulty of cooking has reached a crisis point. And I've partnered with former U.S. Secretary of State Hillary Clinton, Global Ambassador Julia Roberts, and many others to ensure that this issue is on the agenda of advocates, chefs, business owners, and policymakers worldwide.

I've also worked to ensure that my restaurants serve an array of healthy, sustainable, plant-based dishes that everyone can enjoy. My Washington, D.C., restaurant Beefsteak, for example, serves mostly plant-based dishes—putting meat as a side-of-the-plate extra rather than the centerpiece.

Whenever we eat, we make choices. Those choices are wrapped up in family and tradition; they're wrapped up in taste and mood. And whether we think about it or not, they're also wrapped up in what kind of global citizen we want to be. Across the world, millions of people have little or no real choice about how they eat—about how much food they have, how they prepare it, how it's produced. Those of us who do have a choice share in the responsibility to make the right choices. Fortunately, countless people are doing just that, by choosing healthier, safer, more sustainably produced meals—creating a better, cleaner world with every bite.

Named one of TIME's "100 Most Influential People" and awarded "Outstanding Chef" by the James Beard Foundation, José Andrés is an internationally recognized culinary innovator, author, educator, television personality, humanitarian, and chef/owner of ThinkFoodGroup. He is the only chef globally who has both a two-star Michelin restaurant and four Bib Gourmands. Andrés is also a committed advocate for food and hunger issues and is known for championing the role of chefs in the national debate on food policy. His awards and distinctions include the 2017 Lifetime Achievement Award from International Association of Culinary Professionals, the 2015 National Humanities Medal, and the Congressional Hispanic Caucus Institute's Chair's Medallion Award.

SHOPPING FOR A BETTER WORLD

Adjusting to (and sticking with) any diet can be tough if you don't have the right foods handy. By keeping a well-stocked pantry (and fridge) full of protein-packed, plant-based staples, you can ensure success in your effort to easily enjoy eco-friendlier fare.

If you're vegetarian or vegan, these plan(e)t-based pantry items will probably be your everyday staples. If you're a meat, dairy, and egg reducer, at least keep some of these items on deck to help mix up your normal culinary repertoire and ensure success in your efforts to help the planet with every plate. Happy shopping!

PROTEIN 101

We all want well-balanced meals that are as filling as they are healthy. While Americans, on average, *over*consume protein, there's no doubt that combined with a healthy helping of fiber, it helps us feel satisfied after any meal. If you want to mix things up from meat, try packing a protein punch with any of these whole, natural foods.

Tofu: Tofu is made essentially the same way cheese is—except from soybeans instead of milk. Reports suggest that Benjamin Franklin introduced it to America in the eighteenth century, after sending it home from one of his many trips abroad. Here's a hint, though: don't eat it raw! Just as you wouldn't like the taste of raw, unflavored chicken, many people dislike the taste of raw tofu. Cut it up and pop it in any stir-fry, though, and it's great. Broil it on a baking sheet and it puffs up and turns golden brown. Scramble it, mash it, slather it in BBQ sauce and grill it—there are so many delicious ways to prepare tofu!

Tempeh: Tempeh is similar to tofu in that it's typically made from soybeans as well—though instead of being cultured and pressed, like cheese, they're fermented and formed into blocks. It's got a meaty, dense texture and cooks well in almost any format. Try marinating it before cooking it. Tempeh's got a potent taste, and a nice marinade will help it soak up your favorite flavors.

Seitan: This is a magically meaty product made from vital wheat gluten, wheat's primary protein. You can buy it in a plastic tub (like tofu) or vacuum-packed in the refrigerated section of some stores, or make it at home with relative ease. And it cooks up just like meat, too, offering a hearty texture and taking on whatever flavors it's cooked with.

Beans and Legumes: Enough can't be said about beans and legumes. Black beans, pinto beans, garbanzos (chickpeas), kidney beans, white beans, lentils of all colors and types, and more—these are some of the most protein-rich and diverse foods on the planet. You can certainly buy any kind of bean or legume in a can. Want to try your hand at home preparation, though? Buy 'em dried and cook them yourself. Some (like lentils) cook as quickly and as easily as rice. Dried beans, on the other hand, take longer (overnight soaking plus a few hours of cooking)—but preparing dried beans at home really brings out their taste in a big way, and gives you more control over their texture.

TOFU 101

It's versatile, delicious, and protein-rich. But let's face it: to the uninitiated, tofu can be a little scary. In the same way you wouldn't eat an entirely unseasoned chicken breast, you probably won't want to eat raw tofu. And just in the same way raw chicken needs to soak up flavors to taste good, so does tofu. Same principle, different protein. Don't worry! Here are some tips to help ensure a positive tofu experience:

PRESS IT! Pressing your tofu before using it helps it firm up and also improves its ability to take on whatever flavors you're cooking it in. To press tofu, open the packet and pour the water down the drain. Wrap the block of tofu in a clean dish towel or some paper towels. Next, place it on a large plate or tray. Place something flat and heavy on top of it—like a cutting board, heavy skillet, or another plate. (If what you put on top of it isn't that heavy, put something heavy—like a jar of beans or jug of water—on top of that.) Leave it there for at least 10 minutes, or even up to a few hours. If you are working with a 16-oz block of tofu, cut it in half crosswise through the middle first.

FREEZE IT! Freezing your tofu before using it gives it a whole new texture: it makes it firmer and meatier. To freeze your tofu, just take the whole package and stick it in the freezer. Before you use it, thaw the tofu on your counter for several hours. Then once thawed, press a little of the excess water out with clean hands, slice, cook, and enjoy.

BROIL IT! Broiling tofu before you use it makes it puff out and become nice and golden brown, almost like it's deep-fried (but not). To broil your tofu, cut the block into squares (however big or small you want). Place them on a baking sheet and broil in the oven for 15 minutes or until golden brown. Remove from the oven, let cool, then scrape the tofu off the baking sheet with a spatula. From here, you can put the tofu in salads as-is, pop it in some sauce for a stir fry, put it on a sandwich, and so much more. It's like a much healthier (and so much easier) version of deep-frying.

PLANT-BASED "MEATS"

Many people trying to eat more eco-friendly foods start by simply reducing meat and replacing it with the plant-based versions of their favorite items. It used to be that a veggie burger was one of your only options; today, we find a huge range of plant-based meats at grocery stores in virtually every town and city. Of course, like all packaged foods, they have a higher eco-footprint than do whole foods; but from an environmental standpoint, compared to their meaty counterparts, they're the clear winner. So if you want some ready-made options on hand for busy weeknight meals, these are a solid choice.

Chicken: Gardein offers perhaps the best "chicken" tenders on the market (plus all kinds of other bird-free poultry). Try Beyond Meat's chicken strips (and other products)—they have more protein than chicken, and are prepared exactly the same way. Morningstar Farms, Boca, store brand products by Target and Whole Foods, and Trader Joe's offer nuggets and strips as well as seasoned, marinated chicken-free bites. The list of plant-based poultry goes on and on.

A MEAL FOR ALL SEASONS

In addition to eating more whole, plant-based meals, we can lessen our environmental *food*-print by enjoying more seasonal produce, too. Eating seasonally helps cut down on food miles, as produce likely travels a shorter distance to reach your local market when it's in season. Of course, what's in season will change depending on where you live, but as you peruse the recipes, use this as a general guide to help you get started.

	JAN	FEB	MAR	APR	MAY	JUNE	JULY	AUG	SEPT	OCT	NOV	DEC
ACORN SQUASH	●	◐	●					◐	●	●	●	●
ARTICHOKE	◐	◐	●	●	◐				◐	●	◐	◐
ASPARAGUS		◐	●	●	●							
BEETS	●	●	●	●	●	●	●	●	●	●	●	●
BELL PEPPER								●	●	●		
BOK CHOY	●	●	●	●	●	●	●	●	●	●	●	●
BROCCOLI	●	●	●	●	●					●	●	●
BRUSSELS SPROUTS	●	●	●						●	●	●	●
BUTTERNUT SQUASH								●	●	●		
CABBAGE	●	●	●	●	●	●	●	●	●	●	●	●
CARROTS	●	●	●	●	●	●	●	●	●	●	●	●
CAULIFLOWER	●	●	●	●		●	●	●	●	●	●	●
CELERY	●	●	●	●	●	●	●	●	●	●	●	●
CORN						●	●	●	●	●		
CUCUMBERS					●	●	●	●	●	●	●	
EGGPLANT							●	●	●	●	◐	
GREEN BEANS						●	●	●	●			
KALE	●	◐	◐							◐	●	●
LEEKS	●	●	●	●					●	●	●	●
LETTUCE	●	◐	●	●	●	●	●	●	●	●	◐	●
MUSHROOMS	●	●	●					●	●	●	●	●
OKRA					●	●	●	●	●			
PARSNIPS	●	●	●	●						●	●	●
PUMPKINS									●	●	●	
RADISHES			●	●	●	●	●	●	●	●		
RHUBARB				●	●	●						
RUTABAGAS	●	●	●	●					●	●	●	●
SPINACH	●	●	●	●	●	●			●	●	●	●
SPRING PEAS			●	●	●							
SUMMER SQUASH					◐	●	●	●	●	◐		
SWEET POTATOES									●	●	●	●
SWISS CHARD	●	●	●	●	●	●	●	●	●	●	●	●
TOMATOES						●	●	●	●	●		
TURNIPS	●	●	◐	●	●	●	●	●	●	●	●	●
WINTER SQUASH								◐	●	●	●	●
ZUCCHINI	◐	◐	◐	●	●	●	●	●	●	◐		

Burgers: Beyond Meat's pre-made burgers and pre-formed patties (which look, taste, and cook just like ground beef) are best sellers. Gardein's beefless burgers are hard to beat, too. And then there are classics like Boca's Vegan Original, as well as burgers packed with whole grains and vegetables, like Sunshine Burgers and Dr. Praeger's. Find the brand(s) you like best!

Faux fish: Okay, so there's not a ton of fish-free seafood out there. But Gardein makes a stellar frozen, breaded fish fillet that keeps forever in the freezer and tastes incredible. Top it with some lemon juice or a plant-based tartar sauce and you won't know the difference!

Pork without the pig: Tofu Pups and Smart Dogs are two veggie dog brands I like. Field Roast and Tofurky both make an incredible variety of sausages made entirely from plant-based ingredients—creole-flavored, apple sage, spicy chipotle, you name it! Gardein makes Sweet and Sour Porkless Bites and BBQ pulled pork from plant-based ingredients. These items are usually found in the produce sections of grocery stores (by the tofu) and in the freezer section.

Breakfast meats: Sweet Earth makes a vegan bacon that will blow any carnivore's mind, and Lightlife Smart Bacon is another popular brand. Field Roast makes breakfast links as well that are sweet and filled with umami flavor. There are all kinds of other plant-based breakfast meats out there—give them a try and see which ones you like best.

Deli meats: Where tofu is sold, you'll often find a huge array of plant-based deli meats: bologna, ham, turkey slices of all flavors and brands, pepperoni, and much, much more. Want a sandwich in a cinch? Keep a couple of these in your fridge.

FAT = FLAVOR

Animal-based fats tend to be harder on the earth than their plant-based counterparts, because of the inefficiencies associated with factory farming. On the other hand, there are loads of healthy, plant-based fats that are easier on our bodies and gentler on the earth. Try reducing your use of animal-filled fats like butter and lard by swapping for these eco-friendlier fats.

Avocado: Avocado is a fantastic source of healthy fat. You can blend it into sauces and dressings, and even incorporate it into desserts! It's also excellent as a cheese replacement when you want something fatty, tasty, and creamy that isn't dairy on a sandwich or burger.

Oils: Olive oil: We know it. We love it. It's a classic. You can cook virtually anything with it, and it adds a richness and flavor that's fatty and decadent and delicious. But have you tried coconut oil? It's more eco-friendly than animal fat and has a nice, soft taste; it also cooks incredibly well. Try it in place of butter or vegetable oil when cooking. It's solid when cold and liquid when warm, so keep that in mind for storing. Oh, and what about toasted sesame oil? Adds characteristic flavor to any Asian dish—either as a dressing or cooking oil!

Margarine: Try Earth Balance margarine in place of butter once in a while. It's not (by any means) the only plant-based butter on the market, but is likely the most popular. Spreads well, melts perfectly.

WHAT'S THE DEAL WITH PALM OIL?

Palm oil is a significant cause of deforestation, especially in Malaysia and Indonesia, where huge tracts of forests and carbon-rich swamps are being destroyed for palm plantations. This emits massive amounts of greenhouse gases and threatens biodiversity—with orangutans, tigers, rhinoceros, and elephants being killed or displaced by the process.

Mayo: Just Mayo by Hampton Creek has become one of the most popular brands of plant-based mayo—and one of the most affordable. Even the world's largest food-service company, serving millions of meals a day (at universities, ballparks, and more), now uses Just Mayo for 100 percent of its mayonnaise needs nationwide! Plus, it's available everywhere—even the Dollar Tree! Vegenaise is another widely available brand. Even the ubiquitous Hellmann's and Best Foods brands make plant-based mayo, branded as "Carefully Crafted."

MOO-FREE MILKS

Countless people are now drinking nondairy milks. Try a variety of them and see which you like best. You'll find they vary in taste and consistency—that you prefer one brand over another, or one type for baking and another in your coffee (just like you wouldn't bake with half-and-half or drink heavy cream). Here's a short list to get you started:

Soy creamer: Gone are the days of putting regular ol' soy milk into coffee. Now those trying to make their morning joe healthier and more environmentally friendly have all kinds of brands (and flavors!) of soy-based creamers to choose from.

Soy milk: Vanilla, chocolate, plain, unsweetened, sweetened—there are so many types available now. Find the kind you like best. For baking, unsweetened soy milk is best; for drinking or putting on cereal, try vanilla.

Nut milk: Nut milks are gaining in popularity in a huge way. In fact, almond milk is one of the fastest-growing beverages in the marketplace. You can even get almond milk in any espresso drink at Dunkin' Donuts nationwide, and most coffee shops now offer it, too. It's a reliable option, and far more planet-friendly than cow's milk!

COW-FREE CHEESE

Aside from vegans, countless people who continue eating cheese in moderation are now mixing things up with the amazing new plant-based cheeses—cheeses made from almonds and cashews and coconut and tapioca and all kinds of other delicious products that are creamy and fatty and spread well and melt well . . . all while being more eco-friendly to produce. They're available nationwide, and there are always more coming out in the market. By the time you read this, I bet a new plant-based cheese will have hit the shelves!

Miyoko's: Miyoko's Creamery makes higher-end vegan cheeses. Country-style herbes de Provence, aged English sharp farmhouse, high Sierra rustic alpine, and more. They're nutty and incredible.

Field Roast Chao: Field Roast, known for their plant-based meats, dove into the cheese world with a major splash, taking coconut oil and other ingredients and turning them into slices under the Chao brand name. From tomato cayenne to creamy original, these cheese slices are sure to please.

Follow Your Heart: For years, Follow Your Heart was known as the maker of Vegenaise. More recently, it's begun making plant-based cheese products that will knock your socks off. Want a block of cheddar without the eco-harm that comes with industrial dairy production? Follow Your Heart's got your back. Provolone slices, mozzarella shreds, and much more, these dairy-free delights are not to be missed.

Kite Hill: Renowned plant-based chef Tal Ronnen, of Crossroads Kitchen fame, helped create Kite Hill, bringing what some call the most incredible vegan cheeses in history to the market. They make artisanal delicacies like almond milk ricotta and soft, fresh truffle dill and chive cheese, as well as a variety of schmears, like herbed cream cheese.

Daiya: Daiya's cheese uses an innovative ingredient—tapioca—to help it melt and stretch just like dairy cheese. Their cheddar, pepperjack, and mozzarella shreds are especially good on pizzas and for mac 'n' cheese.

Nutritional yeast: Okay, this is not a cheese—technically. It comes as a powder or as flakes. But it has a really cheesy, nutty flavor that can't be beat. And it's a whole food, so its eco-footprint is low. You can sprinkle it on popcorn or pasta like Parmesan, or make decadent plant-based mac 'n' cheese with it. It has a million and one uses.

ESCHEWING EGGS

Want to try egg-free baking? How about a breakfast scramble? Producing eggs is extremely resource-intensive when it comes to protein production, so keep some of these items on deck to use (at least) once in a while if you want to lower your ecological footprint.

The Vegan Egg: From Follow Your Heart, the Vegan Egg comes as a powder that, when mixed with water, scrambles well for breakfast and can be used in any baked good. A quick note, though: if scrambling, try adding some additional flavor—like pepper, sage, or rosemary—to really make it pop.

Egg replacer: Ener-G and Bob's Red Mill brand egg replacers are classic pantry items to replace eggs. Just mix with water to a certain ratio, and you can whip up cookies, cakes and other baked goods that taste and feel just like they have eggs, but are eco-friendlier and healthier.

Applesauce: If you're looking for a whole-foods substitute for eggs in baked goods, applesauce is your best friend. Try substituting ¼ cup of it for each egg called for in a recipe for sweet, baked desserts. Whodathunkit?!

Flaxseeds: Full of omega-3 fatty acids, flaxseeds are a total power food. When ground up into a powder and mixed with water, they make a great egg replacer.

Aquafaba: Aquafaba is a relatively new discovery that's taking the culinary world by storm. You basically take the liquid from a can of chickpeas and whip it for a long time to turn it into a poufy, fluffy, white substance that mimics whipped egg whites perfectly. You can even bake it into meringue! It sounds weird, but Google it and watch some videos—you'll be amazed. Plus, because it's made from an ingredient that would otherwise go down the drain, it's extra eco-friendly!

Chickpea flour: Also called garbanzo flour, gram flour, or *besan*, chickpea flour is full of protein and can be used to mimic eggs in many recipes (like the Rise 'n' Shine Breakfast Sandwiches on page 101).

GO NUTS

Ever tried nuts blended into a creamy sauce? Well, actually, you probably have—if you've had peanut sauce at a Thai restaurant. Other nuts can also be blended into creamy deliciousness. Cashews and almonds work especially well for soup bases and dressings (soak them overnight or for a few hours and blend them up with water). Pine nuts make a rich addition to any pasta dish or salad. Then there are peanuts and macadamia nuts and pistachios and pecans and walnuts and all kinds of others. Keep a bunch in your pantry and, well, go nuts with them!

GRAINS GALORE AND SEEDS-A-PLENTY

White rice is certainly fine, but want something more nutritious and flavorful that'll pack even more protein, flavor, and other goodness into your meat-free meals? Try quinoa. It's a tiny seed that's huge on protein, full of flavor, and cooks in a jiff. Millet, barley, couscous, amaranth, brown rice, wild rice, farina, kamut—these will leave you satisfied and full as you embark on eco-friendlier eating.

ACKNOWLEDGMENTS

Thank you to Josh Balk, Paul Shapiro, and Kristie Middleton. Thank you also to Alex Hodgkins, with whom I started my plant-based journey so many years ago. And to Michelle Geiss, my dear friend and focus group guru, as well as Caitlin Hayes, whose early edits on this book were invaluable. Thank you also, of course, to my father, Parker.

Thank you to Sally Ekus, and everyone else at The Lisa Ekus Group. And to Whitney Frick, Kara Rota, and the team at Flatiron Books. Without them, this book wouldn't exist.

Thank you to my culinary captain and photographer, Jessica Prescott. Her vision for the food and book helped make this what it is. And thanks to Amy Sly, for her on-point design.

Thank you to Staub, Vitamix, and Mauviel for the equipment and to Nouri Zarrugh for the delicious basbousa recipe.

Thanks to all those who contributed essays, blurbs, and photographs.

Thank you to my team of recipe testers: Ali Crumpacker, Amy Webster, Andy Cook, Ann Herbert, Ben Peterson, Bruce Mallory, Eddie Garza, Gabe Wigtil, Hillary Prescott (hey, sis!), Janet Prescott (hi, Mom!), Jim Reilly, Josie Morris, Joyana Hunt (also for the edits!), Justin Leonard, Kamber Sherrod, Karla Dumas, Karla Goodson, Karla Waples, Katie Scott, Lauren Pitts, Marsha Filion, Nicole Nuss, Paul Petersan, PJ Smith, Regan Karlson, Sam Hagio, Terry Hagio, Veronica Martin, and Wanda White.

And finally, thank you to those who helped in other ways: Bernie Unti, Chad Sarno, Cody Carlson, Deb Olin Unferth, Erik Olson, Geoff Orme Evans, Janet Friesen, Jill Soffer, Joe Meloy, Jonathan Kaplan, Karen Bouris, Kat Clark, Lisa Inzerillo, Rachel Querry, Suzanne Barnard, Terri Depaolo, and anyone else I've forgotten here.

ABOUT THE AUTHOR

Matthew Prescott is a leading figure in the global movement to reform how we farm and eat. He's Senior Food Policy Director for the Humane Society of the United States and advisor to the Good Food Institute. A sought-after speaker and thought leader, Prescott has spent over a decade and a half sharing his ideas with Ivy League universities, Fortune 500 companies, consumers, and more. His efforts have directly led to sweeping changes in the supply chains of hundreds of major food companies, impacted countless individuals' diets, and have been covered extensively by the media: his work has been featured by CNN, in the pages of the *New York Times*, the *Wall Street Journal*, the *Boston Globe*, and countless more; his writings have appeared in *USA Today*, the *Washington Post*, *Barron's*, and others; his photographs have been featured in *Rolling Stone* and *Food & Wine*; he's been a guest on national television news programs; and he was even once a guest on NPR's *Wait Wait . . . Don't Tell Me*. He lives in Austin, Texas, with his wife, the writer Lara Prescott.

CITATIONS

1. Lappé, Frances Moore. *Diet for a Small Planet: 20th Anniversary Edition.* New York: Random House, 1991. Print. Page 8.

2. Fryar, Cheryl, Carroll, Margaret, and Ogden, Cynthia. *Prevalence of Overweight, Obesity, and Extreme Obesity Among Adults: United States, 1960–1962 Through 2011–2012.* The Centers for Disease Control and Prevention, 19 Sept. 2014, https://www.cdc.gov/nchs/data/hestat/obesity_adult_11_12/obesity_adult_11_12.htm. Accessed 30 June 2017.

3. "Childhood Obesity Facts." The Centers for Disease Control and Prevention, 10 April 2017, https://www.cdc.gov/obesity/data/childhood.html, Accessed 30 June 2017.

4. Cawley, John, Meyerhoefer, Chad. "The medical care costs of obesity: An instrumental variables approach." *Journal of Health Economics,* 2012; 31 (1): 219.

5. United States. USDA and U.S. Department of Health and Human Services. *Scientific Report of the 2015 Dietary Guidelines Advisory Committee: Advisory Report to the Secretary of Health and Human Service and the Secretary of Agriculture.* February 2015. Web. Accessed 6 May 2016. Available at http://health.gov/dietaryguidelines/2015-scientific-report/PDFs/Scientific-Report-of-the-2015-Dietary-Guidelines-Advisory-Committee.pdf. Accessed 30 June 2017.

6. "Gazpacho." The Humane Society of the United States, n.d. Available at http://www.humanesociety.org/issues/eating/recipes/soups/gazpacho_aha.html?credit=web. Accessed 30 June 2017.

7. "AICR, The China Study, and Forks Over Knives." The American Institute for Cancer Research. n.d. Available at https://web.archive.org/web/20130716220718/http://www.aicr.org/about/advocacy/the-china-study.html.

8. "The Hidden Epidemic: Heart Disease in America." *PBS.* 2007.

9. "Fast Facts: Data and Statistics about Diabetes." *American Diabetes Association,* Dec 2015. http://professional.diabetes.org/sites/professional.diabetes.org/files/media/fast_facts_12-2015a.pdf. Accessed 30 June 2017.

10. Ibid.

11. Anderson, J. W. & Ward, K.: "High carbohydrate, high-fiber diets for insulin-treated men with diabetes mellitus." *American Journal of Clinical Nutrition,* 32: 2312, 1979.

12. Based on calculations from http://www.fao.org/faostat/en/#data.

13. "Farm Animal Statistics: Slaughter Totals." The Humane Society of the United States. 25 June 2015. Web. Accessed 6 May 2016. Available at www.humanesociety.org/news/resources/research/stats_slaughter_totals.html.

14. Dimitri, C., Effland, A., Conklin, N. *The 20th Century Transformation of U.S. Agriculture and Farm Policy.* United States Department of Agriculture Economic Research Service. Economic Information Bulletin Number 3. Page 5, Figure 3. June 2005.

15. Sauven, John. "Why meat eaters should think much more about soil." *The Guardian.* 16 May 2017. Available at https://www.theguardian.com/commentisfree/2017/may/16/meat-eaters-soil-degradation-over-grazing. Accessed 30 June 2017.

16. "Fish Count Estimates." *FishCount.org.uk,* 2014, http://fishcount.org.uk/fish-count-estimates. Accessed 30 June 2017.

17. "Pet Industry Market Size and Ownership Statistics." *American Pet Products Association,* http://www.americanpetproducts.org/press_industrytrends.asp. Accessed 30 June 2017.

18. "Directory of Charities and Nonprofit Organizations." *GuideStar,* https://www.guidestar.org/nonprofit-directory/environment-animals/animal-protection-welfare-services/1.aspx. Accessed 30 June 2017.

19. "U.S. Grocery Shopper Trends 2015 Executive Summary." *The Food Marketing Institute,* 2015. Available at https://www.fmi.org/docs/default-source/document-share/fmitrends15-exec-summ-06-02-15.pdf. Accessed 30 June 2015.

20. Norwood, F. B., J. L. Lusk, and R. W. Prickett. 2007. Consumer preferences for farm animal welfare: Results of a nationwide telephone survey. Working paper. Department of Agricultural Economics, Oklahoma State University, Stillwater, OK. Available at http://cratefreefuture.com/pdf/American%20Farm%20Bureau-Funded%20Poll.pdf. Accessed 30 June 2017.

21. *Journal of Interpersonal Violence.* 2009 Jun; 24(6):1036-56. doi: 10.1177/0886260508319362. Epub 2008 Jun 10. Available at https://www.ncbi.nlm.nih.gov/pubmed/18544751.

22. "How Many Species are we Losing?" World Wildlife Fund for Nature. Available at http://wwf.panda.org/about_our_earth/biodiversity/biodiversity. Accessed 30 June 2017.

23. The United States Environmental Protection Agency. (26 March 2013). *EPA Survey Finds More Than Half of the Nation's River and Stream Miles in Poor Condition* [Press release]. Available at https://yosemite.epa.gov/opa/admpress.nsf/0/26A31559BB37A7D285257B3A00589DDF. Accessed 30 June 2017

24. The Gates Notes. "The Science Behind Plant-Based Protein." Online video. *YouTube,* 19 March 2013. Accessed 6 May 2016. Available at https://www.youtube.com/watch?v=jjlVq5GiHbo.

25. Weise, Elizabeth. "Eating can be energy-efficient, too." *USA Today*. 21 April 2009. Available at http://usatoday30.usatoday.com/news/nation/environment/2009-04-21-carbon-diet_N.htm.

26. Searchinger, T., Hanson, C., Ranganathan, J., Lipinski, B., Waite, R., Winterbottom, R., Dinshaw, A., and Heimlich, R. 2013. Creating a Sustainable Food Future: Interim Findings. Page 4. Available at https://www.wri.org/sites/default/files/wri13_report_4c_wrr_online.pdf.

27. 2013. Gerber, P.J., Steinfeld, H., Henderson, B., Mottet, A., Opio, C., Dijkman, J., Falcucci, A. & Tempio, G. Tackling climate change through livestock – A global assessment of emissions and mitigation opportunities. Food and Agriculture Organization of the United Nations (FAO), Rome. Available from http://www.fao.org/docrep/018/i3437e/i3437e.pdf.

28. Own calculations: (1) based on U.S. total average water footprint per product from Mekonnen, M.M. and Hoekstra, A.Y. 2012. A global assessment of the water footprint of farm animal products. Ecosystems 15:401-15; and (2) whole milk and egg weights from United States Department of Agriculture Economic Research Service in cooperation with the Agricultural Marketing Service, the Agricultural Research Service, and the National Agriculture Statistics Service. 1992. Weights, measures, and conversion factors for agricultural commodities and their products, p. 28 Table 19 and p. 34 Table 21. Agricultural Handbook No. 697. www.ers.usda.gov/media/935958/ah697_002.pdf. Accessed May 6, 2016.

29. NRDC (nrdcfood). "Eating plant-forward dishes can go a long way in reducing diet-related carbon emissions." http://bit.ly/2q6WFI9 via @mindbodygreen. 27 April 2017, 10:00 AM. Tweet. Available at https://twitter.com/NRDCFood/status/857595205679173632.

30. Lia Marie Johnson. "Obama and I have a serious conversation . . ." Online video. *YouTube*, 7 Nov 2016. Accessed 6 February 2017. Available at https://www.youtube.com/watch?v=Dl1stHbyJAw.

31. Grossman-Cohen, Ben. "'Meatless Monday' Too Hot a Potato for USDA." *CNN*. 2 August 2012. Available at www.cnn.com/2012/08/02/opinion/grossman-cohen-meatless-monday.

32. Barclay, Eliza. "Even carnivores are putting more fake meat on their plates." *National Public Radio*. 15 August 2013. Available at www.npr.org/sections/thesalt/2013/08/14/212024490/even-carnivores-are-putting-more-fake-meat-on-their-plates.

33. Scipioni, Jade and Libasi, Matthew. "Tyson Foods CEO: The Future of Food May be Meatless." *FOX Business*. 7 March 2017. Available at http://www.foxbusiness.com/features/2017/03/07/tyson-foods-ceo-future-food-might-be-meatless.html.

34. Black, Jane. "Meat on the Side: Modern Menus Shift the Focus to Vegetables." *The Wall Street Journal*. 31 Oct 2014. Available at https://www.wsj.com/articles/meat-on-the-side-modern-menus-shift-the-focus-to-vegetables-1414784266. Accessed 30 June 2017.

35. Timothy V. "Jamie Oliver Interview—Veganism, McDonald's, Bill Gates." Online video. *YouTube*, 4 Feb 2015. Accessed 21 October 2016. Available at www.youtube.com/watch?v=gAEgSLeepOw.

36. Kennedy, Wally. "Effort to keep CAFO from Arrow Rock mirrors fight to protect parks." *Joplin Globe*. 17 November 2007. Available at www.joplinglobe.com/archives/effort-to-keep-cafo-from-arrow-rock-mirrors-fight-to/article_fe9f629a-3a98-5f27-a49d-ce47c711b6a4.html.

37. "American FactFinder." United States Census Bureau. Accessed 5 May 2016.

38. Kennedy, Wally. "Effort to keep CAFO from Arrow Rock mirrors fight to protect parks." *Joplin Globe*. 17 November 2007. Available at www.joplinglobe.com/archives/effort-to-keep-cafo-from-arrow-rock-mirrors-fight-to/article_fe9f629a-3a98-5f27-a49d-ce47c711b6a4.html.

39. Ibid.

40. Sandy, Jennifer. "Factory Farms: A Bad Choice for Rural America." *Forum Journal*. Vol. 23, No. 2. Winter 2009. Available at: www.preservationnation.org/forum/library/public-articles/factory-farms.html.

41. Gates, Bill. "The Future of Food." *The Gates Notes*. 18 March 2013. Available at www.gatesnotes.com/About-Bill-Gates/Future-of-Food.

42. Kennedy, Wally. "Effort to keep CAFO from Arrow Rock mirrors fight to protect parks." *Joplin Globe*. 17 November 2007. Available at www.joplinglobe.com/archives/effort-to-keep-cafo-from-arrow-rock-mirrors-fight-to/article_fe9f629a-3a98-5f27-a49d-ce47c711b6a4.html.

43. Borgman, Kathy. Phone interview by Matthew Prescott. 11 October 2016.

44. Steinfeld, H., Gerber, P., Wassenaar, T., Castel, V., Rosales, M., and De Haan, C. 2006. "Livestock's long shadow: environmental issues and options" (Rome: Food and Agriculture Organization of the United Nations). Available at ftp://ftp.fao.org/docrep/fao/010/a0701e/a0701e.pdf.

45. Marks, Robbin. "Cesspools of Shame." July 2001. NRDC. Available at: www.nrdc.org/sites/default/files/cesspools.pdf.

46. Steinfeld, H., Gerber, P., Wassenaar, T., Castel, V., Rosales, M., and De Haan, C. 2006. "Livestock's long shadow: environmental issues and options" (Rome: Food and Agriculture Organization of the United Nations). Available at ftp://ftp.fao.org/docrep/fao/010/a0701e/a0701e.pdf.

47. Walker, R., Browder, J., Arima, E., Simmons, C., Pereira, R., Caldas, M., Shirota, R., Zen, S.d., 2009. "Ranching and the new global range: Amazônia in the 21st century." *Geoforum* 40, 732–745.

48. Bianchi, C., Haig, S., 2013. Deforestation trends of tropical dry forests in central Brazil. Biotropica 45, 395-400.

49. Morales-Hidalgo, D., 2006. Tree cover assessment: with special focus on the relative position issue. Case Studies in Open Areas in Costa Rica. Cuvillier Verlag.

50. Rulli, M.C., Saviori, A., D'Odorico, P., 2013. "Global land and water grabbing." *Proc. Natl. Acad. Sci.* 110, 892–897.

51. Devendra, C., Thomas, D., 2002a. "Crop–animal systems in Asia: importance of livestock and characterisation of agro-ecological zones." *Agric. Syst.* 71, 5–15.

52. B. Machovina et al. "Science of the Total Environment" 536 (2015). Pages 419–431. Available at http://dx.doi.org/10.1016/j.scitotenv.2015.07.022.

53. Ibid.

54. Own calculation using: (1) 2014. Eshel, Gidon et al. Land, irrigation water, greenhouse gas, and reactive nitrogen burdens of meat, eggs, and dairy production in the United States. *PNAS.* 19 August 2014. Vol. 111, No. 33. Available at www.pnas.org/cgi/doi/10.1073/pnas.1402183111; with (2) square meters converted to square feet; and for the square footage of an NFL football field (3) Smith, Greg. "A controversial end to an instant classic." 13 Jan. 2010. National Football League. Accessed 6 May 2016. Available at www.nfl.com/news/story/09000d5d815b45a6/printable/a-controversial-end-to-an-instant-classic.

55. Borgman, Kathy. Phone interview by Matthew Prescott. 11 October 2016.

56. Roosevelt, Franklin. *Letter to all State Governors on a Uniform Soil Conservation Law.* 26 Feb 1937. Available at: www.presidency.ucsb.edu/ws/?pid=15373.

57. Ranganthan, J., Vennard, D., Waite, R., Dumas, P., Lipinkski, B., Searchinger, T., and Globagri-WRR Model Authors (2016). Shifting Diets for a Sustainable Future. Page 37. Available at www.wri.org/sites/default/files/Shifting_Diets_for_a_Sustainable_Food_Future_0.pdf.

58. Vaughan, Adam. "Paul McCartney Backs Meat-Free Monday to Curb Carbon Emissions." *The Guardian.* 15 June 2009. Available at: www.theguardian.com/environment/2009/jun/15/paul-mccartney-meat-free-monday.

59. "Climate Actions to Change our World." United Nations Food and Agriculture Organization. 16 October 2016. Available at: www.fao.org/world-food-day/2016/climate-actions/en.

60. Carlson, Cody. Phone interview by Matthew Prescott. 12 May 2016.

61. Lerner, Rebecca. "Toxic Fumes, Blisters & Brain Damage: The Cost of Doing Business?" *The Ithaca Times.* 2 April 2008. Available at: www.organicconsumers.org/news/toxic-fumes-blisters-brain-damage-cost-doing-business. Note: Subsequently, Karen Strecker's father and other residents unsuccessfully sued the dairy for Clean Water Act violations.

62. Ross, Brian and Schecter, Anna. "Got Milk? Got Ethics? Animal Rights v. U.S. Dairy Industry." *ABC News.* 26 January 2010. http://abcnews.go.com/Blotter/animal-rights-us-dairy-industry/story?id=9658866.

63. (1) Lerner, Rebecca. "Toxic Fumes, Blisters & Brain Damage: The Cost of Doing Business?" *The Ithaca Times.* 2 April 2008. Available at: www.organicconsumers.org/news/toxic-fumes-blisters-brain-damage-cost-doing-business; with (2) 157,000 tons converted to pounds.

64. Based on curb weight of a 2015 Ford F-150 4x2. Ford Motor Company. "F-150 Specifications." n.d. Available at: www.ford.com/trucks/f150/specifications.

65. Lerner, Rebecca. "Toxic Fumes, Blisters & Brain Damage: The Cost of Doing Business?" *The Ithaca Times.* 2 April 2008. Available at: www.organicconsumers.org/news/toxic-fumes-blisters-brain-damage-cost-doing-business.

66. Ibid.

67. Hauter, Wenonah. *Foodopoly: The Battle over the Future of Food and Farming in America.* New York: The New Press, 2014. Print.

68. Kilborn, Peter. "Hurricane Reveals Flaws in Farm Law." *The New York Times.* 22 September 1999. Available at: www.nytimes.com/library/national/101799floyd-environment.html.

69. "Corporate Hogs at the Public Trough." *Sierra Club.* San Francisco, California. 1999.

70. Merritt Frey, et al. "Spills and Kills: Manure Pollution and America's Livestock Feedlots." *Clean Water Network.* Izaak Walton League of America and Natural Resources Defense Council. August 2000.

71. "Corporate Hogs at the Public Trough." *Sierra Club.* San Francisco, California. 1999.

72. Merritt Frey, et al. "Spills and Kills: Manure Pollution and America's Livestock Feedlots." *Clean Water Network.* Izaak Walton League of America and Natural Resources Defense Council. August 2000.

73. Hopkins, Elaine. "Dairy Farm Ordered to Clean Up—Inwood Dairy Must Cut Herd Size, Clean Ravine of 2 Million Gallons of Waste." *Peoria Journal Star.* 22 February 2001.

74. Ibid.

75. "Corporate Hogs at the Public Trough." *Sierra Club.* San Francisco, California. 1999.

76. Gordon, Stuart and Lindsay, Alvie. "Polluting Dairyman Gets Jail." *The Modesto Bee.* 14 March 1998.

77. Prince Charles, Prince of Wales. *A speech by HRH The Prince of Wales to the Future for Food Conference, Georgetown University, Washington DC.* 4 May 2011. Available at: www.princeofwales.gov.uk/media/speeches/speech-hrh-the-prince-of-wales-the-future-food-conference-georgetown-university.

78. Environmental Science, Enger and Smith, 6th ed. Fishery management: pages 201-203. Available at: www.mhhe.com/biosci/pae/es_map/articles/article_53.mhtml.

79. United States. EPA. *PA California Dairy Farmer Sentenced for Clean Water Violations.* Press Release. 20 March 1998. Available at https://yosemite.epa.gov/opa/admpress.nsf/0/34ADD4BDC5B8707A852565CD005FD499.

80. Environmental Defense Fund. "Overfishing: Worse than You Might Think." n.d. Accessed 11 May 2016. Available at: www.edf.org/oceans/overfishing-worse-you-might-think.

81. "Fish Count Estimates." http://fishcount.org.uk/fish-count-estimates.

82. Worm, Boris, Barbier, Edward B., Beaumont, Nicola, Duffy, J. Emmett, Folke, Carl , Halpern, Benjamin S., Jackson, Jeremy B. C., Lotze, Heike K., Micheli, Fiorenza, Palumbi, Stephen R., Sala, Enric, Selkoe, Kimberley A., Stachowicz, John J., and Watson, Reg. "Impact of Biodiversity Loss on Ocean Ecosystem Services." *Science.* Vol. 314, Issue 5800, pp. 787-790. 3 November 2006. Available at: http://science.sciencemag.org/content/314/5800/787.abstract.

83. Brown, Culum. "Animal minds: Not just a pretty face." *New Scientist*. 12 June 2004. Available at: www.newscientist.com/ article/mg18224515.200-animal-minds-not-just-a-pretty-face.

84. Oceana. "Responsible fishing: Stopping overfishing." n.d. Accessed 11 May 2016. Available at http://oceana.org/en/ our-work/promote-responsible-fishing/bottom-trawling/ learn-act/more-on-bottom-trawling-gear.

85. Ibid.

86. Harris, Richard. "Whales, Dolphins Are Collateral Damage In Our Taste For Seafood." NPR. 8 January 2014. Available at www.npr.org/blogs/thesalt/2014/01/07/260555381/ thousands-of-whales-dolphins-killed-to-satisfy-our-seafood-appetite.

87. Smith, Z., Gilroy, M., Eisenson, M., Schnettler, E., Stefanski, S. Natural Resources Defense Council. "Net Loss: The Killing of Marine Mammals in Foreign Fisheries." January 2014. Available at www.nrdc.org/sites/default/files/mammals-foreign-fisheries-report.pdf.

88. "Aquaculture." World Wildlife Fund for Nature. Available at http://wwf.panda.org/what_we_do/footprint/agriculture/ aquaculture.cfm. Accessed 30 June 2017.

89. (1) United Nations Food and Agriculture Organization. "Global aquaculture production statistics updated to 2013: Summary information." Table 1. March 2015. Available at: www.fao.org/3/a-i4899e.pdf; with (2) total metric tons converted to pounds.

90. Based on reported weight of 450,000 pounds. The Statue of Liberty – Ellis Island Foundation. "Statue Facts." n.d. Available at: www.libertyellisfoundation.org/statue-facts.

91. Balcombe, Jonathan. Phone interview by Matthew Prescott. 15 May 2016.

92. "Salmon Fishing Problems." Coastal Alliance for Aquaculture Reform. *Farmed and Dangerous*. n.d. Available at: www. farmedanddangerous.org/salmon-farming-problems.

93. Ibid.

94. Crawford, Elizabeth. "Almond milk sales continue to surge, while dairy milk contracts, Nielsen data shows." *Food Navigator*. 15 April 2016. Available at: www.foodnavigator-usa.com/Manufacturers/Almond-milk-sales-continue-to-surge-as-dairy-milk-contracts-Nielsen.

95. Midkiff, Ken. *The Meat You Eat: How Corporate Farming Has Endangered America's Food Supply*. New York: St. Martin's Press, 2004. Print. Back cover.

96. Inzerillo, Lisa. Personal interview by Matthew Prescott. 18 February 2017.

97. Montgomery, Jess. "Delaware's broiler chicken output grows." *The News Journal*. 29 April 2014. Available at: www. delawareonline.com/story/money/business/2014/04/29/ delawares-broiler-chicken-output-grows/8475187.

98. Schuessler, Ryan. "Maryland residents fight poultry industry expansion." *Al Jazeera America*. 23 Nov. 2015. Available at: http://america.aljazeera.com/articles/2015/11/23/maryland-residents-fight-poultry-industry-expansion.html.

99. Kobell, Rona. "Poultry mega-houses forcing Shore residents to flee from stench, traffic." *The Bay Journal*. 22 July 2015. Available at: http://marylandreporter.com/2015/07/22/ poultry-mega-houses-forcing-shore-residents-to-flee-stench-traffic.

100. "Poisoned Waters." *Frontline*. PBS. 21 April 2009. Web. Accessed 10 May 2016. Relevant segment available at: www.pbslearningmedia.org/resource/envh10.sci.life.eco. chickenwaste/chicken-waste-and-water-pollution.

101. Ibid.

102. *Poult Sci*. 2013 Jan; 92(1):64–83. doi: 10.3382/ps.2012-02745.

103. "The Facts." *Cowspiracy*. Web. Accessed 10 May 2016. Available at: www.cowspiracy.com/facts.

104. "Poisoned Waters." *Frontline*. PBS. 21 April 2009. Web. Accessed 10 May 2016. Relevant segment available at: www.pbslearningmedia.org/resource/envh10.sci.life.eco. chickenwaste/chicken-waste-and-water-pollution.

105. Parker, Suzi. "How poultry producers are ravaging the rural south." *Grist*. 22 February 2006. Available at: http://grist.org/ article/parker1.

106. Ibid.

107. Mirabelli, Maria C., Wing, Steve, Marshall, Stephen W., and Wilcosky, Timothy C., "Race, Poverty, and Potential Exposure of Middle-School Students to Air Emissions from Confined Swine Feeding Operations." Available at http://www.ncbi. nlm.nih.gov/pmc/articles/PMC1440786.

108. Pope Francis. *Encyclical Letter of the Holy Father on Care for our Common Home*. 24 May 2015. Available at: http:// w2.vatican.va/content/francesco/en/encyclicals/documents/ papa-francesco_20150524_enciclica-laudato-si.html.

109. Parker, Suzi. "How poultry producers are ravaging the rural south." *Grist*. 22 February 2006. Available at: http://grist.org/ article/parker1.

110. Doujaiji, B. and Al-Tawfiq, J. "Hydrogen sulfide exposure in an adult male." *Annals of Saudi Medicine*. 30(1): 76–80. April 1010. Available at: www.ncbi.nlm.nih.gov/pmc/articles/ PMC2850187.

111. Good, Kate. "How Factory Farming Creates Air Pollution." *One Green Planet*. 10 March 2015. Available at: http://www.onegreenplanet.org/environment/ how-factory-farming-creates-air-pollution.

112. The Pew Charitable Trusts. (29 April 2008). *Pew Commission Says Industrial Scale Farm Animal Production Poses "Unacceptable" Risks to Public Health, Environment* [Press release]. Available at http://www.pewtrusts.org/en/about/ news-room/press-releases/2008/04/29/pew-commission-says-industrial-scale-farm-animal-production-poses-unacceptable-risks-to-public-health-environment. Accessed 30 June 2017.

113. "Air Pollution." Sustainable Table. n.d. Available at: http:// gracelinks.org/media/pdf/air_pollution_tp_20090826.pdf.

114. Curtis Stofferahn, "Industrialized Farming and Its Relationship to Community Well-Being: an Update of the 2000 Report by Linda Labao," Special report prepared for the state of North Dakota, Office of Attorney General, www.und.edu/org/ ndrural/Lobao%20&%20Stofferahn.pdf.

115. Marks, Robbin. "Cesspools of Shame." July 2001. NRDC. Available at: www.nrdc.org/sites/default/files/cesspools.pdf.

116. Pacelle, Wayne. "HSUS 2016 annual report: Transformational progress for orcas and elephants, farm and lab animals, and others." Web blog post. *A Humane Nation*. The Humane Society of the United States, 15 March 2017. Web. Available at http://blog.humanesociety.org/wayne/2017/03/hsus-annual-report-2016-transformational-progress.html. Accessed 30 June 2017.

117. "Per Capita Consumption of Poultry and Livestock, 1965 to Estimated 2016, in Pounds." *National Chicken Council*. 13 April 2016. Accessed 10 May 2016. Available at: www.nationalchickencouncil.org/about-the-industry/statistics/per-capita-consumption-of-poultry-and-livestock-1965-to-estimated-2012-in-pounds.

118. "Chart of U.S. Population: 1790 – 2000." Census-Charts.com. n.d. Available at: www.census-charts.com/Population/pop-us-1790-2000.html.

119. United States. U.S. Census Bureau. U.S. and World Population Clock. Available at: www.census.gov/popclock.

120. "Sales and Trends." *Soyfoods Association of America*. Available at: www.soyfoods.org/soy-products/sales-and-trends.

121. Tropical Smoothie Café menu. n.d. Available at: https://s3.amazonaws.com/tscws/downloads/TSC_Food_Smoothies_Menu.pdf.

122. Beyond Meat. Lightly Seasoned Strips. n.d. Available at: http://beyondmeat.com/products.

123. United States. USDA and U.S. Department of Health and Human Services. *Scientific Report of the 2015 Dietary Guidelines Advisory Committee: Advisory Report to the Secretary of Health and Human Service and the Secretary of Agriculture*. February 2015. Web. Accessed 10 May 2016. Available at http://health.gov/dietaryguidelines/2015-scientific-report/PDFs/Scientific-Report-of-the-2015-Dietary-Guidelines-Advisory-Committee.pdf.

124. United States. Office of the White House Press Secretary. *Remarks by the President at the GLACIER Conference—Anchorage, AK*. 31 August 2015. Web. Accessed 17 October 2016. Available at www.whitehouse.gov/the-press-office/2015/09/01/remarks-president-glacier-conference-anchorage-ak.

125. America's Climate Choices: Panel on Advancing the Science of Climate Change; National Research Council (2010). *Advancing the Science of Climate Change*. Washington, D.C.: The National Academies Press. ISBN 0-309-14588-0. Available at: www.nap.edu/catalog.php?record_id=12782.

126. Davenport, Coral and Robertson, Campbell. "Resettling the First American 'Climate Refugees.'" *The New York Times*. 3 May 2016. Available at: www.nytimes.com/2016/05/03/us/resettling-the-first-american-climate-refugees.html.

127. Ibid.

128. Allen, Leslie. "Will Tuvalu Disappear Beneath the Sea?" *Smithsonian Magazine*. August 2004. Available at: www.smithsonianmag.com/travel/will-tuvalu-disappear-beneath-the-sea-180940704/?all.

129. Ibid.

130. "Tuvalu: Joining forces to tackle climate change." International Federation of Red Cross and Red Crescent Societies. n.d. Available at: www.ifrc.org/Global/Case%20studies/Disasters/cs-tuvalu-en.pdf.

131. Steinfeld, H., Gerber, P., Wassenaar, T., Castel, V., Rosales, M., and De Haan, C. 2006. "Livestock's long shadow: environmental issues and options" (Rome: Food and Agriculture Organization of the United Nations). Available at ftp://ftp.fao.org/docrep/fao/010/a0701e/a0701e.pdf.

132. United Nations Food and Agriculture Organization. "Key Facts and Findings." n.d. Available at: www.fao.org/news/story/en/item/197623/icode.

133. "Fighting Global Warming with Food." Environmental Defense Fund. 27 August 2007. Available at https://web.archive.org/web/20080604070742/edf.org/article.cfm?contentID=6604.

134. "Limit Your Meat Consumption." *Earth Day Network*, n.d. Available at http://www.earthday.org/limit-meat-consumption. Accessed 30 June 2017.

135. Isomaki, Risto. *Meat, Milk and Climate: Why it is Absolutely Necessary to Reduce the Consumption of Animal Products*. Helsinki: Into Publishing, 2016. Page 11. Print.

136. Kandy, Daniel. "The World Mangrove Atlas: Hope Amid Despair." *The World Watch Institute*. 20 August 2010. Available at: http://blogs.worldwatch.org/nourishingtheplanet/the-world-mangrove-atlas-hope-amid-despair.

137. Steinfeld, H., Gerber, P., Wassenaar, T., Castel, V., Rosales, M., and De Haan, C. 2006. "Livestock's long shadow: environmental issues and options" (Rome: Food and Agriculture Organization of the United Nations. Pp. 272). Available at ftp://ftp.fao.org/docrep/fao/010/a0701e/a0701e.pdf.

138. 2003. Pimentel, David and Marcia Pimentel. "Sustainability of meat-based and plant-based diets and the environment." *American Journal of Clinical Nutrition*.78 (suppl): 660S–3S. Available from http://ajcn.nutrition.org/content/78/3/660S.full.

139. Eshel, Gidon. "Grass-fed beef packs a punch to environment." *Reuters*. 8 April 2010. Available at: http://blogs.reuters.com/environment/2010/04/08/grass-fed-beef-packs-a-punch-to-environment.

140. Steinfeld, H., Gerber, P., Wassenaar, T., Castel, V., Rosales, M., and de Haan, C. 2006. "Livestock's long shadow: environmental issues and options." Food and Agriculture Organization of the United Nations, p. 112.

141. Ramanathan, V. and Xu, Y. 2010. "The Copenhagen Accord for limiting global warming: criteria, constraints, and available avenues." Proceedings of the National Academy of Sciences of the United States of America 107 (18).

142. Eshel, Gidon. "Grass-fed beef packs a punch to environment." *Reuters*. 8 April 2010. Available at: http://blogs.reuters.com/environment/2010/04/08/grass-fed-beef-packs-a-punch-to-environment.

143. "Fighting Global Warming with Food." The Environmental Defense Fund website. 24 July 2007. Archived copy available at: web.archive.org/web/20080923070051/http://www.edf.org/article.cfm?contentid=6604.

144. Pine, Joselyn. *Wit and Wisdom of America's First Ladies.* 2014. Mineola: Dover Publications. Print.

145. Scarborough, P., Appleby, N., Mizdrak, A., Briggs, A.D.M., Travis, R., Bradbury, K., and Key, T. "Dietary greenhouse gas emissions of meat-eaters, fish-eaters, vegetarians and vegans in the UK." *Climate Change.* July 2014. Vol. 125, Issue 2, pp. 179–192. Available at: http://link.springer.com/article/10.1007/s10584-014-1169-1.

146. Ibid.

147. 2014. Bailey, Rob, Froggatt, Antony, and Wellesley, Laura. *Livestock – Climate Change's Forgotten Sector.* The Royal Institute of International Affairs. Available from www.chathamhouse.org/sites/files/chathamhouse/field/field_document/20141203LivestockClimateChangeBaileyFroggattWellesley.pdf.

148. 2015. Wellesley, L., Happer, C., and Froggatt, A. *Changing Climate, Changing Diets: Pathways to Lower Meat Consumption.* The Royal Institute of International Affairs. Available from www.chathamhouse.org/publication/changing-climate-changing-diets%20.

149. TED. "The Case for Optimism on Climate Change." Online video. *YouTube,* 14 March 2016. Accessed 30 June 2017. Available at https://www.youtube.com/watch?v=gVfgkFaswn4.

150. Pollan, Michael. "Unhappy Meals." *The New York Times.* 28 January 2007. Available at http://www.nytimes.com/2007/01/28/magazine/28nutritionism.t.html. Accessed 5 October 2017.

151. Katzen, Mollie. *The Heart of the Plate: Vegetarian Recipes for a New Generation.* New York: Houghton Mifflin Harcourt. 2013. Print.

152. Goodall, Jane. *Harvest for Hope: A Guide to Mindful Eating.* New York: Time Warner Book Group, 2005. Print. Page 111.

153. Huget, Jennifer Larue. "Bobby Flay's Recipe for Eating Healthfully." *The Washington Post.* 20 September 2011. Available at https://www.washingtonpost.com/lifestyle/wellness/bobby-flays-recipe-for-eating-healthfully/2011/09/16/gIQA2I8uhK_story.html.

154. Thomas-Wachsberger, Beatrice. "Natalie Portman: a rare bloom." *New Zealand Herald.* 5 May 2011.

155. The White House. (13 Sept 2010). *Remarks by the First Lady in Address to the National Restaurant Association Meeting* [Press release]. Available at https://obamawhitehouse.archives.gov/the-press-office/2010/09/13/remarks-first-lady-address-national-restaurant-association-meeting. Accessed 30 June 2017.

156. Nazarali, Roselina. "Shania Twain is vegetarian." *Foodista.* 3 December 2012. Available at www.foodista.com/blog/2012/12/03/shania-twain-is-vegetarian.

157. Armstrong, Laura and Brankin, Emma. "Leo's Big Misteak." *The Sun.* 19 November 2016. Available at: www.thesun.co.uk/tvandshowbiz/2221787/leonardo-dicaprio-preaches-about-meat-at-a-veggie-talk-but-is-later-caught-tucking-into-lamb-tagine-at-a-steakhouse.

158. "Mario Batali Talks Meatless Monday." *Meatless Monday,* 25 Jan 2016. Available at http://www.meatlessmonday.com/articles/mario-batali-talks-meatless-monday-tuesday-and-wednesday-on-the-chew. Accessed 30 June 2017.

159. Stewart, Martha. *Meatless: More than 200 of the Very Best Vegetarian Recipes.* New York: Random House, 2013. Print.

160. Jenkins, Willis, Tucker, Mary Evelyn, and Grim, John. *Routledge Handbook of Religion and Ecology.* New York: Routledge, 2016.

161. "Sustainable Food." Rachel Carson Council, n.d. Available at http://rachelcarsoncouncil.org/our-work/sustainable-food. Accessed 30 June 2017.

162. TED. "What's Wrong with what we Eat – Mark Bittman." Online video. *YouTube,* 21 May 2008. Accessed 30 June 2017. Available at https://www.youtube.com/watch?v=5YkNkscBEp0.

163. Bessette, Chanelle. "Mark Tercek on Small Changes that Make a Big Difference." *Fortune.* 5 Nov 2013. Available at www.fortune.com/2013/11/05/mark-tercek-on-small-changes-that-make-a-big-difference.

164. Branson, Richard. "Why I've Given up Eating Beef." *Virgin.* 9 July 2014. Available at www.virgin.com/richard-branson/why-ive-given-up-eating-beef.

165. Winfrey, Oprah. "Conscious Eating: What I Learned on the 21-Day Cleanse." *O, The Oprah Magazine.* October 2008. Available at: oprah.com/omagazine/What-I-Know-for-Sure-Oprahs-Vegan-Cleanse.

166. Schwarzenegger, Arnold. "Arnold's Opinion on Vegetarianism: The Oak's Thoughts on Going Meatless." *Flex.* N.d. Available at www.flexonline.com/nutrition/arnolds-opinion-vegetarianism.

167. Agence France-Presse. "Lifestyle changes can curb climate change: IPCC chief." 15 January 2008. Available at www.abc.net.au/news/2008-01-16/lifestyle-changes-can-curb-climate-change-ipcc/1013982.

168. Lantry, Lauren. "My Plate, My Planet." *Sierra Club.* Available at: www.sierraclub.org/compass/2015/05/my-plate-my-planet.

169. Gates, Bill. "The Future of Food." *The Gates Notes.* 18 March 2013. Available at www.gatesnotes.com/About-Bill-Gates/Future-of-Food.

170. Borges, Marco. *The 22-Day Revolution Cookbook.* New York. Penguin Random House, 2016.

171. "Celebrity vegans and the veganism facts you need." MSN. 13 June 2016. Available at: www.msn.com/en-gb/health/nutrition/celebrity-vegans-and-the-veganism-facts-you-need/ss-BBmuG5R#image=5.

172. D'estries, Michael. "Al Gore Says He'll Stay Vegan 'For Life.'" *Mother Nature Network.* 13 March 2014. Available at: www.mnn.com/health/fitness-well-being/blogs/al-gore-says-hell-likely-stay-vegan-for-life.

173. Buckley, Jemma. "I'm going vegetarian 3 times a week says Jamie Oliver." *Daily Mail.* 12 May 2015. Available at: dailymail.co.uk/tvshowbiz/article-3079084/I-m-going-vegetarian-3-times-week-says-Jamie-Oliver-s-got-veggie-cook-book-coming-out.html.

INDEX

Page numbers in *italics* refer to photographs.